Women and the Conquest of California

Women and the Conquest of California, 1542–1840

CODES OF SILENCE

Virginia Marie Bouvier

The University of Arizona Press

Tucson

For Alex —
¡Gracias!
Ginny
1/15/01

First printing

The University of Arizona Press

© 2001 The Arizona Board of Regents

All rights reserved

♾ This book is printed on acid-free, archival-quality paper.

Manufactured in the United States of America

06   05   04   03   02   01   6   5   4   3   2   1

Library of Congress Cataloging-in-Publication Data

Bouvier, Virginia Marie, 1958–

    Women and the conquest of California, 1542–1840 : codes of silence
/ Virginia Marie Bouvier.

      p. cm.

    Includes bibliographical references and index.

    ISBN 0-8165-2025-9 (acid-free paper)

    1. Women pioneers—California—History.   2. Women pioneers—
California—Social conditions.   3. Indigenous peoples—California
History.   4. Indigenous peoples—California—Social conditions.
5. Frontier and pioneer life—California.   6. California—History—To 1846.
7. Women—California—History.   8. Women—California—Social
conditions.   9. Sex role—California—History.   10. Misisons—California—
History.   I. Title.

F864 .B695 2001

979.4′02′082—dc21   00-010603

British Library Cataloguing-in-Publication Data

A catalogue record for this book is available from the British Library.

Publication of this book is made possible in part by the proceeds of a permanent
endowment created with the assistance of a Challenge Grant from the National
Endowment for the Humanities, a federal agency.

Contents

Figures

Acknowledgments

This book has benefited from the critiques of many people. Francine Masiello, who read and commented on many drafts, was a consistent source of inspiration, guidance, and unflagging encouragement. I also appreciate the insightful comments of Margaret Chowning, whose seminars on race and ethnicity in colonial Latin America helped me to situate California within the context of a greater Latin American historiography. Liz Hutcheson, Robyn Muncy, Jane Bouvier, Jean Molesky, Helen Rand Parish, William Simmons, and Mary Ryan also read the manuscript in its entirety and provided me with valuable criticism. Joseph Sánchez, David A. Johnson, Carl Abbott, Stephen Cole, Frederick Luciani, and reviewers for *Colonial Latin American Historical Review, Pacific Historical Review,* and *Colonial Latin American Review* offered helpful suggestions on portions of the manuscript. Discussions and seminars with Gwen Kirkpatrick, Gunther Barth, Alex Saragoza, Frederick Bowser, Linda Lewin, Terry Wilson, James Gregory, Maxine Hong-Kingston, Candace Slater, Dick Walker, Candace Falk, Pilar Alvarez, Karen Bradley, Steve Haskell, Tom Boganschield, and Madeline Kiser all influenced the evolution of this book. I am indebted to the staff of the Bancroft Library, especially Walter Brem, Baiba Strads, and Susan Snyder, for continued assistance during the last decade. Joyce MacKenzie, of the California Parks and Recreation Department, and Elizabeth McClave, from Mayo Hayes O'Donnell Library, facilitated my work in Monterey. Don Garate, from the Tumacácori National State Park, kindly shared with me a copy of his working paper, "Notes on Anza." Santa Barbara Mission Archive-Library director Virgilio Biasiol and his assistant Crescencia Olmstead generously made dozens of documents available to me for consultation. At Mexico's Archivo General de la Nación, Victoria San Vicente, director of administration, and other capable reference librarians assisted my research efforts. My archival work was enhanced by scholars whom I met in Mexico, including Anne Bos, Pilar Gonzalvo at the Colegio de México, Carmen Lugo, and Sonya Lipsett-Rivera from Carleton University. I owe a special thanks to Marcela Suárez from the Universidad Autónoma Metropolitana and to Cristina Iñigo for their help.

The questions raised and recommendations made by my editor, Patti Hartmann, by my copy-editor, Jane Kepp, and by anonymous readers for the University of Arizona Press forced me to refine my thoughts and sharpen my arguments. I thank them for their insightful queries. Thanks also to Louise Nelson for her assistance in tracking down references, to Lisa Bowden for her fine design sense, to Kathryn Conrad and Tappan King for their marketing skills, and to Alan Schroder for his editorial advice.

I was fortunate to receive financial support for various stages of research and writing from the University of California, including a Bancroft Library Study Award, a travel grant from Berkeley's Center for Latin American Studies, the Wilma Seevy Ogden Purse, a Foreign Language and Area Studies grant, the Genevieve McInerney fellowship, and a University of California Regents' fellowship. I also received a Mary McEwen Schimke Fellowship Award and the Horton-Hallowell graduate fellowship from Wellesley College, and a fellowship from the Cushwa Center for the Study of U.S. Hispanic Catholics at the University of Notre Dame. The University of Maryland General Research Board awarded me a two-month grant that enabled me to rethink the organization of my materials, and the University System of Maryland Women's Forum granted me a Faculty Research Award that supported a final research trip to Berkeley prior to publication.

More friends and family than I can name here have helped me financially and emotionally through four computers and more than a decade of work on this book. Thanks Mom, Dad, June, Rose, Jim, Ed, Jackie, Dianne, Michael, Niki, David, Joe, Anna, Dan, Tricia, David, and Kathy. This book is dedicated with appreciation to my husband, Jim, who introduced me to California's history as only a native could, and to our daughter, Maya.

Introduction

In 1989, shortly before beginning the doctoral program in Latin American Studies at the University of California at Berkeley, I accompanied my future husband to a conference in Monterey, California. While he met with fellow architects, I explored the town, visiting the adobes that remained from Mexican times. I listened as docents described the influence of the Vallejos, the Alvarados, the Argüellos, and the Castros in the settlement of California. At the Spanish missions, tour guides raved about the heroic achievements of Father Junípero Serra, who had established the mission system in Alta California. Already this was a new perspective to a Yankee who had ignorantly assumed that California was settled by Anglo-Europeans who traveled across the plains in their covered wagons. But when I asked about the Indian women at the missions who were being trained in notions of Christianity or the Hispanic women whose pictures were on the walls, whose equestrian clothing hung on display, whose cooking implements filled adobe kitchens, and who were often property owners in their own right, the docents could do no more than speculate. What was it like to be a woman living and working on the California frontier? How did race, religion, age, and ethnicity shape these experiences? Was the experience of women at the missions different from that of the men? How did the larger sociopolitical change represented by the independence of Mexico from Spain in 1821 affect the roles of women? My investigations in the archives of California and Mexico began as an effort to address these questions.

In seeking to articulate a female presence on the California frontier and at the missions, I looked toward a variety of sources, including novels of chivalry; mission census, baptismal, marriage, and death records; journals of explorers, missionaries, and foreign visitors to California; nineteenth-century ethnographic accounts; government and ecclesiastical correspondence and documents; legal transcripts and petitions; and oral histories. I found that firsthand female accounts are poorly (and rarely) indexed and tend to be scattered throughout archival collections. Many such accounts have yet to be discovered.

The Bancroft Library at the University of California in Berkeley houses the largest collection of documents related to California. Of particular interest to me were dozens of handwritten oral histories collected in the 1870s from early California settlers (including women who worked at the missions, Spanish soldiers and officers, and a Christianized neophyte); excerpts and transcripts from the Archives of California (the originals burned in San Francisco's 1906 earthquake and fire); chronicles of and correspondence related to the exploration, colonization, and evangelization of California; and microfilms of California-related documents from other major repositories in Spain, Mexico, and the United States. The Bancroft holdings also include somewhat sporadic census, baptismal, marriage, and death records from the missions, which I supplemented with those available at the Santa Barbara Mission Archive-Library. The Junípero Serra Collection and the California Mission Documents in the Santa Barbara Mission Archive-Library also contained correspondence between the California missionaries and church authorities in Mexico that was useful for my study. Finally, I found many pertinent legal documents, petitions, letters, journals, and reports in Mexico's Archivo General de la Nación.

Much of what we know of women's roles on Mexico's northern frontier can be gleaned from mediated sources such as European travel literature, Spanish documents written during or after the conquest, and ethnographic materials collected some two hundred years or more after the initial encounters. Virtually all of the female narratives I located— the reluctant voice of Isidora Filomena de Solano; the poignant testimonies of Toypurina and Delfina Cuero; the insightful interviews given by Eulalia Pérez and Apolinaria Lorenzana; the beseeching petition of María de la Encarnación Castro; and the disturbing testimony of

an Indian girl who was raped by Spanish soldiers—were mediated by
third parties, some of whom were from different cultures and spoke
different languages and almost all of whom were male. Narratives of
non-Christianized, indigenous women are rare, and those of Spanish-
speaking women in colonial Mexico are only slightly more accessible.
These female narratives sometimes allude to the societal constraints of
the day, and they tend to portray women as historical agents, that is, as
people who exercised choices—to marry or not to marry; to live on the
"barbaric" frontier or not; to acquiesce to or to resist the cycles of
conquest; and to adhere to or resist the wishes of mission priests. Bringing these female narratives, filtered as they are, into the chorus of history
and attending to the silences of the historical record regarding women
alter our understanding of the experience and meaning of conquest.

In both content and methodology, my study reflects recent interdisciplinary trends in history, literature, anthropology, ethnic studies,
and women's and gender studies. These fields increasingly draw on each
other in addressing questions of individual and group experiences in
particular local contexts. Given the dearth of female voices, discourse
analysis has been a particularly useful tool for teasing out both female
experience and gender ideologies.[1]

Scholars in Latin American history, U.S. social history (including
that of California and the borderlands region between Mexico and the
U.S. Southwest), and women's studies have each contributed to the
development of this study. The field of Latin American colonial studies
has been opened to new interpretations as a range of black, white,
Indian, mestizo, mulatto, female, and, to a lesser extent, rural voices,
from a variety of geographic regions, have begun to be included in
anthologies of colonial Latin American history and literature.[2] These
heretofore "marginal" subjects have become popular topics of investigation.[3] Recent philological studies have likewise opened the field to a
broader range of sources that contribute to our knowledge of indigenous interpretations of the effects of conquest on some of the major
indigenous groups of Latin America.[4] In the wake of the Columbian
quincentennial, a preponderance of attention has been given to studies
of indigenous peoples and their encounters with the Spanish.[5]

Studies of the Spanish conquest of Latin America traditionally have

sought to explain encounters between the Iberians and the so-called
New World in terms of the timing of the conquest, the charisma (or lack
thereof) of individual conquistadores, geographical considerations, and
the diverse nature of American indigenous groups.[6] Much work re-
mains to be done, however, with respect to gender analysis of the Spanish conquest, a theme that tradition has relegated to the male realm. As
yet largely unexplored are the ways in which gender ideology—that is,
the body of ideas that give meaning to sexual differences between males
and females—shaped the conquest, both directly and indirectly.[7]

In this book, I have drawn on theoretical constructs developed by
anthropologists and social scientists in recent decades that differentiate
sex from gender. I use "sex" to refer to the physiological differences
between males and females, and "gender" to signify a cultural con-
struct—a "set of learned behaviour patterns."[8]

Students of the early modern period have only recently begun to
analyze the significance of categories of gender and gender difference.[9]
Gender analysis, which seeks to break down what the historian Inga
Clendinnen calls the "cultural habit of identifying the male as fully
representative of his female kin" and to analyze the different ways men
and women affected and were affected by history,[10] is already rewriting
the way we understand history.[11] Scholars have begun to analyze female
experiences among the major indigenous groups in preconquest Latin
America.[12] Irene Silverblatt broke new ground in developing a paradigm that helped to explain how gender ideologies and systems shaped
the experiences of both Andean and Spanish men and women in Peru.[13]
Recent studies have elucidated the experiences of Spanish and indigenous women in the early period of contact in Mexico.[14] A variety of
studies analyze the role of Iberian women in expansion overseas.[15] A
small number of studies address the role of women in the Spanish conquest of the Indies, but they tend to lack a framework for moving beyond the "compensatory" approach that incorporates individual women
into history as a kind of postscript.[16] Gender analysis has also contributed to our understanding of later periods of colonial Latin American
history. Almost invariably, these studies explore the intersection of gender and ethnicity, either implicitly or explicitly.[17] Much of the scholarship in this growing field addresses issues of marriage, sexuality, gender,
and the nature of patriarchy in colonial Latin America.[18]

Elsewhere, gender analysis has been fruitfully applied to cross-cultural contact situations in colonial North America. Carol Devens articulated a differential, gender-defined response among the Ojibwa, Cree, and Montagnais-Naskapi communities of the Great Lakes and eastern subarctic regions of the United States to Jesuit missionization.[19] Recent studies have focused on the roles of Indian women as mediators of early European encounters with indigenous peoples in North America.[20] The ethnologist Clara Sue Kidwell has documented the role of Indian women as interpreters, guides, and negotiators in such encounters.[21] Social histories now underscore the multifaceted role of relationships between European men and indigenous women of the forested borderlands region of the present-day United States and Canada, as well as the roles played by their racially mixed offspring.[22] These studies show that despite the lack of indigenous female writings, the presence and participation of indigenous women on the frontier can be traced through documents including company records, correspondence, journals, and demographic reports. Sylvia Van Kirk, Jennifer Brown, and Walter O'Meara each used such documents to analyze the role of female labor in the development of the Canadian fur trade.[23] John Mack Faragher noted that hundreds of Indian women were mediators between Europeans and Indians in the North American fur trade.[24] Although the fur trade might have produced a unique circumstance in which Indians were valued as necessary economic partners, female mediators were far from culture-specific.[25] La Malinche (Doña Marina), Sacagawea, Pocahontas, Molly Brant, Nancy Ward ("beloved woman" of the Cherokees), and Mary Musgrove Matthews Bosomsworth are perhaps the best known of these cultural mediators.

Related to the scholarship on Latin American conquest is a growing literature on the borderlands, a term I use here to refer to the northern frontier of New Spain, a frontier that included the vast lands of what are today the western and southwestern regions of the United States. The borderlands provide a particularly rich archive of conquest experiences that has only recently been tapped with regard to women and gender. Much has been written about the contribution of westering women in the mid- and late-nineteenth centuries.[26] These studies have contributed to theoretical debates over the role of the frontier in shaping American culture and the role of women and family on the frontier.[27]

Current historiography of the U.S. Southwest is deepening our understanding of life on Mexico's far northern frontier, of the Spanish mission system, and of the diversity of indigenous inhabitants and their responses to missionization. Studies of the borderlands have tended to focus on male institutions of power, namely, the Spanish missions[28] and, to a lesser extent, the presidios.[29] A growing number of studies, however, now analyze the complex relationship between gender, class, race, and ethnicity. Antonia Castañeda's work on Spanish-Mexican and indigenous women in California continues to break new ground in the field.[30] Salomé Hernández's work on the role of women in colonization; the work of Victoria Brady, Sarah Crome, and Lyn Reese on female indigenous resistance; and Doug Monroy's work on patriarchy in Hispanic California have all provided new contexts within which to understand women's experiences.[31] Ramón Gutiérrez's analysis of the effects of conquest on New Mexican indigenous societies and Deena González's work on Spanish-Mexican women in New Mexico have set the stage for further gender studies of that region.[32] Other studies of women and gender relations in New Mexico,[33] Texas,[34] and, to a lesser extent, Colorado[35] and Arizona[36] have focused on the Mexican and early American periods rather than on the initial conquest era.

Gutiérrez noted that "no longer is it considered adequate to write the history of men without acknowledging the presence of women, and vice-versa."[37] Yet it is insufficient to acknowledge that women were on the scene without also analyzing the meaning of their presence (or absence) and the ways in which gender and race ideologies might have affected their experiences and the relationship between cultures. Ethnohistories of the missions are beginning to show how the reversal of gender roles introduced by the conquest at some Southwestern missions affected indigenous responses to missionization.[38] In their study, Robert Jackson and Edward Castillo noted that new gender roles that gave Indian men at the California missions the responsibility for agricultural labor traditionally done by women contributed to male "disaffection" and "psychological disorientation."[39] Monroy acknowledged the importance of the "conquest of intimacy" in the psychological conquest of the California Indians.[40] Ana María Alonso analyzed the role of honor and gender in her study of frontier violence.[41] Albert Hurtado investigated cultural assumptions, patterns, and changes related to marriage and sexuality on the California frontier during the late eighteenth and nineteenth centuries.[42]

My own study reflects and contributes to these recent trends in the historiography and places an analysis of male-female roles and relations, marriage and family, and sexuality in the context of the conquest of California and the myths that engendered it. Looking through the prism of gender, we can see new meaning in the exploration of unfamiliar territory, the migration of human beings from one land to another, and the evangelization of an indigenous population. More than a military and religious enterprise, the conquest becomes an ideological and cultural undertaking that dramatically affected everyone involved.

Gender issues were integral to the Spanish conquest in a variety of ways during the Spaniards' exploration, colonization, and evangelization of Alta California from 1542 to 1840. In the context of conquest, by its nature a complex multicultural encounter, a gendered lens raises new questions about relationships between and within each group involved. Gender provides a useful lens through which to analyze frontier dynamics between and among men and women, as well as between settlers, soldiers, and priests or between and among Europeans and Indians.[43] My focus on women and gender adds complexity to a somewhat polarized debate over the role of the missions in Alta California and whether the Franciscans saved or enslaved the Indians.[44] It breaks down the monolithic nature of each side in order to analyze the participation of women—both Hispanic and Indian—in the maintenance of or resistance to the system. In doing so, it explodes simplistic dichotomies that pit the Spaniards against the Indians, and it brings into relief the rifts within the ranks of the colonial authorities and differences among the indigenous groups of Alta California.

My study underscores the way in which notions about gender shaped and in turn were transformed by conquest. I argue that gender ideology was one of the ingredients in the glue that held together the conquest project, albeit in various ways in the different aspects of that project constituted by exploration, evangelization, and colonization. I suggest that gender ideologies also shaped indigenous behavior toward the Spanish conquerors.

In chapter 1, I argue that gender ideologies provided a way to naturalize conquest. I analyze the way in which chivalric romances encoded a gendered paradigm that portrayed conquest primarily as a male venture enacted upon a female land and its inhabitants. The language of imperial conquest and a medieval tale of pagan Amazon women who inhabited a mythic island named California reinforced the chroniclers' feminization of both the land and its inhabitants. In chapter 2, I look at Spanish portrayals of their first encounters with the natives of Alta California and argue that the inscription of idyllic gender relations between the conquerors and the Indians may have sanitized a more violent frontier reality but reflected an initial period of church-state unity at the height of the Spanish golden age of exploration.

In chapter 3, I analyze the accounts of the expedition of 1769, which established the first missions and presidios in Alta California. Slippage between the texts around the issue of gender relations reveals that the Spaniards' abuse of Indian women served as a lightning rod for tensions between the California natives and the Spaniards, as well as between the military and the church. The absence of Hispanic women in the early encounters appears to have influenced some indigenous interpretations of the intent of the European newcomers. Conflictual gender relations in some parts of Alta California prejudiced the possibilities for peaceful evangelization, set the stage for heightened conflict during subsequent colonization, and contributed to building a consensus in New Spain in favor of the participation of women in settling the northern frontier.

In chapter 4, I argue that female participation in the colonization of California was both greater and earlier than historians have heretofore recognized. Christianized indigenous families from the Baja California peninsula served as models for the evangelization of Alta California. An analysis of the journals from the Anza expedition of 1775–76, the first expedition in which women (primarily from the mainland of New Spain) participated, sheds light on the gender ideologies held by Spanish authorities and the ways these might have clashed with those held by the indigenous groups the Spaniards encountered. In chapter 5, I analyze the role gender played in shaping the experiences of men and women at the missions. I find that the missions offered women opportunities and constraints that were circumscribed by ethnicity, religion, age, and marital status and that varied over time and by location. My focus on gender reveals a code of silence regarding the use of force at the missions that intersected with codes of silence about the treatment of women.

In chapter 6, I propose that Franciscan criticism of and efforts to change indigenous attitudes toward sexuality and marriage provided the ideological underpinnings for evangelization and ultimately nourished the roots of indigenous resistance. In chapter 7, I argue that language, religious ceremonies, dreams, dances, dress, and land usage were additional realms in which mission Indians managed to register their dissent and to assert themselves as protagonists in their daily lives, and I analyze the gendered dimensions of this cultural resistance.

A gender analysis of the narratives of exploration, colonization, and evangelization in California reveals numerous codes of silence regarding the use of force at the missions, the treatment of women, ceremonies, sexuality, and dreams. Ironically, these very codes, which served to hide female experiences and female agency, also reveal the gender ideologies of those who created and maintained them. This study of one "contact zone" on the margins of the Spanish empire underscores the importance of considering gender ideologies in our evaluation of conquest and cross-cultural relations in any historic period.

Women and the Conquest of California

I

Mythic Beginnings

Regional idiosyncrasies, the role of the church, the character of the groups encountered, and differences in the timing of exploration and settlement all influenced the dynamics of conquest in Latin America. Gender ideology—that is, the body of ideas relating to gender—shaped each of these factors and, as an independent variable, also influenced the course and discourse of the Spanish conquest of America. Myths that encoded gender ideologies evolved over time to reflect the changing social needs and aspirations of individuals and cultures.

Spain's conquest of California, like that of its other American colonies, occurred in three phases: exploration (often referred to as "discovery"), colonization, and evangelization, the last two overlapping considerably. California's location on the northern margins of Spain's far-flung colony of New Spain meant that it received only sporadic royal attention from the time it was sighted by Juan Rodríguez Cabrillo in 1542 until more than two centuries later.[1] Exploration of the lands that would come to be known as Baja and Alta California began in the 1530s but was never sustained under the reign of the Spanish king Carlos I (1517–56). Even as late as the early eighteenth century, California was believed to be an island or group of islands.[2] Because New Spain's northern frontier was far removed from Spanish administrative centers and settlements and boasted no apparent mineral resources, the Spanish Crown gave exploration there little priority.

The motivations of the Spanish conquest of America were religious, political, and economic. In exchange for colonizing Spanish America, the pope gave the Spanish Crown complete control of the establishment

of the church in the New World under the *patronato real,* or royal
patronage agreement. Yet the initial unity of church and state in conquering the New World exhibited ever-widening cracks and fissures
between competing interests over the course of the sixteenth century.
The main groups involved in the various phases of conquest included
military men, missionaries, and civilians, all of whom acted under the
ultimate authority of the king of Spain.

Spanish interests in the New World grew increasingly multifaceted
during the sixteenth century. As riches were discovered and exploited, a
declining indigenous population proved increasingly incapable of sus-
taining the labor demanded by colonists. New interest groups emerged
and coalesced. Individual colonists gained authority and created their
own fiefdoms far from the metropolis. Races from the New and Old
Worlds mixed. The Crown responded to these social transformations
by creating new administrative oversight positions that more than occasionally obfuscated jurisdictional boundaries between and within ecclesiastical and secular spheres and enabled it to play one group off
against another.

The relatively late discovery (and much later settlement) of California ensured that the Spanish conquest of this frontier would follow a
different path from that pursued in the rest of the Indies (the name
given by Spain to its newly discovered lands). Unlike its earlier practices
in the Caribbean, central Mexico, and Peru, by the time California was
"discovered" in 1542, the Spanish Crown could no longer assure explorers of awards of perpetual Indian labor and tribute, known as *encomiendas.*[3] Under this system, Indians were entrusted to the care of an
encomendero, who was expected to protect and Christianize his charges;
in exchange, the encomendero could exact tribute and labor from the
Indians under his care. The abusive nature of the encomienda system, as
well as the growing power of the recipients, led the Crown to pass the
New Laws of 1542, which abolished the encomienda. These laws were
met with such resistance by landholders in the Indies that they were
quickly modified. Nonetheless, ever more stringent laws limiting the
exploitation of the Indians and requiring encomenderos to Christianize
and provide for the Indians in their care made the encomienda increasingly undesirable, and it was eventually replaced by a combination
of other institutions.

Multiple myths motivated the exploration of the Indies—cities of gold, fountains of youth, water passageways connecting worlds known with those unknown. Most of these myths implicitly codified the role of the male conqueror as the discoverer and ruler of all that he found. Although few of them granted women a role in the exploration of the New World, one myth provided an explicit paradigm that established a gendered dichotomy between the male conqueror and the feminine subjects to be conquered. This was the myth of the Amazons. Strong, independent women who fiercely defended a kind of female utopia, the Amazons taunted a population of male conquerors from afar. Like a chameleon, however, the figure of the Amazon has changed over time and through space. With the first contacts between Europeans and indigenous groups in California, the myth of the Amazons was replaced by new myths, imbedded in chroniclers' reports, of a population of docile, white Indian men and women. These early images and their variations often codified unspoken rules of conquest regarding gender and race relations, and they provided the ideological justifications for a hierarchy of power (sometimes but not always related to gender) within the changing social order advanced by conquest. Scholars have largely failed to reconcile the historical and mythical aspects of the Amazon figure, which traditionally has been presumed to provide evidence of matriarchal societies. Only in the 1990s did efforts begin to be made to understand the evolution of the Amazon figure as a reflection of changing societal needs.[4]

An emblem of "otherness," the Amazon of ancient Greek tradition was associated with the barbarians the Greeks sought to conquer and destroy. The Amazon figure held a special place in the Spanish culture of the early modern period. During the late fifteenth and early sixteenth centuries, Spain's golden age of exploration, rumors spread that lands inhabited by women lay undiscovered just beyond the reaches of charted territory (fig. 1). On his first trip across the Atlantic Ocean, Christopher Columbus wrote of the existence of such an island. He noted that to the east of Yamaye (Jamaica) was "an island where there was nothing other than women by themselves," and that many local people knew of the island.[5] A few days later, he recorded seeing three sirens, "who were not as beautiful as they have been painted, as somehow their faces appeared to be those of men."[6]

Figure 1. Spain's golden age of exploration was marked by the nebulous marriage of myth and reality. Royal instructions often directed conquerors to search for mythic lands ruled by Amazons, shown in the foreground of this 1594 print by Jan van der Straet, "Christophorus Columbus Ligur terroribus Oceani Superatis alterius pene Orbis regiones a fe inventas Hispanis regibus addixit." (Courtesy of the Library of Congress)

Such rumors piqued the curiosity of Spanish monarchs, who began to request that explorers search specifically for these mythic women, whom they called Amazons. In 1524, the Spanish conqueror Hernán Cortés wrote a letter from Mexico to Emperor Charles V regarding his anticipation of finding an island of Amazons northwest of the recently conquered Aztec Empire. The *caciques,* or Indian leaders, of Ciguatán had told Cortés that ten days' distance from their province of Zacatula was an island "completely populated by women, with no men among them," which was visited from time to time by men from the mainland for the purpose of engaging in sexual relations with the island's inhabitants.[7] Cortés solicited support to search for this island of women and wrote to the king that it was supposed to be "very rich in pearls and gold."[8]

These tips may have been mere ruses on the part of the Indians of Ciguatán to encourage Cortés and his companions to go elsewhere. The Indians' observations nonetheless reflected their understanding of what they believed to be important to the conquerors—women and wealth. Cortés's anticipation of the discovery of a mineral-rich Amazon island reflected the dreams and desires of his generation of conquistadores. Nuño de Guzmán, a rival conqueror, detailed the attraction of a similar land. He wrote to King Charles that he hoped to find the wealthy Amazons, "which some say dwell in the Sea, and some in an arme of the Sea."[9] In addition to their mermaidlike affiliation with the sea, Nuño de Guzmán specified that the women he expected to find were "whiter than other women" and considered to be goddesses. His white Amazon warriors admitted males into their company solely for sexual unions, and then only for reproductive purposes. They were highly armed with "Bowes, Arrowes and Targets" and had "many and great Townes." Already, the image of the Amazon was beginning to incorporate notions of a civilization whose social structure was somewhat more evolved, reflecting perhaps the recent discoveries of the magnificent and highly organized Aztec and Inca civilizations.[10]

Tales of the Amazons inspired renowned explorers including Fray Marcos de Niza, Francisco Vázquez de Coronado, and Alvar Núñez Cabeza de Vaca to explore the regions between the Atlantic and Pacific Oceans and from Mexico City north to territories inhabited by Apaches, Comanches, Navajos, Moquis, and thousands of smaller indigenous groups on the northern frontier of New Spain.[11] The name given to the land of California, discovered sometime between 1535 and 1539, explicitly recalled these fantasies of a land inhabited by women. It was almost certainly derived from the popular novel of chivalry *Las sergas de Esplandián* (The exploits of Esplandián), by Garcí Ordóñez de Montalvo.[12] In *Las sergas,* an island named California was located close to the mythical "earthly paradise" (fig. 2). It was inhabited not by white goddesses but by attractive black women whose lifestyle was similar to that of the Amazons. A beautiful infidel queen named Calafia, attired in gold and pearls, ruled over the island.

Ordóñez's California marked the first appearance of a female-ruled land in the romances of chivalry and the first variation to present the

Figure 2. Even as late as the early eighteenth century, California was believed to be an island, as seen in the map "America Septentrionalis." California's name derived from the fictitious land of women ruled by Calafia, the black Amazon warrior queen portrayed in the Spanish novel of chivalry *Las sergas de Esplandián*. (From Jan Jansson, *Novus Atlas,* vol. 3, plate 20 [1646–49]; courtesy of the Library of Congress)

Amazon as black rather than white.[13] The fictional knights considered these black Amazon women to be attractive partners, confirming that Iberian social prejudices of the day, which were particularly vicious against the Muslim Moors and the Jews (who were forcibly expelled from Spain in 1492), were rooted primarily in religious rather than phenotypical difference. Thus, the Christians in *Las sergas* married the darker Amazons, but only after the latter converted to Christianity. In her study of the Amazon, Alison Taufer showed how the literary portrayal of the woman warrior figure shifted from one of a barbarian enemy warranting annihilation in ancient Greece to that of a pagan welcomed into the Christian fold by sixteenth-century Spaniards.[14] *Las sergas de Esplandián* contributed to the evolution of this metaphor.

The tale of the conquest and conversion of the infidel queen and her subjects was undoubtedly familiar to participants in the early exploration of the New World.[15] *Las sergas* was a "folio" romance, typical of the popular literature produced in the early sixteenth century. In 1510, Jacob Cromberger, a German printer, published the work in Seville, billing it as a sequel to the highly successful, four-volume *Amadís de Gaula,* which Ordóñez de Montalvo had translated from its original Portuguese into Spanish.[16] Like its predecessors, *Las sergas*—which featured the adventures of Amadís's son, Esplandián—quickly became a bestseller. By 1525, the Crown granted Cromberger exclusive rights for its sale in the Americas.[17] With the establishment of a printing press in Mexico in 1539, Cromberger was able to sell *Las sergas* to sailors and conquerors embarking for the Californias from either Seville or Mexico.[18] The novel was issued in at least ten editions in the sixteenth century.

Ordóñez de Montalvo's story of Queen Calafia was an epic about the Spanish crusades against the infidels. In the tale, Queen Calafia convinced her Amazon subjects to leave the island to join the Turks in the pagan siege of Constantinople. She promised the women of California great profit, honor, and fame if they would join with other prominent lords and princes in this endeavor. If they did not fight the Christians, the queen cautioned the women, they were destined to inconsequentiality. She told her subjects that "if they remained on the island, doing nothing but what their ancestors did, they were merely buried alive—as though they were dead while they lived, spending their days without fame or glory, like wild animals."[19] In the face of such a dismal future, the metaphoric fate of being female, Queen Calafia's subjects quickly agreed to participate in the siege. The women "were so anxious to extend their fame to other lands that they urged her [Calafia] to hasten to sea right away." Once they arrived in Constantinople, the women fought the Christians brilliantly. They were aided by five hundred griffins, mythical monsters with the head and wings of an eagle and the body of a lion, whom they had trained from birth to devour men. The griffins, which encarnated the virtues of watchfulness and courage, were said to have guarded the fabled gold mines of Scythia and were sacred to the ancient Greek sun god, Apollo. Their presence on the island suggested the wealth that the fictional California was purported to contain.

Calafia's bold ambition led to her ultimate defeat. After routing the Christians, the griffins mercilessly turned on the Turks, thus assisting the Christian victory. Queen Calafia was captured and fell in love with Esplandián, who, already betrothed to his beloved Leonorina, married the Amazon queen off to his cousin. Queen Calafia converted to Christianity, the other Amazons followed suit, and the queen presented the island of California with all its wealth to the Christian victors.

What messages or images did early explorers of the Pacific coast absorb from this fictional fantasy? These imaginative tales told of noble, passionate, and morally pure heroes engaged in the conquest of strange beings who inhabited faraway lands. The melodramatic novels of chivalry captured the imagination of an audience that identified completely with the knightly heroes and their fictional worlds. Ordóñez's tale found a ready audience in a public whose imagination had already been stimulated by the findings of Columbus and his successors. *Las sergas* reinforced the morality of the Spanish conquest of America by underscoring the conquerors' sexual, military, and religious superiority over those they would conquer in the New World. The fictional representation depicting California as an island of women at once desiring sexual engagement with men from the mainland and yet choosing to live in isolation from men tantalized the would-be conquerors from afar. Explorers fantasized that California was a land of exotic women who were desirous of sexual relations, would be easily conquered (as the imagined Amazons had no males among them who might serve as protectors or rivals), and who would welcome the conquerors with gold, pearls, and other riches. Although many explorers had left spouses or lovers in far-off Spain or New Spain to embark on the journey to the unknown, vague rewards of sexual gratification beckoned from beyond the horizon, where fiction and desire were melded in the crucible of the imagination.

Such chivalric writings not only influenced the conquerors but also reflected popular culture and shaped a code of conduct among the populace at large, particularly in Spain. The story of Amadís de Gaula, Esplandián's literary father, has been characterized as "the first idealistic modern novel, the epic of faithfulness in love, the code of honor and courtesy which schooled many generations."[20] Like motion pictures and television in the twentieth century, chivalric romances helped to define the codes of morally acceptable thought and behavior, and they contributed to "artificial standards of value and false attitudes toward reality."[21]

Such tales nurtured a value system based on simplified notions of good and evil that demanded fidelity within marriage and sexual purity before marriage for women, codes of honor among men, and blind faithfulness in matters of courtly love. These social mores provided an ideological framework for the subjugation of those with different values. In the case of California, the legendary sexual practices of the Amazon women of California provided a pretext for a battle between the "good" conquerors and the "licentious"—that is, "evil"—pagan women. Ordóñez's tale told of a conquest in which the enemy would quickly and easily be won over to the advantages of a "superior" civilization. The Amazons were seen as lacking any culture or religious values of their own.

The fictional representation of California as pagan, as well as female, hierarchically governed, and easily subdued, reinforced the conquerors' imagined superiority. Fiction provided the parchment upon which reality would be written. The conquerors believed that California's native inhabitants, like Queen Calafia, would be easily converted once they were exposed to Christianity. Marriage (and the racial mixing it legitimated) was the institution that would perpetuate the new social order and keep the converts in line. Queen Calafia eventually converted to Christianity, was married off to a cousin of the hero (as was her sister), and returned with her spouse to live as a peaceful subject of the Crown in a California that she no longer dominated. Her destiny formed a virtual blueprint for the conquest of the New World.

Before the "real" California was even discovered, literature prefigured history in establishing the ideological parameters that would validate the legitimacy of the Spanish conquest. The romances of chivalry and the fictional California's depiction in *Las sergas* naturalized conquest on the basis of a gendered hierarchy. These myths "masculinized" the conquerors and "feminized" those to be conquered. They justified a priori the subjugation of the native inhabitants on the basis of widely accepted Aristotelian notions of natural law that classified males as innately superior to females, whites as superior to blacks, humans as superior to animals, and so on. These myths pitted Spanish beliefs in their own sexual, military, and religious superiority against a "naturally" inferior opponent.

Chivalric romances and golden-age drama likewise codified appropriate gender roles and relations. Although in Spain both sexes could inherit their parents' estates, Spanish law subjected unmarried women to the authority of their fathers, brothers, or closest male relation.[22] In her analysis of a series of Spanish plays that employed an Amazon motif, the literary critic Melveena McKendrick noted that despite variations in the plot and characters, all of the Amazons fall in love with and marry the male enemy in the end, thus undercutting the female rebel's power and reaffirming "a vote of confidence in normal sexual relations."[23] Other literary critics have drawn similar conclusions.[24]

In the context of conquest, the Amazons inverted Spanish notions of appropriate feminine behavior and thus represented a direct challenge to Spanish gender ideologies. The Amazon myth recognized implicitly that gender relations in the New World were potentially unorthodox, and it explicitly affirmed that such differences, particularly regarding female agency, would not be tolerated. The flagrant refusal of the California Amazons in *Las sergas* to accept male dominion—their nurturing of male-devouring griffins, their interaction with men solely for procreation, and the murder of any male children they bore from such interactions—were challenges to the social order that were easily resolved through conquest. The mission of the noble Spanish explorer-hero was to discover these anomalous societies in order to colonize, evangelize, and reestablish male domination over the female infidels. Racial mixing and marriage were arrows in the knight's quiver. The defeat of the Amazons at the hands of the Christians was not only a religious victory but also a triumph that reinforced gender roles and relations as defined by Spanish society.

Such gender ideologies, in turn, served to naturalize conquest. Myth, language, and culture worked hand in hand to reinforce a gender ideology that dictated male domination of women and provided a paradigm for Spanish domination of the indigenous inhabitants discovered in the New World. The language of imperial conquest shared many features with the discourse of sexual conquest (fig. 3). Land was considered to be female and was often depicted and judged as worthy of possession in

Figure 3. In this 1661 map, "Orbis Terrarum Nova et Accuratissima Tabula," the allegory of conquest is portrayed as an endeavor to bring civilization to the New World and to replace the wanton lust and violence of the natives with idyllic relations of harmony between men and women. (From Johannes van Loon, *Klaer Lichtende,* plate 1, 1661; courtesy of the Library of Congress)

terms of its reproductive capacity—its fertility, barrenness, or virginity. Conquest included the male domination of this land and its inhabitants. Early explorers of California wrote of having "intercourse" with or "taking" the natives and "possessing" the land.[25] "Possessing" and re-naming the lands and their peoples were an explicit part of European discovery.[26] Chroniclers imposed new names on each port of call that masked the earlier identity of each location and marked the territory as belonging to Spain. Similarly, by calling all of the native inhabitants "Indians," the Europeans imposed upon them a new identity that obliterated the great diversity that existed among the many groups native to the New World. Most Native American cultures, on the other hand, viewed land not as a commodity to be owned through discovery or possession but as a sacred space or a place of sanctuary. A feminization of the land, when it occurred among indigenous cultures, was based not on a hierarchy justifying male domination but on the regenerative capacity and wholeness of a feminine earth.[27] Land, though it might be labeled virgin or fertile, was not seen as a body to be ruled, owned, tamed, or transformed.

Yet the conquest was not solely a male endeavor, either ideologically or in practice. Throughout the period of exploration and early Spanish colonization, the Virgin Mary, patroness of the Americas and of the Indians, was a major figure in the symbolic repertoire of the conquest. Conquerors distributed among the indigenous people pictures and statues of the Virgin, symbolizing Spanish power and sovereignty over indigenous deities. Explorers pleaded for the Virgin's intercession and protection on their long journeys into the unknown. In their encounters with new peoples, they appropriated the symbol of the Virgin Mary and its many local variations in the service of conquest.[28] The image was believed to attract and reassure the inhabitants. As early as 1512, the Laws of Burgos, the first Spanish legislation to put forth an official Indian policy, required encomenderos on the island of Hispaniola to place "an image of Our Lady" in the churches they built.[29] In sixteenth-century Spain, soldiers and sailors regularly visited the shrine of the Virgin of Guadalupe upon their return from the New World.[30]

The image of the Virgin, like that of the Amazon, underwent transformations as it crossed the Atlantic Ocean to the New World and traveled to New Spain. In 1531, a humble Aztec convert, Juan Diego, was said to have seen a miraculous apparition at Tepayac, just outside Mexico City, of a dark-skinned Virgin of Guadalupe, who left her image on his cloak. The bishop proclaimed the apparition to have been a miracle and agreed to have a basilica built on the hill reportedly indicated for that purpose by the Virgin. Coincidentally, Tepeyac was also a sacred Aztec site where Tonantzin, the Aztec goddess of fertility, was worshipped. Conversions of New Spain's Indian population purportedly skyrocketed. Friar Toribio de Motolinía claimed that some nine million baptisms were performed in the few months that followed.[31] Wills in Mexico reveal that by 1539, devotion to the Mexicanized, dark-skinned, Indianlike Virgin of Guadalupe was widespread.[32]

Sailors on the expedition that "discovered" Alta California in 1542 pleaded for the Virgin's intercession when they faced a violent Pacific storm that separated the fleet and nearly drove the ships into the rocky coast just south of Point Reyes, not far from today's San Francisco Bay. The men promised to make pilgrimages to the Virgin of Guadalupe's shrine in Spain, stark naked, if she would deliver them from destruction.[33] More than two centuries later, the Virgin Mary would be unanimously selected as the patron saint of Spain's first massive colonization effort in California, an effort led by Juan Bautista de Anza in 1775–76.[34] In the nineteenth-century wars of independence with Spain, her image would be transformed from a symbol of Spanish colonial power and authority into a symbol of rebellion and American identity. More studies are needed of the shifting role of Mary in her many manifestations across time and space. Her image has proved to be amazingly resilient as a symbol both in the service of and in resistance to colonial domination.

The popular myth that the Spanish conquest of the Indies was in practice an exclusively male venture carried out by Spanish men has persisted over time, although the notion has been challenged by modern scholarship.[35] At least 30 of the 330 travelers who accompanied Christopher Columbus on his third voyage to the Indies in 1498 were women. The majority of subsequent expeditions appear to have included women.[36] Some, but not all, of these women were wives of the new colonists. Others were Spanish *conversas* of Moorish or Jewish origins, whose presence violated explicit instructions by the Spanish monarchs that prohibited these "new Christians" from settling in the New World.[37] Another group included African and white slaves, with their masters (both male and female).[38] The white female slaves were Spanish Christians who were sent to the New World as potential marriage partners for the Spanish colonists, who the Crown feared might otherwise be tempted to marry Indian women or Spanish conversas.[39]

From the beginning of the sixteenth century, the Spanish Crown required settlers traveling to the New World to be accompanied by their wives, and it encouraged families to settle in the newly discovered lands.[40] Throughout the sixteenth century, it made repeated provisions for wives who were left behind to be reunited in the Indies with their husbands.[41] The Crown believed that the presence of these women would lend stability to the Spanish colony.[42] Spaniards without their wives were believed to provide poor role models for the natives and to prejudice indigenous conversions to Christianity and a "civilized" lifestyle.[43]

Women served in a variety of capacities in the early exploration and settlement of the Spanish colonies. Some served as soldiers who participated in the subjugation of indigenous peoples. A group of Spanish women successfully defended Santiago de Chile when it was attacked by Araucanians; María de Estrada, a soldier's wife, fought on horseback with Cortés's company in Mexico.[44] Isabel Barreto captured a fleet that was sailing from Spain to Manila.[45] In the early sixteenth century, the Spanish-born Catalina de Erauso would flee her convent in Spain and enlist in the Spanish army as a male soldier, gaining fame as the Lieutenant Nun, and marching from Panama to Peru in the service of the Crown.[46] As the men became incapacitated from hunger in the Río de la Plata region, the women took over their tasks. From Asunción, Isabel de Guevara wrote to Spain's Regent Princess Juana, that the men "were so weak that the poor women had to carry everything, as well as wash their clothes, cure them, make them eat . . . clean them up, guard them, [and] keep the fires going."[47]

Other women contributed to the administration of the new territories. María de Toledo, the wife of Diego Colón, served as vicereine of the West Indies during her husband's absence from 1515 to 1520.[48] Isabel Manrique and Aldonza de Villalobos were governors of the Venezuelan island of Margarita; Beatriz de la Cueva governed Guatemala; Juana de Zarate ruled in Chile; Catalina Montejo succeeded her father as ruler of Yucatán.[49]

Relatively little is known, however, about the participation of women in the early expeditions to California. No ship registers have been located for these expeditions, which departed not from Spain but from New Spain. Even if such registers could be located, women's names would not necessarily be found therein, because captains were required only to make note of the "gente sobresaliente," or "outstanding people," on board.[50] Scattered references show that women apparently participated in some of these early expeditions. During an ill-fated expedition to Baja California from May to October 1596, for example, the Spanish captain Sebastián Vizcaíno reportedly "sent the greater part of the men *and all the women* [emphasis mine] back in the *San Francisco* and the launch, while he decided to make another attempt to ascend the gulf."⁵¹ In his report to the king regarding the expedition, Vizcaíno noted that some five months after the ships had departed from Acapulco, the impending winter had caused him to pull in at the port he named La Paz, where he built a fort, dismantled the flagship, and set off to explore the gulf, leaving behind the "people who were married and most burdensome."⁵² The Spanish phrase Vizcaíno used to describe the people who were married, *la gente casada,* is ambiguous and can refer to either men or women or both. Vizcaíno might have left behind only the married husbands, but this seems unlikely considering the earlier reference to men and women. He might have left behind the pregnant women, probably with their husbands. Or he might have left behind couples who had been brought to establish a settlement at La Paz. That the women on board the ships were Indian women seems less likely given the reference that the women were married, though there might have been Christianized Indian couples present who were brought on board as models for subsequent conversion efforts. These references give women (most probably Spanish-speaking women from New Spain) an undefined role in the early exploration of the California coast—perhaps as wives or daughters of the sailors and soldiers or even as prostitutes, laundresses, or cooks.

As the future explorers of California prepared to set sail, their belief in a basic gendered hierarchy of power, codified in the Amazon myth, remained intact. This unspoken paradigm of conquest as a male venture enacted upon a "feminized" population shaped the attitudes of European explorers, their perceptions of what they found, and their interpretations of the realities they encountered.

2

Exploration

Antonio de Mendoza, the first viceroy of New Spain, reached Mexico City in 1535, at the height of Spanish hegemony in the world. The possibilities seemed endless. Amid tales of Amazon women, undiscovered lands of riches (including the fabled kingdom of Quivira and the Seven Cities of Cíbola, presumed to be located in the lands inhabited by New Mexico's Moqui Indians), the Fountain of Youth, the legendary Atlantis, and the strait of Anián (a fabled waterway that was supposed to link the Pacific and Atlantic Oceans), Viceroy Mendoza ordered preparations for a series of expeditions to survey the lands to the north of Mexico City.[1]

Just as the myth of black Amazon women and visions of great wealth first enticed Europeans to explore the Pacific coast, new myths would be established once they encountered the native inhabitants of California. In this chapter I explore the evolution of these myths and the gender and racial ideologies they represented from the mid-sixteenth to the early seventeenth century. To the extent possible, I suggest ways in which the gender ideologies of the indigenous peoples might have influenced their perceptions and interpretations of the arrival of Europeans on their shores.

Perhaps the first myths to be perpetuated about the exploration of California held the two groups of participants—the Spanish conquerors and the indigenous inhabitants—each to be relatively homogenous. Such stories belied a much more complex reality. The vast land to the north of the recently explored Baja California peninsula was peopled not with Amazons but with natives of both sexes of diverse ethnic backgrounds.

In many of the chronicles, Europeans following in Columbus's wake classified the peoples they encountered simply as "Indians," on the mistaken assumption that Columbus had found the Indies. These Indians were usually catalogued in terms of their relationship to the Europeans and might be described as friendly, hostile, wild, or tame. Once missions were established in Alta California, the Indians there were most often described simply as gentiles (unbaptized Indians) or neophytes (baptized Indians who lived at either the mission or nearby *rancherías,* or Indian villages). This nomenclature perpetuated a myth that masked the enormous ethnic, cultural, and social differences among the New World's indigenous inhabitants—estimated to have numbered 25 million in New Spain alone.[2]

Alta California—the region that extended northward indefinitely from the Baja California peninsula to the fabled Strait of Anián and that is largely occupied by present-day California—was inhabited by indigenous people believed to have numbered in the vicinity of 310,000 in 1770, the earliest year for which any aggregate data are available.[3] Alta California was purported to be the most densely settled land in all of northern New Spain. Its native inhabitants collectively spoke more than 120 languages, over 70 percent of which were mutually unintelligible.[4] Indigenous cultures were as varied as the geography of the region. Native peoples lived in villages scattered along the coasts and in mountain valleys, foothills, high mountains, marshlands, redwood and pine forests, grasslands, savannahs, and open desert. Some dwelled in complete isolation; others merged with neighboring groups of different languages.

The background of the so-called Spanish conquistadores, while not quite so diverse as that of the indigenous population, was far from homogeneous, although all were generally called *gente de razón,* a term meaning "people of reason" that referred to Spanish-speaking Christians.[5] Though many of the conquerors were Spanish, exploring parties were generally assembled in the New World itself and often included Christianized Indians and people of mixed racial descent from Mexico and, later, Baja California. They also took on experienced navigators and soldiers from various regions of Spain as well as from other parts of the Old World, especially Portugal, which had a long tradition of maritime exploration beginning in the late fourteenth century under Prince Henry. To an extent that has yet to be fully documented, women, too, participated in at least some of these early expeditions.

With the chronicles of the first expeditions to Alta California, we find the elaboration of new myths about the relationship of the conquerors and the natives. These contain echoes of the gendered paradigm of conquest seen in the myth of the Amazons in that the chroniclers hold as unquestionably legitimate the power relationship codified in the male domination of a "feminized" land and its population. Obviously, the indigenous populations included both males and females, and as eighteenth-century chroniclers later noted, third genders as well. Yet gender ideologies in this initial phase provided invisible threads that legitimated the dominion of one culture over others. An attentiveness to different gendered responses on the part of the indigenous groups in the first encounters also suggests the particular vulnerability of women to conquest.

On June 27, 1542, a Portuguese navigator, a Spanish and an Italian pilot, two masters (presumed to be from Spain and Portugal, respectively), and a crew of unknown size set sail in two ships from Navidad, in the province of Colima on the west coast of New Spain. Despite their varied backgrounds, the voyagers were united as subjects in the service of the Spanish Crown. Although the original log of Captain Juan Rodríguez Cabrillo (below I bow to the popular usage of Cabrillo's name) has since been lost, a lengthy summary of the document made by one of his contemporaries, probably Juan Páez, is extant.[6] It describes the voyage of the two ships, the *San Salvador* and the *Victoria,* past the bleak sandscape of the lower California peninsula, where Cabrillo constantly searched for signs of indigenous life, probably at the request of the viceroy. After two months without a sign of humanity, the interior landscape suddenly gave way to more fertile valleys, dotted with trees, which hosted a large indigenous population. The ships weighed anchor at a nearby harbor, took possession of this more fertile land, and named the harbor "Puerto de la Posesión," now San Quintín.

Indians from the island who were fishing nearby fled at the sight of the ships, but not before the explorers seized one of them, plied him with trinkets, and released him. When the explorers saw wisps of smoke wafting to the sky, they rowed ashore and found some thirty more Indians. Of these, they brought a young boy and two Indian women on board their ship and gave them trinkets and clothing before releasing them. Sign language failed to establish any communication between the hostages and their captors. Although his descriptions of the Indians were markedly sketchy, Cabrillo's scribe repeatedly used the adjective *quedos,* meaning "quiet," to describe the Indians.

As the voyagers sailed up the coast of Baja California, they found more groups of Indians, including some who appeared to be "de ra-zón," or Christianized. These Indians explained by signs that other men—bearded, armed with crossbows and swords, and accompanied by dogs—were killing Indians in the lands to the east. The explorers headed north, giving names to inhabited and uninhabited places alike and taking possession of the populated zones. On September 28, the two ships anchored in a protected harbor that Cabrillo called San Miguel and that has been identified as today's San Diego Bay.[7] Cabrillo's ships had entered the waters of Alta California, the first European vessels ever known to do so.[8]

Cabrillo's scribe highlighted the fear that the Indians of San Miguel conveyed toward the explorers. He noted that all but three of the Indians fled when the ships anchored in the bay there. That evening, some Indians began to shoot arrows at the explorers as they were fishing, injuring three of them. The narrator did not dwell on this sign of resistance to the European presence but moved quickly to the next morning, when the explorers picked up two boys, gave them each a shirt, and sent them away. He again noted the fear expressed by three large native men who let the explorers know by signs that other bearded and armed men had killed many Indians. Cabrillo, or his interlocutor, did not venture a guess as to the identity of these other explorers, but they were most likely the men accompanying Francisco Vázquez de Coronado. Coronado and some three hundred soldiers and Mexican Indians had left Mexico in 1540 to search for the Seven Cities of Cíbola.[9] A later investigation into that expedition revealed that the Spaniards had "perpetrated robberies, burnings, cruelties, and many other offenses against the native Indians of the lands through which they passed, killing a large number of them, taking their women by force and against their will and that of their husbands and parents," and "lying with them [the women] carnally."[10]

Reports of such abuse of indigenous women likely account for differences in the way Indian men and women greeted the Spaniards in Alta California. Women were sexually vulnerable to the conquerors in a way that their male counterparts were not. Royal orders issued to explorers traveling in the name of the Spanish Crown document continued concern over the abuse of Native American women.[11] The captains of sailing vessels were formally held liable for the behavior of their crews, and royal instructions sometimes explicitly required them to protect public morality.[12]

Sexual conquest, however, was often assumed to be part and parcel of imperial conquest. Cabrillo undoubtedly laid claim to what he believed to be his just rewards. A few years before he traveled to Alta California, Cabrillo had served as a shipbuilder on an expedition to Guatemala under *mayordomo* (administrator) Alvaro de Paz. Bartolomé de las Casas wrote that while in the seaport village of Iztapa, Guatemala, Cabrillo and Paz sent out conscripted press gangs to round up dozens of Indian women and girls to serve the men as bed companions, cooks, and laundresses. Other representatives of the Crown were granted land and allotments of Indians under the encomienda system for helping Pedro de Alvarado conquer the Quiché Indians in Ututlán, the Cakchiquels in Iximché, and the inhabitants of the Tzutuhil capital, Atitlán. Alvarado seized the wife of the Cakchiquel king; Cabrillo took an Indian wife with whom he lived for several years and who bore him at least three daughters. He was reported to have fathered children by other Indian women as well. In 1539, Guatemala's Bishop Francisco Marroquín vehemently protested the sexual activities of Paz and Cabrillo to the Crown.[13]

In this context, it is not surprising that the summary of Cabrillo's log shows that on various occasions Cabrillo recorded seeing women flee as the ships approached.[14] A fearful reaction, if that is what Cabrillo's arrival provoked, would have been a perfectly appropriate response. To single out one occasion in particular, the summary of Cabrillo's log shows that on October 3, Cabrillo and his crew departed from San Miguel; after sailing for four days along a coast characterized by stretches of valleys and plains in the foreground with high mountains rising behind them to the interior, they reached two well-populated islands, which they named San Salvador and Vitoria Islands (now known as the Santa Catalina and San Clemente Islands). The chronicler noted that "a great number of Indians" came out to meet them, shouting and signaling them to land.[15] The Indian women were fleeing, however, and the explorers tried to reassure them. The Indian men put down their bows and arrows and paddled their canoes out to meet the Spanish boats. After giving the Indian men some trinkets, the Europeans pulled ashore, and, the chronicler noted, all the Indians and the women felt safe and secure.

Notably, little of the subsequent historiography mentions the different receptions accorded to the Europeans by women and men in the Santa Catalina Islands. The account of Cabrillo's voyage by the Spanish historian Antonio de Herrera completely overlooked the encounter there; Herrera jumped from September 14 to October 10 with no mention of Cabrillo's anchoring in San Miguel or of the channel islands just to the north.[16] The nineteenth-century historian Alexander Taylor noted that the Indians were greatly alarmed at the appearance of the Spanish ships but were friendly after Cabrillo's prudent treatment.[17] Hubert Bancroft mentioned that Cabrillo and his crew landed on one of the islands, probably Santa Catalina, "after the inhabitants, timid and even hostile at first, [had] been appeased by signs and [had] come off in a canoe to receive gifts."[18] Twentieth-century historians have likewise ignored the different receptions accorded by male and female Indians to the explorers. Charles Chapman noted that the Indians of San Miguel were "greatly terrified" by reports that Spaniards were killing natives to the east, and "here as elsewhere Rodríguez made gifts to the Indians, and gave them no occasion for terror or resentment."[19] He mentioned Catalina Island only in passing. Harry Kelsey justified the Indians' fearful reaction as a sign that they were aware that bearded men dressed in similar fashion had killed many natives.[20]

These historians, who failed to perceive the presence of women in the early encounters, also failed to recognize the role California Indian women sometimes played in defining how the Spaniards would be received. The organization of ceremonies and the distribution of food, often the responsibilities of women, were key elements in determining the nature of relationships outside the confines of indigenous communities.[21] On November 2, for example, Cabrillo and his crew were feted in grand style at the invitation of the elderly female chief of the province of Cicacut, near Point Concepción at the northwest entrance to the Santa Barbara Channel. The chief had called together more than sixteen Chumash Indian villages—Ciucut, Anacot, Maquinanoa, Paltatre, Anacoac, Olesino, Caacac, Paltocac, Tocane, Opia, Opistopia, Nocos, Yutum, Quiman, Micoma, and Garomisopona—to welcome them. After a few days of festivities, in which Indian musicians played their pipes and reeds and European sailors played bagpipes and tambourines, the female chief came aboard the flagship, wrote Cabrillo's interlocutor, where she and many others stayed for two nights.[22]

Subsequent historians have distorted this encounter and disregarded the female chief's position of leadership. The seventeenth-century Spanish historian Herrera noted without reference to gender that the chiefs near Puerto de Sardinas came on board while the sailors replenished their wood and water supply.[23] Two centuries later, Bancroft slighted the woman's power by a passing reference to her age. He noted that the crew anchored at Cicacut, which was "ruled by an old woman who [passed] two nights on one of the vessels."[24] In the early twentieth century, Chapman found nothing worthy of note between October 25 and November 23 besides the storms endured by the explorers.[25] Two decades later, the historian Henry Wagner went to great lengths to "correct" the original chronicler's version of the encounter, which noted that the seamen were "unable to avail themselves of the Indians who came on board with water and fish and displayed great love."[26] In his translation of the original document, Wagner assumed that the author had left out a "no" and claimed that the original Spanish was "a quite absurd statement."[27] His translation "corrected" the original and asserted that the men "*were* able to avail themselves" of the Indians. Yet if we assume the presence of both male and female Indians, the sentence makes perfect sense in its original form and renders Wagner's correction unwarranted. Most likely Cabrillo's log reported the presence on the ship of both male Chumash Indians, who supplied fish, and female Chumash, who supplied water. The chronicler might also have been implying that the Indians did not allow Cabrillo and his crew to take advantage (sexually or otherwise) of the Indian women who came on board.

If the Europeans and subsequent Western historians found it difficult to fathom an alternative gender structure among the Indians, imagine how the Chumash must have reacted to Cabrillo and his crew, who were engaged in tasks (namely, gathering water and wood for the ship) presumed by the Chumash to be exclusively "female."[28] The contrast between indigenous gender roles and those of the newcomers must have been startling for both sides.

On the eve of the seventeenth century, another wave of explorers, led by the Spanish *adelantado,* or merchant-adventurer, Captain Sebastián Vizcaíno, arrived on the California coast.[29] Nearly two hundred men were on board in search of a port between Acapulco and Manila where the galleons could stop for repairs. The chroniclers of the Vizcaíno expedition of 1602–3, Captain Sebastián Vizcaíno himself and Father Antonio de la Ascensión, underscored the docility and generosity of the Alta California Indians, particularly the females.[30] Even more than the sixteenth-century voyagers who participated in the Cabrillo expeditions, these men were interested in the inhabitants and their potential as converts. Vizcaíno was especially impressed by the generosity and friendliness of the inhabitants of the area surrounding the bay at Monterey in northern California. That site offered excellent prospects as a station for ships returning from the Philippines—abundant trees for repairing and building ships, a port safe from winds, and abundant sweet water.[31] Vizcaíno informed the king that the "peaceable and docile" disposition of the natives meant they could "be brought readily within the fold of the holy gospel and into subjection to the crown of your majesty."[32] He also observed the affection for the Virgin demonstrated by the Ohlone inhabitants of the Monterey region. He noted that the natives there "were much taken with the image of Our Lady that I showed them." His crew was received "with signs of friendship" by Indians who were "desirous of trade."

Vizcaíno's indication that the Indians were "desirous of trade" might have accounted for their particular attentiveness to the Catholic symbols and ceremonies, yet the conquerors' depiction of the Virgin as having the power to attract and pacify the Indians is intriguing. The figure of Mary, a nonthreatening, Christian symbol of docility, gentleness, and purity, provided the conqueror with a metaphor for the purity of his mission and a role model of submissiveness for those he would conquer.

During the sixteenth and early seventeenth centuries, European chroniclers of California exploration, following in the steps of earlier explorers of the New World, emphasized the natives' nonthreatening characteristics.[33] Such characterizations must not be taken at face value, however, because chroniclers recorded not only what they observed but also what they expected and hoped to observe at a given moment in time. Perhaps the California natives seemed gentle in comparison with popular culture's depiction of California as a land of aggressive female warriors. Perhaps early explorers hoped that by depicting the Indians as docile and hospitable, they could induce the Spanish Crown to back further efforts to explore and evangelize California.

Father Antonio de la Ascensión, one of three Carmelite friars who accompanied Vizcaíno, served as diarist for the expedition; he expressed amazement at the docility of the Indians. He described the "familiarity, friendship and affability" of the Santa Catalina Indians the voyagers encountered as they made their way north from Acapulco along the Pacific coast.[34] The Indians showed themselves to be "friendly and tame," displayed curiosity about Christian rituals, and seemed predisposed to convert.[35] "When they saw the soldiers praying with their rosary beads, they approached and asked to do the same," recalled Father Antonio.[36]

Ascensión recounted that on November 10, 1602, just outside San Diego Bay, a troop of Indians with their bodies covered in black and white paint approached, brandishing bows and arrows. Seeing the Spaniards prepare their weapons, the Indians retreated to a small hill and then sent what Ascensión described as "two very old, wrinkled women (who had more blotches on their bellies than the sack of a mule-driver)" out to meet the Spaniards.[37] The Spaniards gave these women gifts of abalone beads and biscuits, and the women returned to the Indians on the nearby hill. After showing the newly acquired gifts to the other Indians, the women encouraged their associates to go meet the Spaniards.

As in the mid-sixteenth century, female Chumash Indians on the coast of the southern part of Alta California appeared to set the tone for the reception of the seafarers. At the Santa Catalina Islands, the chroniclers noted that Indian women, children, and men received the Spanish ships with much rejoicing.[38] While the chroniclers avoided direct mention of female indigenous leadership such as that depicted by Cabrillo, one wonders whether the elderly women mentioned in Ascensión's account might have been Chumash leaders, perhaps even related to the woman who ruled the province of Cicacut during Cabrillo's expedition sixty years earlier.

During the exploration phase, conquerors underscored different attitudes toward sexuality both to set themselves apart from the Indians and to illustrate the moral superiority of Indian women over their male counterparts. Dress, or lack thereof, was one arena in which this differentiation was most noted. While Indian men went naked without shame, wrote Ascensión, women covered their flesh with the skins of lions, tigers, deer, and seals, and they were described as being more modest (*honestas*) and extremely fertile.[39]

Father Antonio de la Ascensión's description of the first encounter between the Chumash Indians who occupied the Santa Catalina Islands northwest of San Diego and the Spanish *general*, Vizcaíno, illustrates the role of sexuality in Spanish conquest ideology. Ascensión was the first of many chroniclers of California to represent the generosity of America's indigenous inhabitants as a willingness of the Indian men to share not only provisions but also Indian women with their European visitors. Father Antonio noted in his journal that the indigenous leader of the islands, having been informed of the arrival of the Spaniards, came to offer his land to the Spanish general. The Chumash Indian leader, according to Ascensión, pleaded for the visitors to come ashore, so that he might fulfill their needs. Father Antonio observed that the Indian chief saw no women on their ship and so asked him if they had brought any women with them, "pointing to his private parts and giving us clearly to understand what he meant." Ascensión continued, "The *General* told him he did not have any [women], nor were they necessary. The Indian then importuned the *General* with more energy for all to go ashore, promising to give each one ten women to serve them and please them. This caused us all to laugh very much. The chief, who understood that we were making fun of him, and that we thought he would not do what he promised, renewed his offers."[40]

The priest's interpretation of the encounter tells us as much about the conquerors' attitudes toward conquest and women as it does about what actually occurred. The Spaniards did not criticize the chief's offer as a sign of barbarity but interpreted it as a sign of friendship, suggesting perhaps a perceived commonality of patriarchal power relations between the cultures. The narrative illustrates that conquest was seen as a strictly male endeavor that countenanced the presence of females only in a tangential, subservient, and sexual way. The Indians saw no women among the Spaniards, and Vizcaíno confirmed the absence of women on the ship. In the telling, the priest depicted the Indian women as a commodity to be distributed by the Indian chief for the personal use of the conquerors.

Fray Antonio clearly believed this anecdote to be of some significance, for he repeated the chief's offer in a later summary report.[41] Struck by the large numbers of Indians they found on the California coast, Ascensión wrote in his summary report that the land was so populated that the chief "offered through gestures to give each one ten women if everyone would go to his land."[42] The chief's gesture, suggested the friar, was a sign of the fertility of the natives and "evidence of how populated the whole land is."[43] The friar's representation anticipated the possibility of peaceful relations with such friendly natives and suggested an environment that would favor Spanish colonization and evangelization.

Yet Father Antonio may have completely misinterpreted the natives, particularly given the exclusive use of signs for communication and the different gender ideologies of each culture. Perhaps the Chumash chief was asking why a group of men was traveling so far from home with no female companions. Maybe he was asking how this strange tribe reproduced itself without women. Perhaps he wanted to know where the women leaders were, or he was merely curious about the unfamiliar clothing covering the visitors' "private parts."

Historians have generally accepted Ascensión's tale at face value.[44] However, the denouement of the encounter and some of the contradictions within and between the narratives suggest that conflicting gender ideologies influenced mutual expectations and that the priest's portrayal was either an invention, an embellishment, or a misrepresentation of the encounter. First, according to Father Antonio, the Spaniards held a special council meeting in which they decided to take advantage of the chief's offer; no record of such a meeting exists among the records of the ship's council meetings.[45] Second, Ascensión's full report and his separate summary report give conflicting reasons for the voyagers' sudden departure before the chief returned with the women. According to Ascensión's full report, the visitors decided to postpone the interchange until the return trip, due to changing weather conditions including a favorable southeast wind, "one they had not enjoyed before in all the time they had been sailing."[46] Ascensión's later summary of the trip, however, mentioned nothing of the opportune breezes but attributed the voyagers' precipitous departure to their inability to find an adequate port.[47] Ascensión's full report was more forthcoming in mentioning the rationale for the offer of women, namely "to serve and please" the conquerors, whereas his summary report was more discreet.

The natives' behavior toward the explorers on the ship's return seems inconsistent with their earlier generosity. On their return, Vizcaíno was dissuaded by members of his council on the flagship from stopping at the Santa Catalina Islands, where the Chumash chief had reportedly extended his offer of hospitality. Council members underscored the wretched condition of the seafarers. They argued that Vizcaíno "had no men to furl the sails nor weigh the anchors at time of departure, that the men were dying at a great rate and that if what they wished was done they would all finish there."[48] The harsh voyage had taken its toll on the group, which had lost more than forty-two men by the time it returned to Acapulco.[49] Vizcaíno agreed to abandon his plans to stop on the return. After the ship passed the Santa Catalina Islands, however, three canoes of Indians caught up with it. The Indians then boarded the ship and presented its occupants with many gifts, including sealskins. When the other passengers went to sleep that night, the Indians "perpetrated a remarkable robbery with great cunning and sagacity."[50] Caught with the stolen goods in the morning, the Indians returned to their islands "abashed and ashamed," and the ship continued its voyage.[51] Such behavior is clearly at odds with the generous hospitality of the Indians described by Ascensión during their first encounter, and it suggests that the Spaniards might have misunderstood the chief's offer and its meaning.

Regardless of its veracity, the tale of indigenous generosity with women served an important political function. Spain, enthralled with its military victories around the globe in the sixteenth century, had become heavily indebted, and King Philip II's death in 1598 marked the beginning of a severe economic decline. Ascensión's narrative reinforced not only the notion of the divine mission of the Catholic monarchs to continue to evangelize the New World but also their moral obligation to do so. The parable inherently underscored the moral superiority of the European explorers over the natives.

Race was not the critical variable in the creation of this moral hierarchy. According to Father Antonio, the Indians on the Santa Catalina Islands were "well featured and well built, of good countenance and eyes and modest in their looks and behavior. The boys and girls are white and blonde, and all are affable and smiling."[52] The account of white, blond, European-looking Indians on the Santa Catalina Islands was echoed in Vizcaíno's writings about the Indians of the Monterey Bay region farther north. Vizcaíno described the Indians there as white complexioned and pleasant-looking.[53]

These descriptions of "white" Indians are puzzling. Were these Indians the offspring of earlier explorers? In the mid-sixteenth century, Cabrillo had mentioned his contact with the indigenous groups headed by the female chief near the Santa Catalina Islands. That some white-looking children and grandchildren of mixed racial backgrounds might have been produced by that encounter does not explain the presence of "white" Indians in northern California's Monterey area. The record of landings in Monterey Bay is sketchy and controversial. No explorers prior to Vizcaíno are known with certainty to have reached the Monterey region. Some contend that Cabrillo sighted Monterey Bay in 1542.[54] Only four additional sightings or landings were noted prior to Vizcaíno's landing there in 1602–3. Sir Francis Drake, the English pirate, or privateer, reportedly made an emergency landing in 1579 on the California coast to repair the *Golden Hind,* but there is no record that he came near Monterey Bay.[55] In 1584, Francisco de Gali's Philippine ship inadvertently sighted a "very high and fair land, with many trees and wholly without snow" on its return to Acapulco from Macao (Macau).[56] In 1587, Pedro de Unamuno landed on the California coast in a bay suggested by some to be Monterey but more likely San Luis Obispo.[57] The Portuguese *adelantado* Sebastián Rodríguez Cermeño, likewise coming from the Philippines, was charged by the Spanish

Crown with finding a port of call on the California coast for the Manila galleon; he ran aground near today's Point Reyes in 1595 and discovered what was probably Monterey Bay.[58]

Barring the unlikely possibility that these tribes of "white" Indians were children of some of the European explorers on these expeditions, such descriptions completely subvert present-day understandings of racial categories and suggest that in early California, racial categories were even more fluid and less established than has been imagined. In the California chronicles, there appears to be a direct correlation between the phenotypical whiteness of the native women and how attractive the European chroniclers judged them to be, suggesting that these "whiter" Indians were seen as more desirable mates. In this early phase of exploration, the Spanish desire to form sexual relationships with Indian women and the desire for further exploration of the coast served as prisms that "whitened" indigenous females.[59] In desiring the women, the explorers might have been consciously or unconsciously inventing the whiteness of the Indians in an effort to legitimate intimate relations with native women. Alternatively, if the expectation of these early explorers was to find a country of black Amazons, perhaps the phenotypical descriptor "white" was used to underscore the incongruity between myth and reality.

In Ascensión's narrative, the superiority of the conquerors over the natives rested not on racial characteristics, phenotypical appearances, or even religious differences but primarily on the attitudes (or perceived attitudes) of each group toward gender. First, the explorers used gender relations as an arena in which to establish their superiority. The Spaniards claimed that they did not have or need any women, and they purportedly laughed at their host's offer. Second, Ascensión's account depicted the natives' behavior toward and treatment of indigenous women in a way that asserted the moral imperative of the conquest of the California Indians. While on the surface the sharing of women was portrayed as a gesture of friendship and abundance, the notion that Indian men shared "their" women with strangers, like the treatment dispensed by the mythic Amazons toward "their" men, would have challenged Spanish moral codes of honor at the time. The implied corollary, to be seen in the later mission period, was that Indian women would be better off at the missions than in their own indigenous communities. Such images justified both the conquest in general terms and the rigid sexual discipline imposed on the natives as a form of control at the eighteenth-century California missions. Finally, chronicles of the Indians' generosity with women created an allegory that transformed Spanish sexual violence against indigenous females into compliance with the native males' desires. To narrate that the Indians wanted to share their women with the conquerors neutralized such intercourse, absolved the conquerors of any violations against indigenous women, and established an allegory about the plentitude that America had to offer the Spaniards. This allegory of abundance fueled the expectations of future conquerors and established that the natural rights of conquerors included sexual relations with female Indians.

Ascensión's narrative veiled the more problematical aspects of gender relations between the Spaniards and the Chumash Indians they encountered, encoding them in a tale about indigenous generosity. In the short account of his voyage, Fray Antonio recognized the particular vulnerability faced by women in the conquest enterprise when he wrote to the king asking him not to let women come on future expeditions, "in order to prevent offenses against God, and repulsion between some and others."[60] Fray Antonio advised the king to pacify immediately any encounters "which ordinarily occur in such similar enterprises" and to use discretion in order to prevent "discontent, unpleasantness, enmity, riots, uprisings, or disobedience."[61] His counsel of discretion underscored the silences that ordinarily surrounded such problematical encounters. During the early years of exploration, indigenous groups along California's extensive coastline reacted differently to the arrival of Europeans on their shores. These reactions varied by group and sometimes by gender. The chronicles of the Cabrillo expedition of 1542 and the Vizcaíno voyage in 1602–3 show that indigenous women were present and in some places held important leadership roles within their societies. Yet the gender ideologies of the chroniclers, like those of subsequent generations of historians, rarely permitted these indigenous women to be presented as historical agents. Instead, they transformed the women of Alta California from fierce black Amazons into beckoning "white" Indian women yet to be subdued. These evolving myths set the stage for the next phase of conquest—the establishment of missions and presidios.

3

Evangelization

Black Amazon queens and white Indian women notwithstanding, Spain showed little interest in Alta California following Vizcaino's 1602 expedition. It was not until the 1760s, when Spanish authorities became alarmed by rumors of encroachment by the British, Russians, Dutch, and French, that they turned their attention to the Pacific coast.[1] The English occupation of Havana and Manila in 1762 had served as a vivid reminder of the vulnerability of Spain's American colonies. Russian exploration of the Alaska coast, frequent from 1741 to 1765, seemed more threatening than ever. Heightened fear that foreign incursions would result in the establishment of footholds in northern California from which New Spain could be further attacked prompted Spain's Bourbon king Charles III (1716–88) to act. In 1768, he issued orders to New Spain's viceroy, Carlos Francisco de Croix, Marqués de Croix, for the occupation and fortification of outposts at San Diego and Monterey. Croix, in turn, entrusted José de Gálvez with this task. Gálvez, who had arrived in Mexico in 1765 as visitor-general of New Spain, was a member of the Council of the Indies, the governmental body responsible for the administration of Spain's colonies in the New World, and subsequently minister of state. In keeping with Bourbon reform efforts, Gálvez was charged with reviewing and restructuring the defense and administration of the American colonies.[2] Gálvez is generally credited with initiating Spain's first colonization program for Alta California.[3]

The presence of a stable population base was indispensable to Spain's defensive needs; thus issues of gender and reproduction figured in the Crown's calculations. Gálvez's twofold colonization program aimed to secure the allegiance of the indigenous populations already in California by congregating them into missions for evangelization and to support migration to and procreation of *gente de razón* in Alta California. Gálvez eyed the large indigenous populations living in Alta California with anticipation, hopeful that their transformation into Hispanicized Catholics would complement other colonization efforts to secure Spain's northernmost territory. To this end, Gálvez proposed the establishment of the first missions and presidios in Alta California.

In accordance with Spanish tradition, military men and missionaries would join forces in subjugating the natives of Alta California. The missions, which had long since replaced the encomienda as the conquest institution of choice, would be the Crown's primary instrument for this control, and military guards at the missions, as well as in separate forts, would reinforce missionary efforts. Yet contradictions over the sometimes loose relations between Spanish soldiers and Indian women, on the one hand, and the friars' desire to win over the indigenous population peacefully, on the other, often caused the ostensible allies to collide.

Declining indigenous populations in the sixteenth century had made it necessary for the colonists to reorganize the surviving Indians into larger communities in order to extract labor and tribute and to facilitate evangelization efforts. Like the *reducción* and *congregación* missions cultivated by the Jesuits since the late sixteenth century in South America and Baja California, the Franciscan-established missions in late-eighteenth-century Alta California relocated Indians, forcibly if necessary, into new settlements under missionary administration. These mission communities were temporary agrarian institutions where the Indians would be taught the elements of good citizenship as well as Christian doctrine. As in the other Spanish colonies, initial plans called for the missions to operate for as long as it took to "civilize" the Indians—an estimated ten years. In theory, the missions were to be turned over to the administration of secular parish priests at the end of that time, and the mission land, stock, and herds given over to the Indian converts, who would then form pueblos, albeit still separate from the Spanish population and without full civil rights.[4] In practice, however, it took much longer for the California missions to be secularized, and the timing depended more on colonization plans than on the readiness of the

Indians. Secularization of the Alta California missions was decreed in 1833, and over the next sixteen years the missions were gradually released from church control and the province was opened to private ownership of land.

The Franciscan missions in Alta California differed from other evangelization models and showed variation as civil and religious authorities responded over time to changing social, political, and economic conditions. The Indians of Alta California were not as highly organized as groups of central Mexico. With the exception of indigenous groups living on the fertile floodplains of the Colorado River to the south—who practiced both rudimentary agriculture and hunting and gathering and who functioned as political "nations" in warfare—most Indians of Alta California lived in dispersed communities whose political and social structures were organized loosely around villages or tribelets.[5] Most of these groups obtained their subsistence through hunting, gathering, and fishing; they enjoyed a plenitude of food resources and had no fixed residences that would allow for easy exploitation or evangelization. Gender roles and relations varied throughout California. Although a uniformly rigid division of labor did not develop in California, in many groups, hunting and fishing were considered primarily a man's work, gathering and preparation of foodstuffs were mainly women's work, and both sexes participated in collecting wood and water.[6]

In comparison with the Jesuit missions in Baja California, the Franciscan missions were founded at a time of relative decline of church influence vis-à-vis the state. As the Bourbons sought greater control over the church in the Indies, the influential Jesuit order came under fire. Until 1767, when the Jesuits were summarily expelled from Spanish America, Franciscans, Dominicans, and Jesuits had shared jurisdiction for the evangelization of the Californias. After their expulsion, a new line of demarcation was established a few miles south of the current border between Baja California and Alta California. The Dominicans would take control of the missions in Baja California, and the Franciscans of the College of San Fernando were charged with the dual task of converting the Alta California natives to the Catholic faith and transforming them into loyal and industrious Spanish subjects.

Supreme authority rested with the Crown under the *patronato real.*

The king or his representatives appointed and paid all church authorities and functionaries, built the churches, and oversaw church policies. In return, the missionaries acted as royal agents who accompanied the troops in the conquest.

There are some indications that the Franciscans were initially reluctant to accept the terms dictated by Gálvez for the evangelization of Alta California. Father Rafael Verger, newly elected head of the College of San Fernando in Mexico City, objected to the founding of so many missions at once. He wrote: "If the friars have been sent, it was under compulsion; for we cannot resist him who, without admitting either supplications or protests, commands us with absolute power."[7] Some opposed taking the missionaries' transportation expenses from the Pious Fund, Jesuit monies put aside since the end of the seventeenth century solely for establishing missions in California.[8] Some Franciscans objected that the timing of the 1769 expeditions responded more to political expediency than to spiritual concerns. Finally, Verger noted that the gap between what was expected and what was possible was too wide. The king was to appropriate $1,000 per mission, out of which the friars would be held responsible for the mission's expenses. This sum was supposed to cover the costs of church goods, construction, furniture, tools, cooking utensils, and food supplies, as well as daily rations for any Indians who might come to the missions.[9] The Crown would pay each missionary an annual stipend of $400, and other missions would donate grain and livestock to the new missions.

Whereas the rector of the Jesuit missions had headed the religious, military, and political establishments in Baja California, the Franciscan father-president of the Alta California missions would have authority only in spiritual affairs, and a governor would preside over all military and political questions.[10] This new arrangement left room for many disputes over jurisdictional questions between the military, church, and civilian authorities who would oversee the three major colonial institutions in Spanish California—the mission, the presidio, and the pueblo. As we will see, at times these disputes concerned infractions committed by Spanish soldiers against indigenous women. At other times they arose from questions about who controlled indigenous labor, reimbursement for labor, the availability of priests to service the presidios or pueblos, and so forth.

Presidios, or garrisons, were founded at San Diego (1769), Monterey (1770), San Francisco (1776), and Santa Barbara (1782). Many of the earliest soldiers assigned to Alta California were seasoned Indian fighters from the middle and lower social classes of Mexico and Baja California who had been chosen for their prior experience at presidios along the northern frontiers of New Spain.[11] Others belonged to a regiment of volunteers from Catalonia. About half of the soldiers were assigned to individual missions as bodyguards; the remainder would live at the presidios or, after 1794, in nearby presidial towns. During the entire Spanish period, the military presence would not surpass four hundred men, distributed among four presidios and twenty-one missions.[12]

In 1769, military and religious officials launched the so-called sacred expedition to establish the first of California's missions and presidios, the institutional vanguards of conquest. The Crown's orders to the leaders of the 1769 expedition illustrate both the centrality and the delicacy of gender relations on the frontier. They included specific instructions regarding gender relations. The first order of the day, Gálvez wrote to Lieutenant Pedro Fages, was that "no one offend the Indian women or the other Inhabitants without express orders from the Commanders, or unless they are insulted first."[13] Anyone doing so, Gálvez wrote, would be punished with the greatest severity. In his orders to Captain Vicente Vila, commander of the frigate *San Carlos,* Gálvez reiterated the need for "the strictest discipline."[14] Gálvez reminded the officers that an offense against Indian women was "never forgotten by the Inhabitants of the North of this Peninsula."[15] Gálvez's instructions to Governor Portolá were even more pointed. He urged Portolá to punish any molestations or violence toward the native women "as for an irremissible crime."[16] Gálvez noted that, in addition to such excesses being "offenses against God," they could easily endanger the success of the expedition itself.[17]

By most contemporary accounts of the expedition, early relations with the native inhabitants of Alta California were benign, although later chroniclers suggest otherwise. During the 1769 expedition, as during previous explorations, the chroniclers emphasized the docility and passivity of the indigenous groups they encountered. Father Serra wrote in a letter to Francisco Palou that the Indians were "extremely affable."[18] Portolá recorded in his diary that the natives "seem docile."[19] In only one instance, he noted, did the Indians fail to give them a warm welcome; he attributed their unusual behavior to the fact that they had been given no glass beads.[20] Miguel Costansó, an engineer and cartographer with the Portolá expedition, was equally sanguine. He noted that the Indians' "good nature has given the Reverend Missionary Fathers well-founded Reason to hope to Win them over shortly to the Faith of Christ."[21]

The Spaniards reported that they were supplied with food by the natives. Gaspar de Portolá noted that the Alta California Indians gave the Spaniards fish, grain, nuts, acorns, and seeds. Father Junípero Serra observed that the Spaniards were presented with food by the natives in the area around San Diego.[22] Likewise, Fathers Antonio Rodríguez and Luis Antonio Martínez wrote that the Chumash people who lived in the region where the San Luis Obispo mission was established in 1772 initially maintained the first fathers and those who accompanied them "by means of wild seeds which they had secured for their own use."[23]

Yet the representations of indigenous generosity and affability, although clearly serving the conquerors' needs and interests, cannot be taken at face value. Gifts of food and provisions, or other forms of cooperation with the visitors, although interpreted by the foreigners as a sign of welcome, did not necessarily have the same meaning for the indigenous peoples. Nor did the gifts necessarily reflect the natives' docility. Their generosity toward the Spaniards might have been motivated by fear rather than delight at the Spaniards' presence. The anthropologist Florence C. Shipek found that the Kumeyaay Indians in the San Diego region were skeptical of the newcomers and initially viewed the priests as "constantly stealing, thieves of the worst sort, but also as very powerful witches who must be placated."[24] The Spanish representation of the docility of indigenous groups in Alta California reinforced the Spanish view of the Indians' submissive role vis-à-vis the conquerors, the propriety of Spanish subjugation, and the Spaniards' hope that the Indians would not resist Spanish colonization efforts. By highlighting the openness and receptivity of the Indians to the newcomers, these chroniclers rationalized the imposition of a foreign culture on a people thought to be without a culture of their own.

After establishing the first mission at San Diego, members of the "sacred" expedition divided into two parties and advanced north by land and by sea until they finally located the port of Monterey, where Father Antonio de la Ascensión had celebrated mass some 172 years earlier.[25] Gaspar de Portolá, a Catalán who had served until then as governor of Baja California, and Father Junípero Serra, a Majorcan-born Franciscan who served as president of the California missions from 1768 to 1784, presided over the possession ceremonies. On June 3, 1770, they gathered for mass before a hastily constructed altar adorned with an image of the Virgin.[26] As the congregation prayed to the Virgin, Portolá raised the royal banners and the cross, yanked plants from the earth, threw stones to the four winds, and proclaimed possession of the land in the name of Spain's King Carlos III.[27]

The indigenous peoples' perceptions of the Spaniards were linked in part to their own gender ideologies and to their perceptions of Spanish gender ideologies. The absence of Hispanic women among the con-querors prior to 1774 was striking and created a variety of impressions among indigenous peoples throughout Alta California. According to Lieutenant Pedro Fages, the Chumash Indians they encountered in the San Luis Obispo area interpreted the absence of women on the expedi-tion as an indication that the Spaniards had been banished from their own land and had come in quest of native women.[28] In a plea for more women and families from Baja California to be sent to Alta California, Fages observed that colonization could dissuade the Indians of this idea, for the Indians "would then see men coming here to settle who had their own wives."[29]

The absence of women was perceived by some groups as a sign of the Europeans' aggressive intentions. Elder Kumeyaay in the San Diego region confirmed to anthropologist Florence Shipek that their ances-tors were puzzled by the newcomers because the latter had no women among them.[30] The lack of females made the Europeans appear "more like a war party intent on conquering them than like a trading or visiting tribe," they observed.[31] Nomlaki legends related by the shaman Andrew Freeman in 1936 also noted the absence of women among the first whites to encounter the Nomlaki people in the foothills of the Coast Range in northern California. In one legend, a fortune teller predicted that single men with "awfully light" blood and without wives would

bring illness to the Nomlaki people. The fortune teller, Freeman recalled, prophesied, "They have a four-legged animal which some are
riding and some are packing. They haven't any wives, any of them.
They all are single. They are bringing some kind of sickness."[32] The
prediction reveals a clash in gender ideologies, for it correlates the
absence of women, particularly wives, with a state of illness that would
be unleashed upon the Indians.

Spanish perceptions of indigenous groups, too, appear to have been
linked at least in part to their ideas about gender. Hispanic women did
not participate in the expedition of 1769, although indigenous and Hispanic women alike would be granted an explicit role in the evangelization and assimilation of Alta California natives at the missions. Perhaps
Spanish colonial authorities considered the arduous voyage and the
uncertainty of what would be found on the frontier to pose too great a
risk for women and children. Travel in the late eighteenth century was
not without serious danger. Difficult headwinds and contrary currents
made the northward voyage by water long, exhausting, and sometimes
impossible. Land travel was even more formidable, because the terrain
was virtually uncharted by Europeans. Dozens of participants in the
sacred expedition died en route or upon arrival. By the time Father
Serra established the first of the Alta California missions in San Diego,
more than one-fourth of the expedition's participants had lost their lives
from scurvy, hunger, and hardship.[33]

During the eighteenth-century expeditions to establish the first missions and presidios, chroniclers called attention to the differences between their own gender ideologies and those of the Indians in Alta
California. Though the Spaniards may not have appreciated fully the
wide range of gender roles and relations that existed among the indigenous groups they encountered, they sometimes highlighted the differences between their own views on appropriate gender roles and relations and those they presumed to have encountered among the Alta
California Indians as a whole. As had their predecessors centuries earlier, the California chroniclers used gender variation to underscore the
differences between the newly discovered populations and themselves.
They masked the differences between indigenous groups and, on a
narrative level, appealed to chivalric codes of honor to evoke sympathy

for the female Indians. The chroniclers on the 1769 expedition noted a series of practices, especially male transvestism and indigenous polygamy, that were unorthodox by their standards.[34] They also portrayed indigenous women as objects of war or exchange and as more industrious and modest than their male counterparts.[35]

American Indian tribal groups held beliefs about gender and human sexuality that tended to be much broader than those embodied in the dichotomous categories of male and female. More than two hundred American Indian terms have been used to refer to Indians with alternative gender styles.[36] Such terms often depicted an intermediate status that combined social attributes of men and women in descriptors such as "halfman-halfwoman," "man-woman," "would-be woman," "not-men," "not-women," and so on.[37] These "not-men" and "not-women" were often seen as having a spiritual calling that made them unique, bestowed upon them special powers, and gave them status within the tribal group.[38] The term "berdache," a word derived from the Arabic *bardaj,* meaning slave, and the French *bardache,* used to refer to a boy prostitute or the passive partner in sodomy, was incorporated into English in the early nineteenth century to refer to North American Indian men who adopted the dress and social roles traditionally assigned to women; it was later used to refer to women who adopted "male" dress and roles.[39] This term assigns a pejorative and somewhat narrow meaning to a diverse range of practices. The Spanish translation of the term used by California indigenous groups in the eighteenth century was *joyas,* literally "jewels," a term that perhaps better conveys the great esteem in which these "non-men" and "non-women" were held by their communities.[40]

Joyas, predominantly but not solely males, were to be found throughout Alta California.[41] The widespread presence and acceptance of joyas (interestingly, the Spanish chroniclers noted only the male transvestites) confirm that among indigenous groups there was greater room to express gender differences than there was in the more rigid societies of Spain or New Spain.

The report of engineer Miguel Costansó reflected a scientific curiosity about these joyas. Costansó noticed "a class of men who lived like Women, associated with them, wore the same dress, adorned themselves with beads, earrings, necklaces, and other Feminine adornments, and enjoyed great consideration among the people" in all of the Chumash towns along the Santa Barbara Channel and nearby islands. He observed that the lack of an interpreter prevented the expedition members from ascertaining "what kind of men they were, or to what Ministry they were destined," but that everyone on the expedition suspected "a sexual defect or some abuse among those Gentiles."[42]

Lieutenant Fages censured in even more forceful terms the male joyas in the San Luis Obispo region farther north. He noted the presence in every indigenous community of men who dressed, acted, and lived like women and who engaged in "an excess so criminal that it seems even forbidden to mention its name."[43] These men were "professional sodomites," who "serve these barbarians for the execrable, evil abuse of their bodies." Fages noted parenthetically that all of the Indians were "greatly inclined toward this abominable vice." He believed that this inclination toward "sinning against nature" and "common abuse of the joyas" in every village had an important bearing on the evangelization of the natives, since the Indians would be congregated into reducciones, or villages under mission control (where their activities would presumably be monitored and circumscribed).[44]

Seen in the context of Spanish gender ideologies, one can better appreciate how indigenous practices conflicted with what was admissible in Hispanic cultural norms and traditions. Although cross-dressing existed in New Spain and Spain, it was not accepted by society at large.[45] Golden age drama, in which playwrights exposed and often made fun of prevailing gender ideologies, sheds light on deeply rooted Hispanic attitudes toward cross-dressing. On the stage, representations of the *mujer varonil,* or "masculine woman" (including the Amazon, the *mujer esquiva* who shunned marriage, the female bandit, and the learned woman), were more widely accepted than representations of "feminine" men; the mujer varonil was one of the most popular character types in Spanish golden age drama.[46] In general, the mujer varonil most often gained status through her assumption of a masculine persona.[47] The male character who voluntarily assumed the role of a woman, on the other hand, became an object of ridicule and lost stature on the stage.[48] Such masquerades, however, were only temporary theatrical devices

that were usually reversed with the reestablishment of normative gender roles within the drama.

The Spanish chroniclers of the 1769 expedition viewed male transvestism on the Alta California frontier with disdain. They appeared to
be offended to a lesser extent by the natives' practice of polygamy.
Though polygamy was a crime by Spanish standards, punishable by the
Inquisition in both the New and Old Worlds, the distance between
Spain and the New World often allowed Spanish men to transgress the
law.[49] While Indian men were allowed to have multiple wives, in most
groups only a small minority of chiefs, wealthy men, or prominent
hunters practiced polygamy.[50] Neither Spanish culture nor the indigenous cultures of Alta California permitted women to have more than
one husband.

Costansó, whose journal reflected the relatively scientific "objectiv-
ity" and preciseness of his profession as an engineer, downplayed the
practice of polygamy in his report and noted simply that it was not
permitted among the natives, although the chiefs could have two wives
if they so desired.[51] Lieutenant Fages concurred that polygamy seemed
to be limited to the chiefs, and he complained repeatedly throughout his
account that chiefs could dispose of and take new wives at will.[52] Fages
emphasized the disadvantages and powerlessness of the female Indian
wives, who were subjected to the chiefs' every whim. Likewise, he
criticized the indigenous treatment of women as pawns of war. Because
the Indians were "continually at war with their neighbors," he wrote,
they were constantly sacking and burning villages and stealing both the
single and the married women.[53]

Father Serra related an anecdote that supported the Spaniards' perception that Indian women were at the mercy of the male members of
their communities. He recalled that his party was inclined to stop at a
densely populated ranchería, or Indian village, one day's journey south
of San Diego, until the sergeant told them that the inhabitants there
were "insolent," having tried to tempt him and his companion Cota
with women in exchange for the soldiers' clothing. Because the Spaniards resisted, they saw themselves in great danger and bribed their way
out of the predicament with whatever articles of cloth they could find.[54]

Serra's description of the Indians' desire to exchange their women for clothing and the Spaniards' evaluation that refusing to accept the women put the group in grave danger were echoed by Gaspar de Portolá. Portolá noted that the natives pestered the Spaniards to accept their women, whom "they presented as they would an article of unwanted clothing or food."[55] Though Portolá did not say how the conquerors responded to the natives' offer, he implied that it would have been rude to refuse them. He wrote simply, "We relaxed here for one day."[56] In Portolá's view, the conquerors' acceptance of their host's offer was not only justified but imperative. It was a noble deed, a chivalrous gesture, to rescue these women from men who had discarded them as "unwanted" goods. This representation of indigenous motivations and of Indian women as disposable commodities echoed Father Ascensión's narrative written some 160 years earlier.

A shift in the power relations between religious and military representatives on the California frontier immediately following the 1769 expedition provides an unexpected opening for reevaluating early gender interactions. In the four-year period immediately following the sacred expedition, earlier codes of silence were violated as the treatment of Indian women on the California frontier became a lightning rod for tensions between the military and the church. An analysis of the establishment of three early missions highlights the ways in which gender ideologies might have affected when, where, and how Franciscan missions were established, how the missionaries were received, and how the Indians responded to evangelization.

Franciscan evangelization efforts got off to a slow start, partly because of conflictive gender relations. As the Franciscan missionaries evangelized and sought converts to populate their missions, they viewed the behavior of Spanish soldiers toward Indian women as increasingly problematical, and they began to complain about specific incidents that undermined their ability to attract converts. Complaints of abuse of female Indians were particularly common at the three missions that had the least initial success in securing conversions—San Diego, established in 1769, San Gabriel, established in 1771, and San Luis Obispo, founded in 1772.

The first in the chain of California missions marking the *camino real* (royal road), San Diego mission sat on a hill overlooking the port that

TABLE I

Mission Status in December 1773

MISSION (YEAR ESTABLISHED)	NO. BAPTISMS	NO. LIVING AT MISSION	NO. MARRIAGES PERFORMED
San Diego (1769)	83	76	12
San Carlos (1770)	165	154	32
San Antonio (1771)	158	150	18
San Gabriel (1771)	73	71	0
San Luis Obispo (1772)	12	11	0

Source: Chapman, *History of California,* 246.

Cabrillo discovered and Vizcaíno called "the best [port] to be found in all the South Sea."[57] Though San Diego was surrounded by good land— rich in grapevines, Castilian roses, and a plentiful water supply—the mission fathers had difficulty securing converts from among the local Kumeyaay Indians. One month after its founding, the mission suffered an attack by some Kumeyaays, in apparent retaliation for Spanish inter- ference with their food resources.[58] In the aftermath of the attack, in which an Indian boy was killed and several others injured, the Kume- yaay offered stubborn resistance to evangelization. No conversions were registered for at least a full year after the arrival of the Spaniards.[59] In comparison, San Carlos de Borromeo, the mission that was first estab- lished at Monterey and later moved to Carmel, did somewhat better, registering its first baptism six months after being established. After five years of occupation, the Franciscans had succeeded in converting only some 83 people at the San Diego mission (table 1).[60]

When success was forthcoming, the chroniclers often noted favorable indigenous responses to the Virgin. The Indian women of the San Diego area apparently were quite taken with a painting of the virgin and child and offered their breasts to feed the infant.[61] Perhaps her image afforded an appealing contrast to the violence perpetrated against women in that region.

Consciously or unconsciously, the Spaniards' insistent use of the im- age of the Virgin (with and without child) reflected a notion that the

Figure 4. "Father Garcés and the Indians." Note the image of the Virgin and child on the banner. (From Soulé, Gihon, and Nisbet, *The Annals of San Francisco,* 1855; courtesy of the Bancroft Library)

Indians would be attracted to what the Spaniards must have considered a universal maternal symbol (fig. 4). The image of Jesus on the cross, on the other hand, disrupted traditional Spanish gender ideologies by displaying a man characterized by defeat, humility, and servitude. His image took a backseat to that of the Virgin Mary in the Franciscans' evangelization of America.

Problematic gender relations may have accounted in part for the lack of evangelical success in the San Diego region. Father Luis Jayme wrote a letter in 1772 to the head of the Franciscan College, Father Rafael Verger, that provides detailed testimony on the seizure and rape of Kumeyaay Indian women living in that vicinity.[62] Jayme wrote that he had received numerous reports from at least four rancherías near the

San Diego mission where soldiers had raped indigenous girls.[63] Many of the Indians from the rancherías were fleeing to the mountains so that the "soldiers would not take their women."[64] The problem was pervasive. There was not a single mission, wrote Jayme, where the soldiers had not "scandalized all of the Gentiles." Furthermore, it was well known that the soldiers were "committing a thousand wrongs, particularly with regard to sex." There were, he wrote, "very many soldiers who deserved to be hung for the continuous abuses they commit, seizing and violating women." Jayme did not accuse all of the soldiers of misbehavior but suggested that those who behaved well would provide a good example that would enhance Franciscan evangelization efforts.

Jayme limited himself to commenting on what he had seen and heard at San Diego since his appointment there in mid-1771.[65] On that basis, he predicted that the Spanish soldiers' behavior would provoke fatal retaliation. His subsequent death on November 5, 1775, in a Kumeyaay attack on San Diego mission attests to the accuracy of his prediction.

Of the various general charges made by Luis Jayme, only one specific case during that time period—the rape of two young Indian girls at the Soledad ranchería near the San Diego mission in 1773—appears to have produced a trial. Sergeant Mariano Carrillo, the investigating officer, noted that the local priests had notified him that three soldiers had raped two very young Indian girls, one of whom died as a result.[66] Before four witnesses and via an interpreter, the surviving girl testified that three soldiers had followed the two girls into the canyon where they were digging plants. In an effort to escape, the girls headed up a nearby hill, where two of the soldiers trapped the witness, pushed her to the ground, and "sinned against her" while the other soldier pursued the other girl and injured her spine while raping her. The latter died two days later.[67] In June 1773, Lieutenant Pedro Fages, now commander of Monterey, informed the viceroy of the incident; not until some fifteen months later did Attorney General José Antonio Areche process the overlooked letter in Mexico City.[68] Two of the soldiers, Francisco Avila and Sebastián Albitre, were imprisoned in the San Diego presidio; the third, Matheo Ygnacio de Soto, under the pretext of illness, returned home to the mission of San Fernando de Velicatá in Baja California, where he mysteriously disappeared.[69] The opportunity to make an example of the guilty soldiers, belated though it might have been, was not lost on the attorney general. He recommended that the guilty soldiers be turned over to the governor for judgment, and he noted that an "exemplary" response to such a crime would create a strong impression upon the Indians.[70] After a "rigorous and extended" prison term, however, the two soldiers were released and sent as settlers to Monterey, away from the scene of the crime.[71]

Such sexual violence became an issue of contention in the internal tensions between the church and the military and was used by the church to assert its moral authority. Serra, long embroiled in a feud with Fages, used the San Diego incident to secure the military commander's removal in 1774. He recommended that Fages's replacement be instructed to listen to the friars' complaints, and he urged that Fages's successor remove the "soldier or soldiers who give bad example, especially in matters of licentiousness."[72] The incoming officer should recall such offenders to the presidio and replace them with "another or others who are not known as immoral or scandalous," advised Serra.[73] Serra pleaded for discretion in such cases, invoking the need to keep such offenses out of the public eye in order to protect the conquest endeavor. The friars who lodged the complaints should not be required to divulge the scandalous behavior in order to be heeded, since in certain cases it was "not advisable to give the reason, either to prevent making public a hidden sin, or for other reasons that can easily be imagined."[74] Serra's instinct to keep such incidents hidden from public view for fear that they would hinder evangelization efforts was supported by the viceroy, who granted Serra's request.[75]

San Gabriel mission was the fourth mission to be established in Alta California. On August 6, 1771, Fathers Somera and Cambon, fourteen soldiers, and four muleteers headed north from San Diego.[76] They found a fertile, wooded site near the San Gabriel River some forty leagues north of San Diego and nine miles east of present-day Los Angeles that was promising for its pastoral and agricultural possibilities. According to Father Serra, the Indians of the region around San Gabriel initially welcomed the missionaries with open arms. He noted that the indigenous women of the Los Angeles Basin area were particularly taken with a painting of the Virgin Mary, to whom they brought offerings of grains, seeds, and food.[77] Palou was more candid about initial indigenous resistance to the missionaries. He noted that the Indians of the San Gabriel Valley were divided under two chiefs and tried to prevent the establishment of the mission. Like Serra, however, he emphasized the impact of the image of the Virgin on the indigenous women. In Palou's account, the symbol of the Virgin purportedly transformed the reception given to the missionaries. When one of the priests held up a painting of Our Lady of the Seven Sorrows, the Indians were won over. They all cast aside their bows and arrows and paid homage to the Virgin, marking the beginning of more cordial relations with the Spaniards.[78]

In September, the priests and soldiers established the San Gabriel mission. Several weeks later, as they worked with some of the local Indians gathering willow poles, timbers, and tules for construction of the mission building, a large number of armed Indians attacked, and the Indian chief shot an arrow at one of the soldiers.[79] Using his shield for protection, the soldier escaped the angry chief's arrow, but the incident provided the pretext for a military engagement. A fight ensued in which the Spanish soldiers killed and decapitated the Indian chief and displayed his head on a pole. Following this incident, attendance at the mission predictably sloughed off. Serra, apparently blind to the true motivations behind the attack, attributed the indigenous unrest to Fages's efforts to restrict access to the mission compound. Palou, clearly more knowledgeable (or less discreet) than Serra, attributed the incident to the actions of "a soldier [who] had raped an Indian girl from the ranchería" and noted furthermore that the wronged girl was the wife of the Indian chief.[80] Historians have largely accepted Palou's interpretation. Bancroft noted that there was "little doubt that their [the Indians'] sudden hostility arose from outrages by the soldiers on the native women."[81] The mission historian Zephyrin Engelhardt also blamed the soldiers and observed that the soldiers' misconduct "destroyed the good impression made by the Fathers, delayed the acceptance of the Gospel, and created lasting hatred for the military."[82]

Tensions at San Gabriel mission escalated over the next two years, and Serra became more vocal about (and perhaps more aware of) the abuses of indigenous females. In August 1772, he protested to Father Rafael Verger, the guardian of the Franciscan College of San Fernando in Mexico, that at the newly founded mission of San Gabriel, the "secular arm . . . was guilty of the most heinous crimes, killing the men to take their wives."[83] Eight months later, Serra reported that he had received letters from the mission priests indicating vulgarities that he declined to detail.[84] In May 1773, Father Serra informed Viceroy Bucareli that a group of muleteers at San Gabriel were using their lassos to catch Indian women "to become prey for their unbridled lust."[85] When some Indian men tried to defend their wives, wrote Serra, they were shot with bullets. Paradoxically, Father Serra's portrayal of the Indian men defending their wives is at odds with earlier representations that depicted Indian males as disloyal and uncaring.

Hugo Reid, a Protestant Scotsman who married Bartolomea Comicrabit, a Christianized Gabrielino Indian woman, echoed Palou's belief that violence against Indian women marred the evangelization effort. Reid noted that the soldiers' behavior affected not only the fabric of indigenous society but also indigenous perceptions of the Spaniards. He affirmed that the Spaniards' abuse of Indian women, along with their cruel treatment of animals, was seen by the Indians as proof of the newcomers' mortality.[86] In a series of letters to the Los Angeles *Star* that were published weekly beginning on February 21, 1852, he depicted indigenous life during the early colonial period and challenged interpretations of the early encounters as harmonious.[87] According to Reid, when the first Spaniards came to the Los Angeles County region, the women "ran to the brush and hid themselves."[88] When the second group of Spaniards arrived, they tied "the hands of the adult [Indian] males behind their backs" and made signs that they wished "to procure women." According to Reid's account, the Indians did not offer their women to the newcomers, who obtained what they sought through "harsh measures." Such sexual violence sometimes resulted in pregnancy and the rejection of both the violated women and their offspring. Reid wrote that these women were considered "contaminated," and they were "put through a long course of sweating, drinking of herbs, etc." Any white children born as a result of these relations were "secretly strangled and buried." Although the Indians "necessarily became ac-

customed to these things," Reid concluded, "their disgust and abhor-
rence never left them till many years after."

The initial tensions over gender relations between Spanish soldiers
and the indigenous peoples of the San Gabriel region had repercussions
beyond the immediate environs of San Gabriel mission. When new
missionary and soldier recruits came through San Gabriel on their way
to establish another mission at San Buenaventura, they had to remain
at the former mission as reinforcements, given the tremendous hostility
of the natives there. The first mission on the Santa Barbara Channel, San Buenaventura, was thus delayed by twelve more years.[89] Likewise, the diversion of military personnel to San Gabriel delayed establishment of missions at San Francisco and Santa Clara until 1776 and
1777 respectively.[90]

In 1772, the missions of Carmel and San Antonio de Padua were near
starvation. Recalling the Cañada de los Osos, a valley with plentiful
game discovered by Portolá in 1769, their friars sent out a hunting party
to look for food. The explorers found the marshy valley with its plentiful game and returned to the missions with nine thousand pounds of
salted and jerked bear meat and twenty-five loads of edible seeds secured by barter with the local Indians.[91] Father Serra set out immediately with soldiers, muleteers, pack animals, and farming implements
to establish a new mission near the valley. San Luis Obispo mission was
thus founded on September 1, 1772, some three miles from the coast on
a low hill by a stream overlooking the Cañada de los Osos. It was the
fifth mission to be established in Alta California.

Relations between the Spanish soldiers and the native inhabitants at
San Luis Obispo were fraught with difficulties from the start. During
the 1769 expedition, "disorderly" soldiers had passed through the area
and, according to Father Pedro Font, had taken liberties with the Indian women there because the women were "so affable and friendly."[92]
In June 1771, soldiers again "made use of the San Luis women," and
Font noted that Commander Fages did nothing about their lewd conduct.[93] In 1772, Serra expressed concern that among the soldiers assigned to San Luis Obispo were some "notorious molesters of Gentile
women."[94] The following year, Serra wrote to the viceroy that the "enemy" had already infiltrated the mission camp at San Luis Obispo in the

form of a "bad soldier, who shortly after arriving was discovered in fla-grant sin with an Indian girl."[95] By the end of 1773, the friars there had succeeded in baptizing only twelve Indians.[96] Sexual violence, though considered by some soldiers to be appropriate masculine behavior in the conquest of the native female population, had conflicted with the need to win the hearts and minds of the native people.

By 1773, the total Spanish population in Alta California numbered sixty-one soldiers (including six who had married native women), eleven friars, and occasional craftsmen, but no Hispanic women.[97] Fages at-tributed his difficulty in keeping a rein on the soldiers at least in part to a lack of families or female companions on the California frontier. He pinpointed the presence of women and families as one of the necessities for normalizing relations between the indigenous and Hispanic cul-tures.[98] By the mid-1770s, the benefits of such a presence, which presum-ably would have a civilizing influence on the soldiers, seemed to out-weigh its potential costs. Spanish-Mexican women in Alta California would purportedly defuse the explosive sexuality on the frontier, thus diminishing tensions between the Indians and the military, as well as between the church and the military.[99] The underlying assumption was that the Spanish men, with women of their own on hand, would be less likely to attack Indian women.

Ironically, while the military commander, Fages, favored the im-migration of Hispanic women, the missionaries—chief complainants about the soldiers' behavior—were somewhat ambivalent about bring-ing women to the male-dominated California frontier. Serra lamented the "disorder" that a female presence could create at the missions, which were "daily becoming more infected with lewdness."[100] Father Serra, adept at framing religious needs in politically expedient terms, was nonetheless a strong advocate for colonization when the colonists could be attached to the missions in some way. He repeatedly opposed the establishment of pueblos of Spaniards and people of mixed racial de-scent, but he supported incorporating such respectable people as could be found into new and existing missions.[101] An increase in population on the California frontier could only help the missions, which suffered severe isolation and food shortages. Serra promoted marriage as one way to maintain order and decency on the frontier. He requested that

married soldiers be allowed to return to their families in Mexico and
that the unmarried soldiers be encouraged to take wives among the
Indians.[102] He urged the Crown to organize a northbound expedition to
Alta California with a large number of Spanish families. Such a project
would, he argued, "serve the missions well, populate the land, and
facilitate the spiritual and temporal conquest" of Alta California.[103] The
soldiers "need not all be married," wrote Serra, so long as each mission
was sent two families of "honorable" background.[104]

By 1773, a major colonization project that would bring Hispanic
women to the frontier missions and presidios had the support of all the
leading frontier actors. The military believed the female presence would
keep the soldiers in line. The friars welcomed the prospect of new
subjects at the missions. Colonial Spanish authorities counted on the
presence of Hispanic women from New Spain to establish a stable
population base of settlers who could then secure Alta California against
external threats. They hoped the women's presence would also help
assuage tensions between the various groups on the frontier.

The Anza expedition, a brief two years later, marked the conver-
gence of these religious and political goals and provides a useful case
study for evaluating the roles that gender and gender relations played in
the colonization of the frontier, as well as the ways in which they were
inscribed. Spain's first colonization project, supported by military and
clergy alike, was about to begin.

4

Colonization

The first women to go to the Alta California missions under the sponsorship of the Spanish Crown were Christianized Indian women who arrived with their families. Selected because of their ethnic, civil, and religious status, these Indian women of Baja California arrived in Alta California as early as 1772. In that year, one of the priests from the San Diego mission traveled to Baja California for provisions and upon his return brought with him two Christianized Indian families.[1] The arrival of these first—and to us, largely anonymous—Baja California families caused quite a stir among Christians and non-Christians alike, who "did not know what to make of these families, so great was their delight."[2]

One of these early immigrants may have been called María Dolores, but little is known about her or the other Baja California women who contributed to the evangelization efforts in Alta California. In 1769, Sebastián Taraval, María Dolores's husband, had accompanied the sacred expedition to San Diego. He subsequently returned to Baja California and then to Alta California, perhaps with María Dolores, to work at the San Gabriel mission. It is unclear exactly when his wife joined him there from the Santa Gertrudis mission in Baja California, but it was prior to November 15, 1772, when María Dolores was listed as the *madrina,* or godmother, at the baptism of a one-year-old infant at the San Gabriel mission.[3] In August 1773, Sebastián Taraval, María Dolores, and a Baja California companion ran away from the mission. María Dolores and her companion both died when they were forced to hide in the desert to avoid capture.[4] No documents have yet been uncovered that might confirm the reasons for their fugitivism, but conditions must have seemed bad enough that they were willing to risk their lives in fleeing. After their unsuccessful attempt to escape from the mission, Sebastián Taraval, who survived, apparently returned to the service of the Spaniards, acting as a guide for the first Anza expedition and later serving as a *padrino,* or baptismal sponsor, at the San Gabriel mission.[5]

In 1772, as the Franciscans were discussing the imminent transfer of their Baja California missions (initially ceded to them after the expulsion of the Jesuits) to the Dominicans (in exchange for exclusive evangelization rights in Alta California), they negotiated the transfer to Alta California of some of the Baja California Indian families and animals.[6] Father Palou, acting president of the missions in Serra's absence, recommended that twenty-five families be sent to Alta California. Given the potential problems of fugitivism, Palou stressed that the families go "of their own free will and with enthusiasm."[7]

In early 1773, Serra, who had written to Viceroy Antonio Bucareli and recommended sending more Christianized Indian families north from Baja California, stressed the utility of such a measure.[8] It would accomplish two purposes, he noted. It would provide needed Indian laborers, and, more importantly for Serra, it would placate the Indians, who "until now have thought it very strange to see all these men without any women among them."[9] Serra also hoped that the presence of Christian Indian families from Baja California would encourage the Alta California Indians to marry and bear more children.

In May 1773, Palou began recruiting Indian families, whom he planned to escort from the Baja California missions to the Franciscan missions in Alta California. From the mission at Loreto, Palou recruited three bachelors and a Christianized Indian couple;[10] at the Santa Gertrudis mission, he selected three married couples and two bachelors;[11] at San Borja mission, he chose seven more families and several young boys.[12] When news reached him that the ship with the food and supplies for the Alta California missions had had to turn back because of a broken rudder, Palou discontinued his recruitment efforts and contented himself with arranging the trip for ten families.[13] On July 21, 1773, under the leadership of Sergeant José Francisco de Ortega, fourteen

soldiers and these ten Indian families left San Fernando de Velicatá.[14]
After walking for nearly six weeks, they reached San Diego mission.[15]
Palou left only one family there, in order that "the woman might teach
the Indians to sew and to knit the wool which was already beginning to
come in from the sheep that the mission had."[16] In these new Alta
California missions, production of food and clothing was in its infancy
and required human labor. On September 26, Palou, the remaining
Indian families, and some new missionaries left San Diego mission and
headed for other missions farther north.[17]

The following week, the group arrived at San Gabriel mission, which
continued to suffer the consequences of the soldier's earlier assault on an
Indian chief's wife. Indians had been slow to return to the mission since
that time. Given the lack of neophytes, Palou left six Baja California
families and most of the men there.[18] Eleven months later, Nicolás
Torres and Gertrudis María, one of the Indian couples who had come to
San Gabriel from the Baja California mission in San Borja, had a son,
Mariano Enrico Torres; Antonio María Lisboa and his wife, María
Salomé, also from San Borja, served as godparents for the newborn.[19]

On October 25, 1773, Palou and the remainder of his group arrived at
San Luis Obispo. Like that at San Gabriel, the recently founded mission
at San Luis Obispo boasted fertile land and an abundant water supply
but lacked workers. Palou thus left the remaining three (or possibly
four) families and a handful of bachelors there.[20]

Given the difficulties both in recruiting families for the uncharted
frontier and in keeping them in Alta California once they arrived, the
Crown soon turned from Baja California to the mainland of New Spain
(Mexico) for additional recruits. On January 23, 1774, the Spanish frigate *Santiago* (formerly called the *Nueva Galicia*), set sail from the port of
San Blas.[21] After forty-nine days of relatively easy sailing, the ship
landed in San Diego and then proceeded to its disembarkation point at
Monterey, where it arrived on May 9, 1774. According to Bancroft, the
voyagers included Father Serra, Juan Soler (a storekeeper for Monterey), José Dávila (a surgeon) and his family, three blacksmiths and
their families, and three carpenters.[22] Bancroft gave no names of the
female participants on this voyage. In her study of women on the frontier, Antonia Castañeda compiled a list of the female members on board,
garnered from marriage and baptismal records. They included Ana

María Hurtado, the wife of blacksmith Fernando Antonio Chamorro, and their two daughters—María del Carmen, eighteen, and Cipriana, twenty; Josefa Chavira de Pedro y Gil, the wife of Rafael (storekeeper-designate for San Diego presidio), with her servant, María Teresa de Ochoa; and Josefa María Góngora, Dávila's wife.[23] A ship's list from San Blas in the Mexican archives, however, indicates that the group of voyagers was larger than either Bancroft or Castañeda suggested; it shows a much larger contingent of twenty-three persons plus a crew of eighty-eight.[24]

The group on the *Santiago* seems to have included at least seven Mexican women of mixed backgrounds, primarily from Tepic and Guadalajara. It included single, married, and widowed women and their children. Few of these women continued on to Monterey, the *Santiago*'s final destination, which may help to explain their absence from later California records. María Teresa de Ochoa, the Mexican from Tepic who was supposed to be a servant for the storekeeper and his wife, married Lorenzo de Resa, a second pilot of the expedition, despite the vehement objections of her prospective employers.[25] María Josefina Dávila, a native of Guadalajara, settled at the San Gabriel mission, where she was baptized on June 6, 1774.[26] A few months later, she served as madrina for an infant from a nearby ranchería.[27]

Female motivations for participating in these expeditions were not recorded. But whether these women migrated to California reluctantly to be with their families, enthusiastically in search of new and better opportunities, or for other reasons, virtually all of these seven women from the *Santiago* contingent returned home after the expiration of their husbands' contracts or terms of office.[28] Only María del Carmen Chamorro, who married José Marcelino Bravo, corporal of the Carmel mission guard, in a ceremony on August 30, 1774, settled permanently in Alta California.

At about the same time, an additional group of soldiers and perhaps half a dozen or more of their families arrived in Alta California. Headed by Fernando Rivera y Moncada, who would replace Fages as the new governor of California, this group totaled some fifty-five persons. They traveled north from Sonora and arrived in San Diego on September 26, 1774.[29]

Other preparations were under way for Spanish colonization. In

1774, Juan Bautista de Anza, the military commander of the presidio at Tubac, had charted a new overland route from Sonora, New Spain (Mexico), to Monterey, California, and back, a distance of over three thousand miles.[30] Thirty-four men, with 140 horses and 65 cattle, participated in Anza's 1774 scouting expedition. Delayed by Apache raids, Anza and his soldiers, two Franciscan friars, and some Indian interpreters and guides had mapped the desert and opened the land route to others who would follow. They had established an alliance with Salvador Palma, a leader of the Yuma tribe that occupied the strategically critical banks of the Gila and Colorado Rivers. Viceroy Bucareli would later give Palma full credit for the success of Anza's two expeditions to Monterey, as well as for "the attachment of the neighboring tribes to the Spaniards, and the observance amongst themselves of peace and quietude which they lacked before."[31]

Following his scouting expedition in 1774, Anza returned to Mexico City, where Antonio María Bucareli y Ursúa, the viceroy, governor, and captain-general of New Spain, acting at the behest of Carlos III and José de Gálvez, entrusted him with the task of organizing another overland expedition to establish a port on San Francisco Bay and to select sites for two missions and a presidio there.[32] Bucareli assigned twenty-eight men with their lieutenant and a sergeant to found San Francisco.[33] He ordered Anza to lead this expedition of troops, who, he indicated, would be required to "bring their wives and children in order that they become better attached to their domicile."[34] The requirement that the troops be married and with families responded to Father Serra's earlier pleas. The Spanish Crown desired not only greater numbers of people on the frontier but also greater stability. Without women, the viceroy believed, men would be mere vagabonds, unlikely to make permanent their homes on the frontier.[35] The presence of women and families was seen as the key to ensuring that the men would settle in far-off California.

Women and children constituted the majority of the participants in the Anza expedition. The 165-day journey from Sonora, Mexico, through Arizona, across the Colorado River, and over desert and mountain to the San Gabriel mission and beyond was undertaken by Spain's largest colonization force ever, and it was the first to be accomplished by land. The Spaniards had hoped that an overland route would prove a viable alternative to the long, dangerous, and unpredictable sea route, which until then had been the only path connecting California to Mexico.

The recruits for the Anza expedition came primarily from Sonora and Sinaloa, poor desert provinces on the western coast of the mainland of northern New Spain.[36] In a letter to the viceroy, Anza recommended that people from the *alcaldías,* or municipalities, of Culiacán, Sinaloa, and Fuerte, in the province of Sonora, were "best suited for the purpose and most easy to obtain without being missed in their own country."[37] Anza believed that in addition to being the most expendable, such individuals would most appreciate an opportunity to begin anew, and he noted that he had little doubt that such inhabitants, "submerged in the greatest poverty and misery," would "eagerly and with great willingness embrace the advantages which your Excellency may deign to afford them."

Ignaz Pfefferkorn, a German Jesuit who served as a missionary in Sonora for eleven years, documented the desperate conditions of the regions from which California would draw its early colonists. In two published volumes of a proposed three-volume work, written following his order's expulsion in 1767, Pfefferkorn noted that military recruits were easily found in Sonora; more than were needed "gladly volunteer in order to receive board and clothing without doing any work."[38]

For the most part, the recruits were not only impoverished but also caught in the ravages of a civil war that had been going on for decades. Until 1751, when a general uprising among the Pima and Papago Indians wiped out most of the Spanish inhabitants and Jesuit missionaries, Sonora had been a mixture of Indian and Spanish villages dedicated to cattle raising and the mining of gold and silver. In 1760, when he put down a rebellion of one thousand Papago Indians, Juan Bautista de Anza was given command of the presidio of Tubac.[39] There he also engaged in pacifying the Seris, Sibubapas or Suaquis, and Comanches. "Before the horrible ravages of the Apaches and Seris filled the entire country with fear and terror," wrote Pfefferkorn, "many Spaniards lived on their own estates at some distance from the villages."[40] Driven from their estates, some fled to garrisons, some to the missions, and some to the *reales de minas,* the mining communities situated near the gold and silver mines. By the time the Spanish Crown expelled the

Jesuits from Spanish America in 1767, the haciendas were long gone and even the mines had been abandoned. The region was ripe for recruitment.

In early 1775, Anza opened a recruiting office for the Crown in San Felipe de Sinaloa. He offered incentives including mules, horses, cattle, and transportation costs for the soldiers, settlers, and their families. Moreover, the Crown was prepared to give each participant two year's pay and five year's rations, as well as a full set of clothing.[41] Each woman was outfitted with two skirts, one underskirt, three blouses, three white cotton petticoats, two pairs of shoes, linen material for two jackets, two pairs of Brussels stockings, two pairs of hose, two *rebozos* (shawls), a hat, and six yards of ribbon.[42] The men and children were likewise clothed down to ribbons, hats, and blankets. The participants would begin to receive their payments and rations on the day they enlisted. The Crown would finance the entire package of clothing, food, tents, armaments, presents for the Indians, and animals and their feed.

Recruitment efforts appear to have reached the intended audience— the poor, marginalized inhabitants of the targeted provinces. The colonists came from presidios, villas, pueblos, mining communities, and ranches between Culiacán in the south and the Pimería Alta in the north. Of those who participated, the majority came from Sinaloa (part of the province of Sonora between the Sierra Madre Occidental and the Gulf of California), and a few were from north of the Yaqui River (near the Pimería Alta and the area of the Indian raids).[43] Yet recruitment was less successful than the planners hoped. Whereas early budgets had anticipated the participation of 180 children, evenly divided between the sexes, the final tally of participants included just 115 children.

These early California pioneers were primarily of mixed racial descent, as were all but a handful of the inhabitants of the provinces from which they came.[44] With the exception of the governor, the officers, and a few merchants, pure Spaniards were few and far between in Sonora. These exceptions notwithstanding, most of those who claimed to be Spaniards were probably of mixed blood.[45] The Anza delegation included a few Spanish soldiers who returned to Tubac, but those who settled in California were primarily of humble Spanish and Indian (mestizo) or African and Spanish (mulatto) families from Sinaloa and

Sonora.[46] Noncommissioned officers tended to be of mixed lineage, and the wives of the soldiers were often Indians.[47] Of the twenty-nine soldiers, seven were mulattos.[48]

On April 5, 1775, the first three recruits and their families signed on.[49] Among those who followed them, attracted by the frontier opportunities or, more likely, pushed by their desperate economic situation and the ravages of war, were María Feliciana Arballo de Gutiérrez (sometimes written María Feliziana Arsayo) and her husband, the Spanish lieutenant José Gutiérrez.[50] Feliciana, age twenty-five, had married the Spanish soldier when they were barely teenagers, and they had a four-year-old daughter, María Tomasa, and a one-month-old, María Eustaquia.[51] Just before Anza's expedition was due to leave, however, Lieutenant Gutiérrez died. Father Pedro Font, one of the priests who would accompany the expedition, tried to convince Feliciana to remain in Sinaloa, but to no avail.[52] On September 30, she and her daughters set out from Culiacán in Sinaloa, Mexico, for San Miguel de Horcasitas, where most of the group was assembling. From there, they proceeded to Tubac, where they joined the remaining participants of the expedition. In Anza's roster of October 20, 1775, Feliciana was listed as part of the family headed by Agustín de Valenzuela, age thirty, and Petra Ignacia de Ochoa, age twenty.

The roster of the delegation as it prepared to leave the Tubac presidio in Sonora included 3 military officers, 3 missionaries, 1 purveyor, 20 muleteers, 38 soldiers, 29 wives of the soldier recruits, 136 additional members of the soldiers' families, 3 cattle herders, 4 servants, and 3 Indian interpreters.[53] All told, 30 families including a total of 34 women and 115 children participated in the 240-member trek.[54] It was a particularly young group: only 11 of the colonists were aged 40 or over, 125 of them were 18 years or younger, and 92 were 12 years of age or under.[55] Of the 30 soldiers in the Anza delegation who remained in Alta California, only Lieutenant José Joaquín Moraga was unaccompanied by his wife, María de León, who was ill.[56] In addition to the soldiers and their wives, settler families participating in the expedition included 4 couples and their children, 3 bachelors, and 22-year-old Isabel Berreyesa and her 15-year-old brother, Nicolas Antonio Berreyesa.[57]

At three o'clock on the afternoon of October 23, 1775, a caravan of

240 people and several hundred animals halted by the Tubac River at a place called La Canoa, in the province of Sonora, Mexico.[58] One hundred sixty-five pack mules were loaded down with provisions—arms, ammunition, baggage, and glass beads and other presents to win favor with any Indians encountered on the journey. More than three hundred head of cattle and an equal number of horses accompanied the group. Half of the cattle would feed the expedition along the way, and the remaining half would replenish the stocks at the missions of Alta California. It was the first day of a sixteen-hundred-mile journey through the barely charted wilderness, mountains, and desert between Tubac, Sonora, and Monterey, California. The group had set out at eleven o'clock that morning and traveled some fifteen miles on its overland journey northward.

At a time of awakening international interest in the Pacific coast, women's roles as wives and mothers were fundamental in establishing a stable population base on a far-off frontier. These women were directly tied to Spanish expansion as settlers, primarily through marriage or kinship relations. Many were soon to be residents and workers at the presidios and at the Franciscan missions in Alta California. Others would help to populate the pueblos that were established in Alta California during the following decades. Only three days after the trek began, Father Font married three couples.[59]

In addition to voluminous correspondence in anticipation of the venture, five diaries were written during the journey by the military and religious participants—Captain Juan Bautista de Anza,[60] Father Pedro Font (who kept two journals),[61] Father Francisco Garcés,[62] and Father Thomas Eixarch.[63] These documents attest to women's presence on the overland trail. They tell of the roles that the organizers of the journey envisioned for women and, at times, of female resistance to those roles. Inadvertently, they give us considerable information about female contributions to the settlement of Alta California.

In keeping with the state's desire to increase the population on the California frontier, the official diarists of the Anza trek of 1775–76 made note of pregnancies, miscarriages, and births along the way. Don Juan Bautista de Anza, the commander of the expedition, was punctilious in recording information. On the first day of the trip, he recorded the labor endured by the wife of one of the soldiers, the successful birth of a lusty boy that evening, and the ultimate death in childbirth of the mother.[64] Father Pedro Font, one of the chaplains accompanying the expedition, wrote in his diary of the same event that "the delivery was so irregular that the child was born feet first, and the woman died in childbed early in the morning."[65] Although the mother's name was not mentioned in the diaries, in a separate report on the colonists Anza identified her as María Ignacia Manuela Pinuelas, the thirty-one-year-old wife of Vicente Feliz, age thirty-four, and the mother of six other children ranging in age from four to twelve years.[66]

Expedition leaders also documented at least five miscarriages along the way. On November 10, 1775, Anza noted one such death. He wrote, "The wife of a soldier having suffered a miscarriage, with the infant dying, she appears to be faring badly as a result."[67] Anza identified the woman only by her relationship to her husband, a soldier, and her pregnant condition. On the following morning, Anza was obliged to delay the march. He noted that the woman "was not in a condition to travel today, for she awakened this morning with her whole body swollen."[68] In his entry for that day, Father Font noted that the woman had "given birth to a stillborn baby on the second of the month."[69] On November 19, another soldier on the expedition reported that his wife had gone into labor.[70] Anza suspended the march for three days while Dolores, one of the few women mentioned by name in the journals, gave birth and recuperated. Father Font baptized the newborn and "named him Diego Pasqual, because it was the octave of San Diego and because the place where we were was called San Pasqual."[71] On November 24, Anza halted the journey for yet another woman who was suffering labor pains. In his journal entry for that day, Father Font recorded Anza's kindness toward the woman and noted that Anza had provided food to satisfy her cravings.[72] A few weeks later, Anza justified his tardy arrival at the Colorado River in a letter to the viceroy written while on the road at Laguna de Santa Olalla. He wrote that in addition to the change of temperature, which had caused much illness, the greatest delays had been caused by women giving birth or miscarrying, because it was impossible for the new mothers to mount horses for four or five days.[73] In addition to explaining intermittent delays, such details reflect the importance of women's reproductive role within the colonization enterprise.

There was little room on that journey for the "fainting hearts of the timid women and children" that Zoeth Skinner Eldredge described in his history of California.[74] Women, like their male counterparts, endured, surmounted, and survived the difficulties posed by the harsh climate and topography of the land before them. After a march of thirty-seven days through what is now Arizona, the group reached the junction of the Gila and Colorado Rivers. It took a day to clear a path through the thicket. At the river junction, Yuma allies aided the party in crossing, as they had aided Anza's scouting expedition the year before. The Colorado River had risen so much that the Spaniards had to be carried across on rafts built for the occasion. The Yuma women, whom Anza described as "more skillful swimmers than the Men," helped the Spaniards transport their belongings across the deluge, as they had on Anza's earlier scouting mission.[75] The women placed the Spaniards' possessions in baskets on top of their heads as they swam back and forth across the river twelve times in the course of a single day. As a reward, the Spaniards gave them glass beads and trinkets. Anza noted that one woman who carried about two bushels of beans on her head had asked for only two strings of glass beads in exchange for her labor.[76] As in many other chronicles of conquest and encounter, the Spaniards recorded their surprise at finding people whose value systems differed from their own, particularly with regard to material possessions.

Shortly thereafter, the group split into three divisions in order to cross the Colorado desert.[77] The first two groups marched through with relative ease, but the third division met with bitter cold in which many of the horses and cattle froze to death.[78] Ahead loomed the San Gabriel Mountains and the most difficult part of their journey.

On December 19, the pioneers began their ascent. It rained or snowed constantly for the entire eight days it took them to cross the summit. In the bitter cold that Christmas Eve, a woman went into labor and delivered the third child to be born on the journey.[79] Father Font's description once again added details that inadvertently provide a window onto the difficulties the female pioneers encountered. He wrote: "In the afternoon they called me to hear the confession of the wife of a soldier. Since yesterday, she had been suffering labor pains; she was the same one I mentioned on Nov. 24 who was having cravings, and she was very fearful of dying. Having consoled her and cheered her up as best I could, I retired to my tent, and at half past eleven at night she happily and very quickly gave birth to a boy."[80]

Father Font played down the difficulties and dangers of pregnancy and childbirth while highlighting his own role in consoling and heartening the woman. We see this again in his description of the new baby's baptism on the following day: "Shortly before midnight on this holy night of Christmas, the wife of a soldier (the one whom I mentioned yesterday) happily gave birth to a boy, and since the day was very raw and foggy, it was decided that we should remain here today. Thus I said three Masses, and afterwards I solemnly baptized the child, naming him Salvador Ygnacio."[81]

The group resumed its march on the following Tuesday morning, because the mother was better and felt up to it, but Anza expressed concern that the cold, rainy weather and the steep terrain might injure her.[82] On December 26, the travelers felt an earthquake that Anza recorded as having lasted for four minutes.[83] On the following day, the group marched through the summit of the pass without further ado.[84] The worst of the trip was over. On January 4, 1776, the group reached San Gabriel mission.[85] Heavy rains and fog accompanied them throughout the remainder of their journey to Monterey, but the terrain on that final segment was much less grueling. On March 10, 1776, after sixty-two days' march, Anza and his entourage arrived at Monterey.[86] The original group had lost only the woman who died giving birth on that first day's journey from Tubac, four deserters and two servants who remained at San Gabriel mission, and Carlos Gallegos, age thirty-four, and his seventeen-year-old wife, María Josepha Espinosa, who had "obtained permission to return to their country of Sonora."[87]

From Monterey, Anza himself returned to Tubac, and part of the expedition continued to San Francisco. This journey was narrated by two participants in the event—Father Francisco Palou and the commander, Lieutenant José Joaquín Moraga.[88] On June 17, 1776, Lieutenant Moraga, three other officers, and sixteen soldiers headed north from Monterey to found a presidio in San Francisco.[89] All but the commander were accompanied by their wives and families. In addition to the eight women who had already given birth or miscarried during the trip, still others had children on the way.[90] Father Palou mentioned making several stops "in order not to fatigue the little children and the women, especially those who were pregnant."[91] Moraga mentioned that three days after leaving Monterey, one of the pregnant women fell ill.[92]

Although women and children composed a majority of the delegation members, their presence, when acknowledged at all, is relatively sketchy. It tended to be amorphous, often nameless, and mentioned almost exclusively in relation to childbirth.[93] To our knowledge, none of the female participants kept a journal, and all were probably functionally illiterate. The more than one hundred children who participated in the expedition were barely mentioned in the journals. The concerned paternalism of the authorities allowed little room for female voices to be heard, much less recorded. In some instances, however, female resistance to patriarchal expectations was acknowledged, if only inadvertently.

The experience of the widow Feliciana de Arballo is illustrative of both the new opportunities and the patriarchal continuities offered by the frontier. Despite her husband's death and the opposition of Father Font, Feliciana chose to take her family on the challenging journey to a new land. In his journal, Font complained about the "somewhat discordant" and "very bold widow" who accompanied the expedition.[94] In particular, Font was dismayed by the widow's contribution to a *fandango* dance celebration. "Applauded and cheered by all the crowd," wrote Font, Feliciana "sang some verses which were not at all nice."[95] Others shared Father Font's disapproval. The priest observed that the man with whom Feliciana had gone to the dance became justifiably angry and punished her. When Anza protested such treatment, he and Father Font had a falling out in which Font defended the right of Feliciana's companion to punish her. Captain Anza retorted that Feliciana was merely boosting the morale of her fellow colonists. Font later conceded that his own ill health might have caused him to overreact to the situation.

On other occasions, however, Font came to the defense of women, particularly if male efforts to circumscribe their activities impinged upon his evangelical mission. On one occasion, the priest noted that he had reprimanded some of the soldiers, "who were so jealous of their wives that besides not permitting them to talk with anybody, they even prohibited them from coming to hear Mass."[96]

Perhaps the restrictive atmosphere was what prompted Feliciana and her daughters to separate from the expedition at the San Gabriel mission. There, according to church historian Francis Weber, Feliciana caused "a minor sensation" when she deserted the expedition to marry Juan Francisco López, a young soldier who had come to California years earlier with Father Serra.[97] They married in early 1776 at San Gabriel, with the reinstated Sebastián Taraval as their witness.[98] Feliciana continued to serve the state in its conquest effort, taking on a new role as an overseer for the San Gabriel mission's dormitory for young Indian girls. Mission records note that she and her new husband served as padrinos for the young daughter of Isidro Martínez and Petra María from the Indian village of Juyuvit.[99] The infant was given the baptismal name María Feliciana, after her new godmother. Feliciana and Juan Francisco López later had two children of their own.[100]

Many of the earliest Hispanic females to arrive in Alta California were related to soldiers, and some worked at the military presidios. In a letter to Viceroy Bucareli, Father Serra complained that too many of the soldiers' wives were reserved for the presidio, leaving none for the work at the missions. In particular, the women were needed to help educate the Indian women, because this work "presents obvious difficulties to the Fathers."[101]

State financing of colonization schemes in Alta California provided many poor women with new options for economic survival. Nonetheless, many Spanish-Mexican women were reluctant to relocate themselves or their families to the far-off frontier. Some wives chose to remain behind. Father Font complained that Doña Ana Regina Serrano, Anza's wife of fourteen years, devised all sorts of machinations to postpone her husband's departure, including persuading the priest himself to ask Anza to delay the trip until Font's health improved.[102] The Anza expedition of 1775–76 was initially postponed, according to Father Font, simply "because his [Anza's] wife wished it and he had the opportunity to give her this pleasure."[103] The reasons for Ana Regina

Serrano's decision not to join her husband on the northward journey are unclear. In the colonial period, many other wives of Spanish officials would choose to accompany their husbands to their new posts.

Worthy of mention here is the case of Eulalia Callis de Fages, the wife of Pedro Fages, who was appointed governor of California in 1782. Eulalia initially resisted accompanying her husband to the California frontier but was apparently convinced by Fages's predecessor to move north with her son.[104] By 1784, after she had given birth to another daughter, Eulalia had declared her intent to take the children back home. Her husband refused to accede to her wish, whereupon she banned him from her house for three months. When the governor did not respond to her pressures, she accused him of having an affair with a Yuma servant girl and publicly demanded a divorce. Fages called in the friars, who intervened on his behalf, and under the threat of her husband and the missionaries, Eulalia was temporarily sequestered to and silenced at the San Carlos mission. She filed a confidential legal complaint against the priests, who threatened to gag, beat, and handcuff her.[105] In her petition for legal separation, Callis charged that she was held at the mission incommunicado and under guard for several months.[106] The couple was reconciled in 1785, but Eulalia continued to pressure her husband to leave California. Five years later, Fages asked to be relieved of his duties, and the family returned to Mexico.

Family and economic considerations appear to have been central to some women's decisions to go to California. María de León petitioned Spanish authorities on at least two occasions for assistance in joining her husband, Lieutenant José Joaquín Moraga, at the San Francisco presidio.[107] Having been gravely ill at the time of her husband's departure with the Anza expedition in March 1776, María de León was then unable to follow in her husband's "loving company."[108] In the first of the two petitions, she asked that the Crown allow her husband to come home in order to accompany her to California. Several years later, government authorities had not yet responded to her letter. María de León communicated once again with Commander General Teodoro de Croix, the governor and commander general of the Provincias Internas, an administrative unit of northern Mexico. She informed him that she and her husband had made arrangements for her and their son to join an expedition to Alta California being led by Captain Fernando de Rivera y Moncada, and she asked that the four hundred pesos in expenses needed to prepare for the long journey be deducted from her husband's salary. The letter, signed by María de León but written by an anonymous hand, stressed the petitioner's eagerness to leave Sonora. "The supplicant is ready and prepared [to depart], and nothing short of her becoming incapacitated will stop her from doing so," the scribe wrote.[109]

Similarly, a petition from another woman underscored the familial and economic factors that motivated her desire to live in California. In 1783, María de la Encarnación Castro dictated a letter to Manuel Ramón de Goya, a *factor,* or company agent.[110] Highlighting the patriarchal nature of Spanish society in California, she narrated that "with the approval of my Parents and the permission of the governor," she had married Joseph Joaquín Dávila, the presidio surgeon in Monterey.[111] Native to Sinaloa, the Castro family had come with Anza to settle at the presidio of San Carlos in Monterey, California. When María de la Encarnación's husband was granted permission to go to the viceregal court in Mexico, she accompanied him. Shortly after their arrival in Mexico City, he died, leaving her stranded and destitute in the capital city. María de la Encarnación wrote, "After one month he died, leaving me a widow, in a foreign land, with a one-and-a-half-year-old baby, and with no protection other than that of God." A lengthy note scribbled in the margins of this document indicates that José Joaquín Dávila died on January 24, 1783, and that Colonel Felipe de Neve, the royal assessor and governor of the peninsula of California, had distributed a military pension, including some 431 pesos, 6 reales, to Dávila's widow on the following day, but that the total barely covered the costs of Dávila's protracted illness, his burial, and the wake. The widow appealed to the Crown for assistance, recalling the long-time service to the Crown of the men in her family. She begged in the name of "Christian Piety and the charitable Breast" to be allowed to return to California to see her family, as "only love for my Husband could have taken me away from them." In a note of his own, Manuel Ramón de Goya stressed the woman's destitute condition and ill health since her husband's death and observed that she survived only "thanks to the Charity of a Brother-in-law of her deceased Husband, who, for the Scarcity of his resources, barely manages to give her something to eat."

These petitions are a poignant reminder of the extreme dependency of women, particularly widows, on their husbands, male family members, and the Crown. In such letters, women emphasized the patriarchal aspects of society that were most beneficial to them, namely the state's obligation to take care of them and their own desires to be with their families, particularly with their husbands or fathers. Caution must be exercised in interpreting women's motives, however, given the goal-directed orientation of these letters, which were dictated to or written by third parties on behalf of the women.

While most of the colonists who accompanied Anza and his predecessors settled around the presidial posts and missions, some (including just over a dozen fresh recruits guided to Alta California by Rivera y Moncada from the Mexican mainland) established the first pueblos in California. San José and Los Angeles were founded in 1777 and 1781, respectively, under the auspices of Governor Felipe de Neve. (An additional pueblo, Branciforte—later known as Santa Cruz—was established by Governor Borica in 1797.) Governor Neve envisioned these pueblos as agricultural settlements that would help to alleviate the severe food shortages being experienced by the settlers in Alta California. Until mission agriculture could flourish, the settlers were totally reliant on ships from San Blas, Mexico, for their food supplies.[112]

The majority of families who would undertake the daunting journey from Mexico to Alta California—numbering some six or seven hundred men, women, and children—had already arrived by 1781.[113] In that year, an uprising of thousands of indigenous peoples of the Colorado River valley against the Spanish presence altered the course of colonization of Mexico's northern frontier.[114]

Some of the ways in which gender and sexuality intersected power relations in Mexico's northern territories may be gleaned from an analysis of Spanish-Yuma relations. Yuma women initially appear to have been particularly receptive to the Spaniards. They actively collaborated with the Spaniards, giving them food and helping them to survive the harsh conditions of the frontier. Father Thomas Eixarch, who traveled with the Anza expedition as far as the Colorado River, noted the attentiveness of the Yuma women. In his journal, he recorded that "the Indian women brought a great quantity of beans, maize, calabashes and some wheat, and to show my pleasure and happiness I gave them glass beads and tobacco."[115] The Yuma women brought him so many provisions that they "filled up the house." Eixarch gave them more beads and dismissed them.[116]

The Spaniards showed disdain toward the Yuma men for their practice of sharing their women with the guests and with each other. Father Font noted that the women were "held in common," and the favor shown to guests was to give them women with whom to sleep.[117] He characterized the Yumas as the most shamelessly and excessively promiscuous of any nation in the world, and he noted that the young people especially "live with whomever they want" and leave the women "whenever they feel like it."[118] Father Eixarch observed that the Yumas were more immodest than any other group he had ever encountered. He noted that there was "not a youth who does not have plenty" of women.[119] Father Eixarch wrote that Pablo, one of the Yuma leaders, was "like all the rest with regard to wives, a matter so contrary to natural reason that there is no nation to which it is not repugnant."[120]

Eixarch believed that the Indian women might be more receptive to evangelization than the men. Like Father Serra a few years earlier, he granted a slight moral edge to the Indian women, because, unlike the men, "the women at least covered themselves."[121] Such modesty was viewed by the Spaniards as a sign of sexual restraint, civility, and cultural superiority.

Father Font agreed. He related a humorous exchange he had had with the daughter of Salvador Palma, the Yuma chief and intermediary favored by the Spaniards. Palma's daughter had helped them cross the Colorado River and was a great swimmer.[122] She wore red ochre paint on her body that was completely waterproof, even after a day's swimming. Face and body painting, used decoratively and as a sunscreen, was more common among the Colorado River groups (Yuma, Mohave, and Halchidhoma) than anywhere else in California (fig. 5).[123] Father Font urged her and the others to follow the example of the Spanish Christians and reject body painting. He insisted that Palma's daughter wash herself to get rid of the paint. The spirited woman replied that she did

Figure 5. Face and body painting, used both decoratively and as a sunscreen, was common among the Colorado River groups encountered by the Anza expedition. ("Mohave Indians of the Big Colorado River," from H. B. Möllhausen, *Diary of a Journey from the Mississippi to the Coasts of the Pacific,* 1860; courtesy of the Bancroft Library)

not know how to wash herself and that Font should do it for her. Font wrote, "To her great pleasure and that of those assembled I did give her a good soaping, and succeeded in removing the paint." He then gave her a mirror, and "looking at herself, she broke out laughing." Font had less luck with the men, who were "so enamored of their paints that it will be very difficult to succeed in taking them . . . for they consider it gala dress to go around painted and dirty like devils." Father Font's anecdote manifests the women's openness to change and a willingness to laugh at themselves. Body politics, sexuality, and gender relations were arenas in which the Spaniards could attest to differences in underlying ideologies that sometimes varied by gender.

One wonders to what extent the hidden realm of sexuality, "misunderstandings" about the exogenous sharing of women, and the transformation of codes of sexuality might have influenced the violent denouement of the Yuma-Spanish encounter. Sexuality, in some ways the

most visible and concrete manifestation of religious and cultural conversion, was a touchstone for determining with which Yumas the Spaniards allied themselves. Anza and his men had cast their lot with Salvador Palma, a Yuma leader who ruled by reason of primogeniture and
who presumably maintained a monogamous marriage.[124] They favored
Palma over other indigenous leaders, such as Pablo, who were unwilling to change their polygamous practices, and over female shamans,
whom they considered to be witches.

In late 1776, Captain Anza penned a letter to the viceroy on behalf of
Salvador Palma. Its ostensible purpose was to demonstrate the legiti-
macy of Palma's authority among his own people, to flaunt Palma's
Christian credentials and loyalty to the Spaniards, and thus to establish
Palma's suitability as the single intermediary between the Yumas and
the Spaniards. Despite, or perhaps because of, these considerations,
Palma's petition also demonstrates the centrality of gender issues in the
negotiation of power between the two groups.

To dispel any suspicions that the viceroy might have about his character, Palma, through Anza, first described the qualifications that he
believed would enable the Spanish viceroy to judge his worthiness and
good faith. Palma asserted his position as the Yumas' supreme authority,
which he had inherited from his ancestors with the "universal applause
of his subjects," an interpretation that later events would challenge.[125]
He then described his efforts to care for his tribe and to establish and
enforce laws to that effect. In his petition, Palma sought to represent his
worldview, particularly his attitudes toward female religious leaders
and sexuality, as synchronous with that of the Spaniards. He denied ever
having more than one wife and condemned polygamy in no uncertain
terms. He asserted that he had always "looked with horror on Polygamy," and although he might not condemn such a generally accepted
practice in others, he would never accept it for himself, for he had
"never known any woman other than the legitimate one which I have at
present, and who has given me six children, five girls and one boy."[126]
He told Anza that he "considered witchcraft to be the worst of crimes,"
and thus he "imposed the death penalty on witches." Other crimes, he
noted, were punished with whippings or beatings, "in proportion to
their seriousness." Palma's representation of his own sexual practices

was challenged by other documentation, however. In a journal entry some months earlier, Father Eixarch had noted that Palma boasted that he "used to have many wives, but that since they gave him the [ruler's] staff he has put them away; and now he has and lives with only one, by whom he has six children."[127]

Palma's prevarication illustrates his perception of sexuality and gender as central issues in the negotiation of power. His narrative shows either how indigenous leaders manipulated gender ideologies to be in conformity with Spanish ideologies or how Spanish domination, inadvertently or otherwise, reconstructed indigenous gender relations. In any case, Palma clearly hoped that his self-portrayal as someone who shared Spanish ideas about gender would help him to get arms from the Spaniards and legitimate his authority, at least in their eyes. In fact, it may have done just the opposite.

The Spanish alliance with the Yumas broke down as the Spaniards gradually adopted a more hostile attitude toward the Indians and failed to fulfill the many promises made by Palma on their behalf.[128] The Yuma revolt of 1781, which the historian Charles Chapman called "a disaster of almost unprecedented proportions in the history of Spain's conquest of the northern frontier,"[129] cost the Spaniards the lives of some fifty-five men, twenty women, and twenty children; the Indians captured an additional five soldiers, four settlers, and sixty-seven women and children.[130] Without the support of the Yuma people, crossing the Colorado River became impossible. The revolt spelled the end of the overland colonization route only recently established by Anza.

By 1790, the total number of whites, mestizos, and mulattos in Alta California had reached about 970. Most of these people were pioneers who had come to Alta California between 1769 and 1781, and their descendants.[131] Alta California was a highly mixed society. In 1790, in the town of Los Angeles alone, 49 adults headed up 31 families and included 22 persons who were identified as Spanish, 11 identified as mestizo, 7 as mulatto, 6 as *coyote*,[132] and 3 as Indian.[133] Among those who were married, interethnic marriages prevailed, with 19 mixed couples, 7 Spanish couples, 2 Spanish widows with Spanish children, 1 mestiza widow with Spanish children, and 1 Spanish widower with mestiza children.[134] Of the mixed couples, 3 had no children.

Opportunities for social mobility on the removed California frontier, and indeed, in the Spanish colonies as a whole, were plentiful in the eighteenth century.[135] Spanish efforts to enforce a strict racial caste system, which placed Spaniards on top, American-born creoles and those of mixed background in the middle, and Indians and Africans at the bottom, continued but showed increasing flexibility as economic pragmatism overshadowed social considerations and the Bourbons allowed wealthy people of mixed racial backgrounds to purchase certificates of racial purity. Many individuals of racially mixed backgrounds were reclassified (or reclassified themselves) as Spaniards in the first decades of settlement. In his review of census data from 1785 to 1792 in Los Angeles, Santa Barbara, and San Jose, Jack Forbes found many examples of persons whose race changed over time.[136] In January 1796, California's governor, Diego de Borica, instructed frontier officials on the prices of these certificates: it cost five hundred reales for *pardos* to buy a new ethnic identity and eight hundred reales for a *quinterón* to change status.[137]

Beginning in the 1790s, Spanish authorities in California and Mexico began a formal recruitment policy to help increase the population on the California frontier. In 1797, Viceroy Branciforte notified California Governor Diego de Borica that volunteer soldiers from Cataluña would be permitted to marry Christian Indian women in order to establish residency and increase the population on the California frontier.[138] Governor Borica responded that the neophytes at the missions were not a reliable source of wives, "because it was difficult to induce the Indian women to separate themselves from their relatives" and "because the missionaries objected to marriages of this kind, unless the proposed husbands were of exemplary habits." Thus, Borica asked the viceroy to send Spanish women to marry the soldiers stationed in Alta California.

Viceroy Branciforte supported programs to recruit artisan families, convict-settlers, and, later, orphans and single women for Alta California. Women were central elements in each of these programs.[139] The government authorities believed that the artisans and convicts would be more likely to stay in California if they were accompanied by their families. Commutation of prisoners' sentences for exile was conditioned upon the wife's petitioning the authorities and upon her willingness to accompany and take responsibility for her convict husband in Alta California.[140] Female orphans and single women were needed as wives for the soldiers at the presidios.

The Crown's efforts to recruit permanent female settlers for the California frontier were not a complete success. Many wives stayed behind in Mexico City with a stipend from their husband's wages. Few of the tailors, masons, carpenters, weavers, pottery makers, tile layers, blacksmiths, chair makers, and ribbon makers and their wives remained in California after their contracts expired. Few of the convict families who went to California remained there, and many of the orphan girls participated only reluctantly in the government's colonization schemes.[141] The historian Daniel Garr noted the divergence between Spanish policy aspirations that called for the settlement of California with "respectable and industrious soldiers and settlers, accompanied by their families," and the reality of settlement practices, which channeled "a reluctant and frequently unstable population" to the distant hinterland while simultaneously removing "undesirables" from the Mexican heartland.[142]

By 1800, the settlers had increased in number to about 1,200.[143] After 1800, despite repeated requests for settlers from California authorities, the Crown appears to have been unable to sustain the necessary political will for further colonization or to entice many new settler families to its far-off frontier. An exchange of letters between the governor of Baja California and the auditor (*fiscal*) of the Royal Treasury indicates that the Spanish authorities responded more in this period to petitions for population from Baja California than to petitions from its northern neighbor. Governor Felipe Goycochea wrote in 1805 that the primary need of Baja California was the "increase of its population," and he suggested that the problem of idle youths in the cities of Mexico could be easily resolved by rounding up such youths "of both sexes," as well as families and those who had been detained for minor crimes, for the colonization effort.[144] The treasury officials adopted the idea and agreed to send youths from poor houses and orphanages to the Californias and the Provincias Internas, but the policy was apparently never put into practice.[145]

In 1817, Governor Pablo Vicente Solá, the last Spanish governor of California, requested that five hundred Spanish families be sent to California because they were essential for the development of agricultural and commercial resources there.[146] In another report that same year, he called for the introduction to California of more than one thousand families. These colonists, he wrote, were the country's most pressing need and would be the key to the defense of California's extensive coast.[147] Governor Solá's pleas for more colonists, as well as subsequent pleas from the frontier, went largely unanswered during the remaining few years of Spanish rule, as war for independence raged in Mexico and Spain struggled to tighten its grip over its American colonies.

In 1821, Mexico declared its independence from Spain, and California temporarily disappeared from even the margins of the new republican agenda. Following Mexico's presidential elections in March 1833, however, California gained greater prominence as the liberal leader Valentín Gómez Farías, acting chief executive for the caudillo Antonio López de Santa Anna, announced legislative reforms that stressed primary education, the colonization of Mexico's relatively deserted frontiers, and new secularization decrees.[148] José María Padrés lobbied Mexican officials to pay attention before they lost "the most precious pearl of their necklace."[149] He personally recruited families and tried to get the Santa Anna government to send its political enemies to California, "considering that this would rebound to benefit the proscribed ones and the country."[150] Juan Bandini, José María Híjar, and José María Padrés created the Cosmopolitan Company, a trading company designed to "develop California agriculture and manufacturing and promote the export of its products to world markets."[151] The Cosmopolitan Company provided one of the ships that would be used in the colonization efforts.

In April 1834, the Híjar-Padrés expedition (named for two of its leaders, but really the brainchild of Gómez Farías) departed Mexico City for California. Participating in the expedition were some 239 colonists, including 105 men, 55 women, and 79 children.[152] Instructions from Mexico's foreign minister, Francisco María Lombardo, approved by California governor José Figueroa, directed José María Híjar to occupy the properties of the California missions and to select sites where the quality of soil, water, and air would favor settlement. The towns were to include both Indians and other inhabitants—a departure from

the Spanish *sistema de castas,* which for centuries had dictated the separation of races in the American colonies. The Mexican federal government would pay each colonist a per diem and give each family a plot of
one hundred square yards of land in town and land outside of the town
for additional crops or cattle raising. It would also provide each family
with "four cows, two yoke of oxen or two bulls, two tame horses, four
colts, four fillies, four head of sheep—two female and two male—and
also two plows ready for use."[153] Some of the mission properties would
be distributed among the Híjar-Padrés colonists, and the remainder
would be sold to help pay for costs of the colony, including stipends for
the missionaries, salaries for schoolteachers, and the costs of school
supplies and farm equipment.[154]

Antonio Coronel, who came to California with his family on that
expedition, observed that many people, more than the Mexican government could support, wanted to come to California. He noted that the
"enthusiasm and interest was so great that if the government had had
sufficient resources, it would have been able to send more than 1,000
families—families of a decent social status—to colonize California."[155]

Almost exactly the size of the Anza expedition, the Híjar-Padrés
venture was the first and only major colonization effort sponsored by
the Mexican government. Political infighting and insufficient government support led to the disbanding of the colony shortly after the participants reached their final destination of Sonoma. The church resisted
the secularization of its land and the release of the neophytes from mission control and protection. Political leaders of Alta California, while
favoring the secularization of the missions, were reluctant to share the
spoils of the missions and political power with Mexican political refugees. The president of the Republic of Mexico, who believed the Cosmopolitan Company leaders were out to set up a liberal stronghold in
California and feared they would secede from the republic, sent orders
to disperse the colonists. José Figueroa, governor of the territory, initially supported the colony but turned against it because of the subversive activities of some of the colonists. Although the Cosmopolitan
Company disintegrated soon thereafter, some two hundred of the expedition members remained in California.[156]

Whereas women's reproductive capacity was central to the design of

Spanish colonization efforts, it appears to have been somewhat less important in the Mexican colonization of California. Only one woman, Guadalupe Díaz, age twenty-two, was noted as having given birth during the voyage from San Blas to Monterey in 1834. Educators, agricultural workers, garment workers, and artisans predominated in the Híjar-Padrés expedition. Of the women known to have participated in the expedition, twelve were seamstresses, nine were teachers, and the remainder were listed as wives, daughters, mothers, midwives, or without classification.[157] In 1834 there were no schools for girls in Alta California, and according to Governor José Figueroa, no attempt had ever been made to give the girls of the territory a good education.[158] The teachers of the Híjar-Padrés expedition would be distributed throughout the territory and paid from municipal funds and from cash or produce from the missions. Whereas women in the Anza expedition were needed primarily in terms of their reproductive roles as mothers, to serve as cultural models and acculturators at the missions, and to assist at the presidios, the short-lived colonization efforts in the Mexican era offered promise of a wider range of roles for women in the construction of a new republican society on the Alta California frontier.

5

The Missions

Between 1769 and 1823, Spanish friars established a chain of twenty-one missions, each a day's journey from the next, along 650 miles of Pacific coastline from San Diego in the south to Sonoma in the north (fig. 6). The missions were developed in two clusters, each radiating outward from one of the first two missions established in 1769–70, those at San Diego and Monterey (later moved to Carmel). In the decade from 1770 to 1780, additional missions were founded at San Gabriel, San Luis Obispo, San Antonio, San Juan Capistrano, San Francisco (popularly named Mission Dolores), and Santa Clara. In the following decade, the gap between the northern and southern clusters was narrowed with the opening of three missions along the Santa Barbara Channel—San Buenaventura, Santa Barbara, and La Purísima Concepción. During the last decade of the eighteenth century, the gaps between the missions were reduced with the founding of missions at Santa Cruz, Soledad, San José, San Juan Bautista, San Fernando Rey, San Miguel, and San Luis Rey. The last three missions—Santa Inés, San Rafael, and San Francisco Solano (Sonoma)—were settled in 1804, 1817, and 1823, respectively. The mission farthest inland was Soledad, established in 1791 some thirty miles from the Pacific coast.

With the construction of the missions, a new architecture was imposed upon land and inhabitant alike. Earth, stone, seashells, straw, and branches provided the materials for the pillars, arches, and walls of the mission structure. Spaniards, Baja California Indians, mestizos and mulattos from Mexico, and the newly Christianized Indian neophytes of Alta California participated in fabricating these mission structures. Gardens provided mission residents and their occasional visitors with

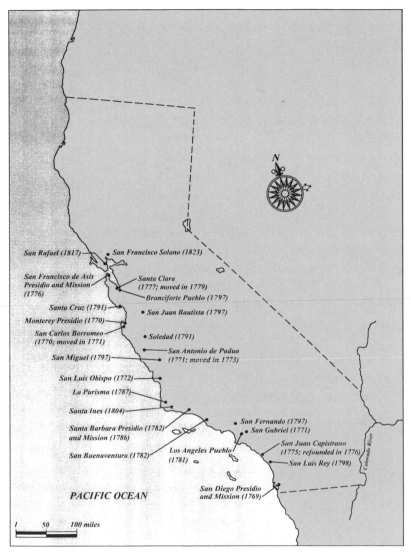

Figure 6. Missions, Pueblos, and Presidios in Alta California. (Artist: James N. Lyons)

food. Between 1782 and 1832, California missions produced nearly 2.5 million pounds of wheat and other agricultural products. By the end of that period, mission corrals were filled with more than 308,000 head of cattle, sheep, goats, swine, horses, hogs, and mules.[1]

Mission architecture embodied Franciscan attitudes about gender.

It symbolized simultaneously protection, isolation, opportunity, and imprisonment for those who lived within its confines. Built like a military fortress, the main mission building generally formed a quadrangle with adobe walls six to eight feet thick. Its various compartments could be individually locked from the outside to provide both protection and control of the residents therein. A separate guardhouse with its own kitchen usually housed the five or six soldiers who were required to accompany the priests on their search for potential Indian converts and escapees. A palisade or wall often enclosed the main mission quadrangle, its separate buildings, and sometimes the adjoining rancherías of thatched huts, adobe houses, or long barracks, where the married neophytes and their families lived.

One of the first structures to be built was often the *monjerío,* the separate dormitory where neophyte girls and single or widowed neophyte women slept under lock and key.[2] Until they reached adolescence, usually sometime after age eleven and sometimes at an earlier age, young Indian girls lived with their Christianized Indian parents in the nearby rancherías. When they reached adolescence (presumably when they began menstruating), the girls were brought to monjeríos, ostensibly to "safeguard their virginity and help them to prepare for Christian marriage."[3] The girls left the mission compound only after they were married, when they returned to the rancherías with their husbands. The Indian men at the missions were sometimes housed in separate quarters called *jayuntes,* where they were only occasionally kept under lock and key.

Roles and experiences at each mission varied over time and were circumscribed by gender, religion, ethnicity, age, and marital status. The missions offered both opportunities and constraints for the women who came to Alta California from Mexico and Baja California. The role of the female newcomers to Alta California was initially an ideological one. Christian women—both Indians and Hispanics—would be role models for the neophytes at the Alta California missions. They were to acculturate women to both Christian and Hispanic ways, theoretically instilling in the neophyte population European habits of personal hygiene. As early as 1774, Father Font noted that the young women at San Luis Obispo mission had been taught to sew "and to keep clean; and they already do so very nicely, as if they were little Spaniards."[4] Father President Lasuén likewise reported "neatness and cleanliness" among the neophytes at San Buenaventura mission.[5] When the English ship captain Frederick Beechey visited the San José mission in 1826, he was impressed by a religious procession in which the Christianized female Indians were "neatly dressed in scarlet petticoats, and white bodices, and walked in a very orderly manner to the church, where they had places assigned to them apart from the males."[6] Not all visitors reported such "successful" adaptation on the part of the Indians. On his visit to the missions in 1792–93, George Vancouver found among the neophytes in San José and San Francisco a "horrid state of uncleanliness and laziness."[7]

The Hispanic acculturation of the Indians included the deliberate inculcation of a European work ethic. Archibald Menzies, a Scottish naturalist who accompanied the Vancouver expedition, noted that the purpose of the missionaries was to create for the state "valuable and industrious subjects, reard [sic] up in the paths of virtue and morality."[8] Such values were seen as essential to the priests' mission and were imposed in part through a rigorous work regimen.

The priests and women from Baja California and Mexico trained the neophyte girls in a number of practical tasks, such as sewing and weaving, designed to cultivate industriousness and to prepare the girls for Christian marriages. The single or widowed females at the monjerío carded, cleaned, and spun wool. They also wove and sewed. Those who were married lived at the rancherías with their families, attending to domestic duties.[9] At the monjeríos, the girls were taught to be useful subjects and wives. Vancouver noted that in addition to being taught how to manufacture wool, the neophytes were instructed in "a variety of necessary, useful, and beneficial employments, until they marry, which is greatly encouraged." Then the girls retired "from the tuition of the fathers to the hut of their husband."[10]

Religious and cultural considerations were more important than ethnicity for the task of acculturation. Although there was some fluidity between Hispanic and Indian women in terms of their labor, a definite hierarchy of responsibility put the priests squarely in charge, followed by Hispanic women (when they were available) who oversaw other Christianized Indian women, who oversaw Indian neophytes. Older

Indian women, as well as Hispanic and Baja California women, served as teachers and role models for the new female converts. At the San Luis Obispo mission, the wives of the soldiers sometimes served as guards at the monjeríos.[11] At the San Diego mission, older Indian women watched over the female neophytes. These indigenous supervisors reported directly to the priest, without a Hispanic intermediary.

Apolinaria Lorenzana, one of the foundlings who came to California in 1800, observed, "The unmarried Indian girls were cared for by an elderly Indian woman who served as the matron. The latter watched over them very closely, taking them to bathe. She never let them out of her sight. In the afternoon, after dinner, she locked them up and gave the key to the Priest."[12] Eulalia Pérez, a self-described daughter of "pure white" parents from Baja California, served as the *llavera,* or housekeeper, of the San Gabriel mission. Pérez recalled that an Indian woman named Polonia, whom the girls called "Mother Superior," was in charge of securing the girls in the monjerío.[13] At the Santa Barbara mission, Angustias de la Guerra Ord, the daughter of the Spanish *comandante* at the nearby presidio, recalled that the female overseers were "ever so ladylike."[14] The Santa Barbara mission priests entrusted neither the Indian nor the Hispanic women with the keys, however. The nunnery at Santa Barbara mission, Ord noted, had three locks and three keys, which were held by the prelate, the *alcalde mayor,* and the corporal of the mission guard. Without the consent of the three officials, no one could enter the monjerío.[15]

At the monjeríos, these Christianized (and usually Hispanicized) Indian women taught female neophytes the ways of Hispanic culture and played a pivotal role in the ideological conversion of their peers. The priests relied on Christianized Indian women to bring female newcomers into the fold and to socialize them in the ways of mission life. Guadalupe Vallejo observed that "when heathen Indian women came in, or were brought by their friends, or by the soldiers, they were put in these houses, and under the charge of older women, who taught them what to do."[16]

Female labor was not limited to social acculturation but served a socioeconomic role as well—a role that expanded with the growing prosperity of the mission enterprise. The testimonies of Eulalia Pérez and Apolinaria Lorenzana, obtained as part of an oral history project conducted in the 1870s at the behest of Hubert H. Bancroft, shed some light on the changing roles and relationships of Baja California and Mexican women at the California missions. Lorenzana and Pérez amply documented the contribution that women made in the supervision, teaching, and execution of basic household tasks such as cooking, cleaning, sewing, caring for the sick, laundering, and managing the daily affairs of the missions. Such tasks were monumental when one considers that a single mission household might include hundreds of neophytes.[17]

Four-year-old Apolinaria Lorenzana arrived with her mother in Alta California from Mexico City in 1800. Shortly thereafter, her mother remarried and returned to Mexico, leaving Apolinaria a virtual orphan. She was taken in by Lieutenant José Raimundo Carrillo and Doña Tomasa Lugo in Santa Barbara, and when Carrillo was promoted to captain of the San Diego presidio, she accompanied them there. Lorenzana had learned catechism and to read at a very young age, and she taught herself to write when she got to California. She recalled, "I learned to write all by myself, using any book I could find to do so. I imitated letters on whatever paper I could get—empty cigar cartons, or any blank paper that had been tossed away. That is how I learned enough to make myself understood in writing when I needed something."[18] After a few years, she moved in with Sergeant Mercado and Doña Josefa Sal. After the sergeant died, his widow opened a girls' school. Because Josefa's time was consumed with running her large estate, Apolinaria was given virtually exclusive custody of the school, where she taught girls reading, catechism, and sewing.

A few years later, she was brought to the mission, where she served as the nurse for the newly constructed mission hospital. As in other places and times, frontier priests in colonial California sometimes discouraged women from engaging in the healing arts. Although Apolinaria Lorenzana was put in charge of the patients in the mission hospital, the priests tried to limit her activities to administrative duties. She managed to exercise her skills as a *curandera* nonetheless. She narrated proudly that she took care of the sick people "even though Father Sánchez had told me not to do it myself, but to have it done, and only to be present so that the servant girls would do it well." Despite the priest's objections, she noted, "I always, as best I could, gave a hand, and attended to the sick."[19] Her friend María Ignacia Amador also knew how to cure sick people and was described by Pérez as a "good curandera."[20]

Faced with a shortage of doctors and medical supplies on the frontier, Hispanic women frequently engaged in such healing activities (sometimes learned from indigenous healers).[21] Apolinaria Lorenzana and Eulalia Pérez both engaged in midwifery, assisting in childbirth for both the indigenous and the Hispanic communities. Juana Machado de Ridington spoke Spanish and the indigenous language of the region and worked with the local doctor and priest to minister to the population in and around the San Diego area.[22] When midwives, caught in the often precarious moment of childbirth, took it upon themselves in the absence of a priest to baptize a newborn, the priests often reprimanded them and invalidated their work by repeating the baptismal ceremony themselves. Such was the case of María Gertrudis del Castillo, the midwife of the town of San Diego, who "badly baptized" the infant born to Jacoba Bernal and Chrisistomo Galindo. Soon thereafter, Father Domingo de Carranza blessed and rebaptized the child.[23]

Women were often given roles as supervisors and teachers at the missions. Pérez emphasized that her responsibilities included supervising men as well as women. She oversaw the men involved in making soap, working the wine presses, and producing olive oil, and she directed the Indian servant who delivered food and supplies to the troops and servants.[24] Lorenzana was responsible for stocking the mission from the cargo ships. She used to take servants with her on board to receive those items that were needed at the mission, and she was authorized to add to the list the priests had given her any additional items she deemed to be useful. Although Lorenzana never married and had no children, she served as a baptismal and confirmation sponsor to some 200 *ahijados,* or godchildren, of all backgrounds. She taught the Indian girls at the San Diego mission to sew, and she personally supervised the making and laundering of the church vestments. She wrote, "Everything was done under my direction and care. I took care not only of making clothing for the church, but saw that the Indian girls laundered it as well."[25] In the 1840s, Lorenzana was the beneficiary of two land grants from the Mexican government; she later bought a third.[26] In the wake of the Mexican-American War, Lorenzana lost her land to speculators.[27]

Eulalia Pérez (fig. 7) was married to Miguel Antonio Guillén, a soldier from the Loreto presidio in Baja California, where she gave birth to three sons (two of whom died) and a daughter. When her husband was reassigned to Alta California, she accompanied him to his new post at the San Diego presidio. There she served as a midwife for eight years, and she complained that she was unable to leave the presidio to visit relatives because her husband refused to accompany her and the presidio commander would not let her leave, owing to the shortage of midwives in the area. After her husband was transferred to serve as a guard at the San Gabriel mission, the family moved north. When her husband died, Pérez returned to San Diego, where she lived temporarily with Lieutenant Santiago Argüello and his family at their home, the only house in the area. Three years later, her son took a job as a mission guard at San Gabriel mission, and Pérez and her five daughters relocated there.

Because she was a widow "burdened with a family," Pérez recalled, "the priests wanted to help me out."[28] The priests originally hired her in 1821 to teach the Indians at the San Gabriel mission (male and female alike) to cook. In the course of more than a decade there, Pérez assumed increasing responsibility for the supervision and administration of the mission. After one year, she was promoted to llavera and assumed responsibility for distributing the rations of food and clothing to the neophytes. At San Gabriel mission, the population grew from 1,201 in 1810 to 1,636 in 1820, and it then declined to 1,320 neophytes by the close of 1832.[29] With 26,342 cattle, sheep, goats, hogs, horses, and mules, its corral in 1832 was second only to that of San Luis Rey mission; the agricultural production of San Gabriel surpassed that of every other mission.[30] Pérez and her five daughters were responsible for cutting and sewing the clothing for the neophyte *vaqueros* who rounded up the livestock. When her daughters were unable to fulfill the clothing needs of the mission, they would ask the priest to contract other women from the nearby pueblo of Los Angeles to assist them.[31]

Many of the women working and living at the missions felt a certain

EULALIA PERZ, 139 YEARS OF AGE.

Figure 7. Eulalia Pérez was born in the presidio at Loreto in Baja California, where she married a soldier when she was fifteen. She later moved with him to the San Diego presidio. There she served as a midwife. She later served as *llavera* at the San Gabriel mission for more than a decade. (Courtesy of the Bancroft Library)

loyalty toward the priests. Pérez was so grateful for their assistance that she found it difficult to reject their counsel, even when it involved making decisions about marriage. When one of the San Gabriel priests urged her to remarry, she confessed that she had no desire to do so, but she "acceded to the father's wishes because I didn't have the heart to deny him anything when Father Sánchez had been like a father and a mother to me and to my family."[32]

Women from Baja California and Mexico taught the Indians how to cook, and they assisted in the preparation of lemonade for the Indian workers and delicacies such as chocolate paste and preserves for the missionaries.[33] Culinary skills were rather rare in the San Gabriel region. Eulalia Pérez recounted that when she arrived at the mission, only two other women in that part of California knew how to cook—María Luisa Cota, the wife of mayordomo Claudio López, and María Ignacia Amador, the wife of soldier Francisco Javier Alvarado.[34] Pérez trained two Indians to cook for the missionaries' kitchen and distributed the daily food rations to the mission Indians. Pérez's description of María Ignacia Amador clashes with many popular stereotypes of poor, colonial women as illiterate. Amador could cook and sew, and like Apolinaria Lorenzana, she could also read and write, and she taught others to do so in her home.

Despite the opportunities open to women on the frontier, there were still limitations on their activities. In an interview in 1874, eighty-one-year-old Dorotea Valdez, whose father had been one of the first settlers of San Diego and who was born in Monterey, referred to these limitations when she noted that because she was a woman, she "was denied the privilege of mixing in politics or in business."[35] At the missions, women were further limited by ecclesiastical concerns about impropriety. Church authorities in New Spain advised the Alta California priests to limit their contact with women at the missions. Appearances could take on their own reality. In an 1807 circular to the priests at the California missions, Father Vicente Francisco de Sarria, the prefect at the College of San Fernando in Mexico City, cautioned the missionaries to keep in mind "how wicked it is to deal with persons of the opposite sex in a familiar way."[36] The order demanded that the priests not "keep suspicious company, nor take advice from women, desiring not only that we be chaste, but that we appear to be so before [other] men." For this reason, Sarria continued, "ministers must refrain from having female servants indoors, and instead avail themselves of men or boys." Sarria repeated his instructions ten years later. The Franciscan order called for particular caution with "Persons of the opposite sex," and

Sarria reiterated that contact with women should be limited to rare occasions and only when others were present.[37] Women were an integral part of the mission project, however, and the instructions from New Spain were sometimes subordinated to the requisites of frontier life. Women, including both the wives and widows of soldiers working at the presidios or the missions and indigenous women, provided institutional support that kept the mission operations running from day to day.

The opportunities and constraints offered to indigenous women at the missions were partly a function of how and why these women had come to the missions in the first place. Twentieth-century anthropologists have concluded that, often in tandem with the use of coercion, indigenous motivations for coming to the missions included a variety of factors, such as environment, the availability of material goods and food at the missions, a belief in and fear of the supernatural powers of the newcomers, a desire to learn how to fight the diseases brought by the strangers, and a shift in the basis of indigenous self-esteem.[38] Although scholars agree that the Indians effectively gave up their freedom once they were baptized, they disagree about whether gentile Indians voluntarily chose conversion or were forced into it.[39] Scholars also disagree on the nature and degree of force exercised to maintain the Indians at the missions and to punish recalcitrant behavior.

The missions of California were built on patriarchal notions that cast the priests as parents of the indigenous "family" to be evangelized (fig. 8). Charged with the "management, control, punishment, and education of baptized Indians," the Spanish priests in Alta California believed their subjects were like children.[40] The task of the fathers in Alta California, as they defined it, was to transform a "savage race" into "a society that is human, Christian, civil, and industrious." This model would rely on persuasion whenever possible and on force when necessary.

Typically, a mission was established in the midst of an indigenous village. One or two missionaries, accompanied by bodyguards, would venture forth from the mission where they were based to nearby native villages in search of new converts. As populations were converted, particularly after 1800, soldiers participated in expeditions into the interior of California in order to capture non-Christianized Indians, who were then brought to the coastal missions for baptism. In the initial recruit-

Figure 8. "The Reverend Father N. Durán and Child," probably done at Mission San José, where Durán served as a missionary and head of the mission system in California from 1825 to 1827 and from 1830 to 1838. This image provides a metaphor for the patriarchism of the mission system. The priests were fathers charged with the care, conversion, and discipline of the infantilized and often "feminized" Indians. (Unsigned, from Duflot de Mofras's expedition in 1844; courtesy of the California State Library)

ment phases, evangelization stratagems included capturing indigenous women and children in order to attract their parents or spouses. Indigenous accounts, generally obtained from Christianized mission Indians, are not particularly forthcoming about the use of force in the recruitment phase. Lorenzo Asisara, a Christianized neophyte at the Santa Cruz mission who sang in the choir and became a manager (*mayordomo*) and keeper of the keys, discussed how missionaries tried to lure children to the missions in order to attain the loyalty and conversion of the entire family. The children were captured first. "The padres would erect a hut and light the candles to say mass," observed Asisara, "and the Indians, attracted by the lights—thinking they were stars—would approach, and soon be taken."[41] Once the young people and their parents were at the mission, their relatives and friends would follow them.

Asisara was somewhat reticent about the role of coercion in these recruitment practices, noting merely that the stratagem for attracting
family members to the missions—taking the children first so that family
members would follow—met with some success.[42]

A report by the military commander José de la Guerra described the
same child-focused strategy. In 1804, Father Juan Martín and his body-
guard made an unauthorized visit to a native village called Cholan,
some fourteen leagues east of the seven-year-old San Miguel mission,
established in the southern reaches of the Salinas Valley. Eager to evangelize the Salinan population that dwelled on the swampy shores of
Lake Tulare, Father Martín asked Guchapa, the chief of all the villages thereabouts, "to give him some children in order to make Christians out of them."[43] The chief balked at the priest's request and "told
the Father and the soldier to get out at once or it would go badly for
them, as he 'was not afraid of the soldiers, who were cowards, and he
knew with certainty that they would die like everyone else.' "[44] Apparently, the priest returned empty-handed.[45] Soon thereafter, de la Guerra
dispatched fourteen soldiers to bring in the uncooperative leader; they
took the chief's son in exchange for Guchapa's promise to "bring in all
the Christian fugitives in his jurisdiction."[46]

The focus on the evangelization of children was common at the
frontier missions. In New Mexico, which was missionized some two
hundred years before California, Franciscan friars fostered a unique
relationship with Pueblo youths that undermined cross-generational
loyalties and indebted the youths to their new "fathers." Gifts for
the youths, accompanied by practices that intentionally disgraced the
Pueblo parents before their children, disrupted preexisting familial relationships among the Pueblo Indians.[47] Franciscan efforts to recruit children in Alta California were based on the same paternalistic ideals,
which emphasized the opportunities and provisions, generally including an annual gift of a new shirt and blanket, that baptism would bring
to Indian children.

Much of the information we have about the use of force in the initial recruitment of converts in Alta California comes from later accounts by foreign visitors traveling under the auspices of Spain's rivals
in conquest. Following his visit to the California missions during 1826

and 1827, the English rear admiral and geographer Frederick Beechey noted that women and children were "generally the first objects of capture," and subsequently, their husbands and parents would "sometimes voluntarily follow them into captivity."[48] Beechey described how the mother of one little boy fled her captors before they could enroll her in the mission list. She "was shot while running away with him in her arms," and the boy was sent to the presidio, where he was "given to the *alférez* [ensign] as a reward for his services."

In memoirs first published in 1829, fifty-three-year-old Kirill Khlebnikov, the Siberian-born administrator of the Russian American Company office in New Archangel from 1816 to 1832, asserted that coercion was always used during the Spanish conversion of the Indians, but that the Indians often went to the missions voluntarily, "sometimes on account of their relatives, sometimes driven by hunger."[49]

The Scotsman Hugo Reid confirmed that recruitment practices among the Gabrielino Indians in the Los Angeles area were built not only on force but also on Spanish notions of motherhood and family. Reid observed that on two separate expeditions to recruit new converts, the soldiers "tied and whipped every man, woman and child" they found. Once back at the mission, the male prisoners were further humiliated, as they "were instructed to throw their bows and arrows at the feet of the priest, and make due submission."[50] After the men were humiliated into submission and had turned in their weapons, the priests baptized the infants and children under eight years of age. The infants were left with their mothers, but other youngsters were isolated from their parents. The women consented to baptism, we are told, "for the love they bore their offspring," and the men followed suit, "for the purpose of enjoying once more the society of wife and family."[51]

Gaps in the statistical record and intentional codes of silence within the church account in part for the debates over the nature and extent of the use of force. The existing data do not show the degree to which Indians came voluntarily to the missions or were coerced. Data are virtually nil for the mission populations before 1786 and only partially available for the years from 1786 to 1798.[52] Generalizations about patterns of recruitment among males and females are difficult to make, because statistics on baptisms were not always broken down by gender.

Furthermore, Franciscan policies promoted codes of silence regarding the use of force at the missions in general and the punishment of females in particular.

Authorities at the Franciscan college in Mexico tried to ensure that all complaints of mistreatment of the Indians would be channeled to them. In 1775, Father Francisco Pangua, guardian of the San Fernando College in Mexico, sent instructions to Father President Serra and all of the missionaries in Alta California that explicitly prohibited the priests from reporting anything concerning the missions, Indians, or soldiers to the viceroy or the archbishop.[53] All information was to be sent to the college instead, where it could be evaluated, responded to, and silenced if necessary.

In turn, the California-based father-president of the missions wanted control of his subordinate priests at each mission and could punish those who broke the codes of silence. The church was particularly sensitive to foreign critics and did its best to keep negative impressions from outsiders. Critiques of the monjerío and the Spanish gender ideologies it represented were part of the effort to undermine Spanish authority in California. Foreign visitors to the missions frequently commented on the priest's confinement of the Indian girls. Georg Langsdorff, a physician and naturalist who was counselor to the emperor of Russia, accompanied the first voyage of the Russians around the world, led by Count Nikolai Petrovich Rezánov. On his visit to the San Francisco mission in 1806, Langsdorff charged that the girls and widows were kept in separate houses under lock and key, not only at night but frequently during the day as well.[54]

Some observers portrayed female confinement as a political ploy. Captain George Vancouver, the first Englishman to visit San Francisco Bay, noted that Indian women were virtual hostages at the missions. On his voyage around the world from 1790 to 1794, Vancouver spent the better part of a year in California, where he visited several of the Spanish missions, including the San Francisco mission. There he observed that, given the affection of the Indians for their women and girls, the Spaniards kept the latter at the missions "as a pledge for the fidelity of the men, and as a check on any improper designs the natives might have for the missionaries, or the establishments in general."[55] According to Vancouver, the priests believed that the Indians would be less likely to attack the Spaniards if Indian women resided at the compound. A female presence at the mission proper was thought to ensure both the loyalty of the male converts and the safety of the Spanish colonists, as well as to deter both Spanish and Indian men from "unauthorized" sexual contact with the Indian women.

The church's response to foreign critiques was to increase its secretiveness about how it treated the Indians. In 1806, Franciscan authorities at the college in Mexico City instructed the California mission priests never to punish neophytes in the presence of foreigners or to communicate anything to foreigners regarding punishments given to the Indians.[56] The instructions established a maximum sentence of twenty-five *azotes* (lashings). If the priests determined that twenty-five lashes were insufficient in proportion to the severity of the crime, they could repeat the punishment one week later, or even daily, and supplement it with other punishments, such as the stockade (*cepo*) or shackles (*grillos*). The priests were forbidden to work the Indians for more than five to six hours in the winter and six to seven hours in the summer. Treatment of women was a particularly sensitive issue. The Franciscan authorities explicitly admonished that the punishment of women should be applied in "hidden locations" and by another woman "as one has been accustomed to doing until now."[57] The Frenchman Jean de La Perouse had observed this practice on his visit to Monterey in 1786, when he noted that women were "never whipped in public, but in an enclosed and somewhat distant place that their cries may not excite a too lively compassion, which might cause the men to revolt."[58]

The college's instructions about the punishment of women responded to complaints by some unnamed priests about corporal punishment. Sarria ordered the priests to halt the "commotion which, for some infractions on the part of your Ministers, have reached not only my predecessors and me, but the Viceroyalty of this Capital as well."[59] Sarria was critical of the infraction—committed not by the priests who were whipping the Indians but by those who had informed the religious and secular authorities in Mexico City of what was happening at the missions. A code of silence had been broken, and college authorities sought to reestablish it: the punishments could continue, but silence must be maintained.

Civil authorities on the California frontier also promoted a policy of discretion on issues related to the use of force against indigenous women. After several Indian women were given twenty-five lashes each in a public flogging at Mission San José in 1808, Governor José Joaquín Arrillaga registered his objections. What he was concerned about was not the punishment, however, but its public nature.[60] Church and civil authorities thus concurred that force against women could be an effective way to ensure Spanish domination of the Indians, but if exercised publicly, it could be a double-edged sword. Frontier authorities feared repercussions from either Crown authorities or the indigenous communities themselves.

Shortly after Father Antonio de la Concepción Horra arrived from Mexico at the San Miguel mission in July 1797, he criticized his fellow prelates for cruelty and mismanagement of mission affairs.[61] Soon thereafter, Father President Lasuén had the priest expelled from California on unsubstantiated charges of insanity, which Bancroft called "absurd."[62] Upon his arrival in Mexico, Concepción fired off a missive to the viceroy, reiterating his criticisms and complaining of the retaliation enacted upon him. "The treatment given to the Indians," he wrote, is "the most cruel I have ever read in history. For even the slightest offense, they beat the Indians, shackle them and put them in the stocks with such cruelty that they hold them there for days without giving them even a sip of water."[63] The viceroy asked Governor Diego de Borica to investigate the charges, and Borica sent a questionnaire to the commanders of the four presidios and then forwarded the responses to Lasuén. Lasuén was furious and charged his accuser with being of an "unstable mind."[64] In his response to the charges made by Concepción and their corroboration by the presidio commanders, Lasuén expressed his clear preference for dealing with internal criticisms behind closed doors. "There is no defect that could not be remedied better by charitable correction than by a blatant accusation," Lasuén protested.[65] With regard to the treatment of women, he noted after consultation with Fathers Estevan Tapis and Juan Cortés that stocks for women were located only inside the monjerío at Santa Barbara mission.[66] There the women were "ordered to be flogged if they deserve it," according to Father President Lasuén.[67] He affirmed that, as required by law, punishment of the women at Santa Barbara mission was always carried out

by other women. The missionaries' comportment toward women responded to their perceptions of female nature. Lasuén noted that wom-
en's "right to privacy is always respected," in order that "the modesty,
delicacy, and virtue belonging to their sex" might be instilled in them.[68]
In 1805, after a lengthy investigation in which presidio commanders
substantiated many of Concepción's charges, the viceroy nonetheless
dismissed Concepción's complaints as "the emanations of an unsound
mind" and cleared the other priests of any wrongdoing.[69]

Nearly two decades later, with church power in decline and a new
climate sparked by Mexico's independence from Spain in 1821, charges
by another priest received a different hearing from that granted to
Concepción de la Horra. In 1823, Father José Altimira, who had been
scouting out the possibility of transferring the mission in San Francisco
to a place with a more amenable climate, visited Indians in the Suisun
region north of Carquínez. In a letter to José Señan, president of the
missions from 1820 to 1823, Altimira charged that, according to the
Indians of the region, Father Narciso Durán of Mission San José "was in
the habit of making raids for converts in that region, forcibly seizing the
gentiles, and even killing those who resisted."[70] Señan apparently shared
Altimira's concerns with Father Sarria, who responded to Altimira
directly. Sarria pointedly did not accuse Altimira of acting in bad faith,
expressed concern about the violent means apparently necessary to carry
out the transfer of the Indians to the new San Rafael mission, and noted
that while all were zealous for new conversions, they should be accomplished with moderation, regularity, and wisdom.[71] He issued instructions to José Darío Argüello, the military commander, that no force was
to be used to secure new converts.[72]

Military raids became increasingly common during the Mexican period, as soldiers and priests ventured into the interior in search of recruits to replace the dying mission populations. All of the indigenous
populations, both at and outside of the missions, suffered tremendous
declines as a result of exposure to European diseases and epidemics. In
the decade from 1801 to 1810, seven thousand children of neophytes
were baptized; sixteen thousand Indians died during the same time
period.[73] Overall death rates rose from 50 percent of baptisms in 1800 to
72 percent in 1810 and 86 percent in 1820.[74] Indigenous women and

young children were hit the hardest. Venereal disease in particular negatively affected reproduction and birth rates and was largely responsible for elevated death rates.[75] The birth rate was about forty-seven per thousand in 1779 and about thirty per thousand in 1829, a decrease of approximately 35 percent.[76] Available data in the aggregate suggest that women made up roughly half of the total mission population in the first decade of mission life (1770–80), reflecting the pre-mission parity between the sexes.[77] Yet the ratio grew increasingly imbalanced over time as women experienced higher death rates than men.[78] Surgeon Major Rollins, who visited San Carlos mission with La Perouse in 1786, reported that "independent of the maladies which the women share in common with the men, they are subject to several peculiar to their sex, particularly those which attend on childbirth, haemorrhages from the uterus, or loss of blood, abortions, &c."[79] By the end of the mission period in 1834, there were only three women to every four men, owing to a "differential death rate between males and females during adolescence and maturity."[80]

In what were perhaps disingenuous and sometimes futile attempts to stabilize sex ratios at the missions, women appear to have been particular targets of some of the raids during the Mexican period. Indian women were often brought in disproportionate numbers to the missions for conversion; the men often escaped or were killed, or perhaps were absent from the villages when they were raided.[81] In one account, Beechey described a retaliatory expedition against the Cosemenes village in 1826. He noted that the commander in charge, Ensign Sánchez, "made a triumphant entry into the mission of San José, escorting forty miserable women and children, . . . and other trophies of the field."[82] Following their capture, the Indian women were brought to the chapel at the San José mission. There, the captive Ohlone women "could see the costly images, and vessels of burning incense," meant to convince them of the benefits they, too, would enjoy as Christians.[83] The absence of male prisoners here is striking.

Within the context of evangelization, native women often became pawns of war. The narrative of a visiting Frenchman, Auguste Duhaut-Cilly, about a similar expedition early in the Mexican period repeated this motif of the capture of female proselytes. Duhaut-Cilly noted that when the harvesting season in 1827 or 1828 was over, the priest at San Francisco Solano mission at present-day Sonoma gave permission to eighty of his Christian Indians to visit their old native villages.[84] The neophytes were navigating up the Sacramento River in a large boat, Duhaut-Cilly wrote, when the "savages"—that is, nonmission Indians— attacked them unawares "in a confined spot where they could neither flee nor defend themselves" and killed more than forty of the neophytes.[85] As in the case discussed by Beechey, a retaliatory incursion was ordered and led by José Sánchez, a veteran Indian fighter from Sonora. Members of Sánchez's expedition took out their anger on the native women and children, killing thirty of them. The soldiers returned, wrote Duhaut-Cilly, "in shameful triumph, with two young girls and a child whom they brought as prisoners, as a token of their victory." In this incident, women were not only proselytes to be captured for conversion but also objects of revenge, receptacles of wrath, and symbols or trophies of victory.

Duhaut-Cilly was a French Catholic who felt himself to be a spiritual brother to the predominantly Spanish missionaries, most of whom he considered to be "men of distinguished merit and great discretion." He noted that he got on well with the padres, particularly by virtue of shared "complaints against the [Mexican] government which had taken the place of the royal authority." Duhaut-Cilly needed the trust and assistance of the priests in order to pursue his own commercial interests, because the priests gave him information about the credit-worthiness of those with whom the Frenchman hoped to trade. Although Duhaut-Cilly implicitly sided with those taken "in shameful triumph," he was careful not to implicate the priest in the retaliation.[86]

Once Indians were baptized, church-state cooperation and the nature of mission life made it difficult for them to flee. For women, confinement in the monjeríos made escape even more difficult than it was for the men. In principle, force was allowed to maintain Indians at the missions once they had been baptized, and in practice, the close collaboration of the cross and the sword procured this end.

In his journals, the Frenchman Jean de la Perouse noted that the carefully watched Indian women at the California missions attempted to flee their restrictive conditions at the risk of severe corporal punishment. He observed that when neophytes tried to escape from the missions, the Franciscan missionaries asked the governor to intervene. The latter would order soldiers to seize the escaped convert, sometimes "in the midst of his family," and return him to the mission for punishment.[87] Perouse's reference to the violation of the family heightens the reader's indignation and suggests that gender ideologies, while used by the priests to justify their paternal role, provided both images and language to critics of the missions as well.

A Russian visitor likewise played up the effects of Spanish coercion on the family. The otter hunter Vassilli Petrovitch Tarakanoff, who was captured and held by the Spaniards for more than a year, described the thwarted escape of one group of neophytes, who "were all bound with rawhide ropes and some were bleeding from wounds and some children were tied to their mothers."[88] Tarakanoff's image of the indigenous children and their mothers served as a metaphor for the helplessness and vulnerability of the mission population as a whole, and it attests that women and children participated in escape attempts. The decision to flee the missions allowed some family members to stay together, but it undoubtedly created divisions as well, as other family members and friends were left behind. Although the head of the missions attested that women were "not so much given to running away,"[89] examples of female escape attempts abound. Mission census records sometimes show the names of such women crossed out from the rolls. Among twenty-one neophytes who escaped from the San Francisco Solano mission in 1826 were Jacinta Atamapi, a Caymus Indian, who fled with her husband, Bertran Pilawspi; the widow Dionisia Lemancitipi, age forty, who fled with her two children (Ysidoro Cholla, twenty, and María Trinidad Chiaipi, fifteen) and her thirty-five-year-old sister-in-law, Estefania Nanaiamitipi Canijosmo; and a Caymus widow, Venancia Octola.[90]

Soldiers who participated in the recovery of escaped neophytes sometimes left memoirs that confirm female resistance to mission life. Inocente García, who described his parents as "pure white" from Sonora, Mexico, served as a mission guard at San Miguel, La Soledad, and the Carmel mission in Monterey before becoming mayordomo at the San Juan Bautista mission. There, sometime between the years 1811 and 1812, García was assigned to participate in a military campaign in search of some Indian women who appear to have fled from San Juan Bautista. Under the command of Sergeant José Dolores Pico, García and five other soldiers accompanied Father Arroyo de la Cuesta and some thirty armed Indians from the San Juan Bautista mission to the southern Ohlone rancherías of Jayaya and Tapé, adjacent to the mission. They went "in search of some *monjas* [Indian maids] that the Captains of other rancherías had offered," noted García. The raid for the women had been previously arranged by Padre Arroyo and the Ohlone captain Jayaya.[91] Nonetheless, upon arriving at the first ranchería, García and his company found the Indians "well armed and ready for battle."[92] The chief of Tapé was absent and had not informed his Indians about the Spaniards' expedition. A melée ensued.

A gender analysis of García's narrative raises questions that challenge traditionally held assumptions about the nature of the evangelization project on the California frontier. García's narrative, collected as part of an oral history project in the 1870s, testifies to the military-religious collaboration in raids whose ultimate purpose was the capture of women. García's assertion that an agreement had been made between the friar and the Indian chiefs of two villages for the hand-over of the girls attests to the patriarchal nature of decision-making structures in both the Spanish and the southern Ohlone communities—or at least to the Spaniards' belief that they were dealing with people whose social structure reflected their own in terms of gender hierarchies of power.[93] That the sergeant brought thirty armed Indians from the mission with the expedition shows that the Spaniards anticipated resistance and that the envisioned outcome of the raid (i.e., the procurement of the Indian girls) was determined to outweigh the costs of military confrontation. The use of force to capture these Indian women suggests that, Laws of the Indies notwithstanding, the presence of women at the missions was, in at least some cases, involuntary.

García's account provides no clues regarding the names or specific tribal affiliations of the females in question, so we do not know whether they belonged to the rancherías where they were being sought. Their being referred to as *monjas,* the chief's mysterious absence from Tapé, his alleged failure to inform the village about his arrangement to return the girls to the mission, and the village's readiness for battle all suggest that the Indian women had been Christianized, had fled the San Juan Bautista mission and sought refuge at Tapé and Jayaya, and apparently enjoyed the support of the community that took them in.[94] That the expedition specifically sought female Indians highlights the vulnerability of the women, raises the possibility of a gendered resistance to mission life, and suggests the likelihood that gender partially determined the nature of indigenous experiences at and resistance to the missions.

Narratives by other Spanish soldiers likewise attest to the capture of women. José María Amador, a Spanish soldier who lived at the San José mission and who later became brigadier general of the Mexican army, argued that it was the male mission Indians who initiated the capture of women and children. He described a military campaign in 1837 in which he was second-in-command, accompanied by some seventy soldiers and civilians and two hundred mission Indians, or "auxiliaries."[95] In this retaliation campaign against Indians who had stolen nearly one hundred head of stock from his ranch, Amador attested that he oversaw the slaughter of some two hundred Indians in cold blood. His version of what happened next would lead us to believe that the mission Indians who participated in the campaign suddenly began calling the shots and insisted on going back across the river to capture the ranchería, kill the remaining men, and take the wives and daughters of those who had just been shot. Amador asserted that it was the mission Indians who "made me cross the river swimming with them" and who instigated the killing of 40 men and the capture of 160 women and children at the ranchería.[96] Although accompanied by a sizable Spanish force, Amador depicted himself as powerless to control the mission Indians under his charge, suggesting, at the very most, his reluctant complicity in the raid.

In this case, there was an intersection between what the neophytes purportedly wanted and what Amador wanted. As Amador described it, the San José mission gained 160 new female and young proselytes from the raid. The desires of the Indians who brought the women back to the mission may or may not have been the lustful ones that Amador attributed to them. There is evidence that Indian men at the missions sometimes collaborated with Spanish soldiers for the procurement of women.[97] Father Serra noted that the priests at San Gabriel mission had written to him with proof that Indian alcaldes were doing so, and in

1780 he complained to Governor Felipe de Neve that Nicolás, the Indian alcalde at San Gabriel mission, "was supplying women to as many soldiers as asked for them."[98] If such were the case here as well, then Amador's anecdote would illustrate a convention of behavior toward women shared by Spanish and Indian males and a collaboration across ethnic borders forged by gender. Even if we admit to a certain dissimulation on the part of the Indians and entertain alternative rationales for indigenous actions, the raid underscores the vulnerability of women and children both in the mission endeavor and within the old order.

The capture of native women, either inadvertently or intentionally, exacerbated tensions among the Indians themselves. The involvement of male neophytes in such expeditions contributed to antagonism between mission and nonmission Indians. Beechey wrote that although the capture of women furnished proselytes, it also prolonged "a perpetual enmity amongst the tribes, whose thirst for revenge is almost insatiable."[99] He observed that animosity between the converted and unconverted Indians made nonmission Indians less likely to assist escaped neophytes and that it was "of great importance to the missions" because it checked desertion. Furthermore, he noted, such animosity was "a powerful defence against the wild tribes, who consider their territory invaded, and have other just causes of complaint."

Use of the neophytes in raids to recover escaped mission Indians provoked frictions between civil and religious authorities as well. In 1799, Viceroy Miguel José de Azanza ordered the missionaries to refrain from including neophytes in efforts to capture runaways from the missions.[100] The practice appears to have continued into the Mexican period, however.

The presence of female captives from the raids added to the ethnic mixture already present at the missions, where Indians from many different tribes, with a variety of relationships among them, cohabited. Lorenzo Asisara noted that at the Santa Cruz mission where he lived, there were members of about thirty different bands, who were often unable to understand each other.[101] The atmosphere of distrust or hostility among the Indians, exacerbated by raids for women and the lack of a common language, gave the priests added insurance that the Indians would not unite in rebellion against them. The Laws of the

Indies prohibited the forced conversion of the Indians unless the Indians caused harm to the Spaniards. The capture of Indian women, like the abuse of Indian women by Spanish soldiers, often provoked retaliation, which enabled the Spaniards to justify their use of arms in "self-defense"—which then allowed them to bring new recruits to the missions.[102]

Rhetorical critiques of the indigenous division of labor contributed to and reflected ideologies that legitimated conquest in general and the mission system in particular. Missionary priests believed that the mission would provide protection for Indian girls within the mission's walls, and they extolled the benefits of missionization for the female indigenous population. The Spaniards' assumptions derived in part from their gender ideology and its conflict with the ideologies of indigenous groups. The priests believed that the mission offered women an easier regime of labor than that experienced in pre-mission days. They were quick to underscore what they saw as the inequities of the pre-mission division of labor for women. Father Gerónimo Boscana noted, "It was the duty of the women to gather the seeds, prepare them for cooking, and perform all the meanest offices as well as the most laborious, whilst their lazy husbands were either at play or asleep. Frequently, they would receive ill-treatment in return."[103] This contrast between the hardworking "squaw" and her lazy husband formed part of a rhetoric that suggested that women were better off at the missions.

Father President Fermín Francisco de Lasuén agreed that the indigenous division of labor was unfair to women, and he noted the abuse given to the indigenous wives by their spouses. He observed, "In their native state they [the women] are slaves to the men, obliged to maintain them with the sweat of their brow. They are ill-treated," he wrote, "trampled on by them even to the point of death if, on returning to their huts after spending the entire night in raids or in dancing, the entire morning in play, and the entire evening in sleeping they find that the women have made no provision for food for them." Conditions were better for women at the missions, according to Lasuén, who pointed out that the women "never object or show any dislike for the work we assign."[104]

In the pre-mission period, California Indians had seldom engaged in subsistence agriculture, and then only in the extreme southwest.[105] For most indigenous men and women of Alta California, sedentary agriculture at the missions and the lifestyle it entailed represented a marked departure from days of yore, when the Indians "neither cultivated the ground, nor planted any kind of grain; but lived upon the wild seeds of the field, the fruits of the forest, and upon the abundance of game."[106] In pre-mission days, women in most California tribes had primary responsibility for the collection of foodstuffs. They gathered acorns, roots, seeds, berries, and grasshoppers. They shelled the acorns, dried them, and ground them into flour for bread.[107] The acorn permeated indigenous societies and provided the inhabitants of Alta California with their principal sustenance before the mission period.[108] Its value extended beyond the merely nutritional. The year was measured from "acorn to acorn," or from "seed to seed."[109] The northern Ohlone Indians at San José mission distinguished the seasons of the year by the rotations of the moon, the rains, the weather, and the ripening of the acorn seeds.[110] Spring was marked by the appearance of flowers; summer was when the grasses became dry and the seeds matured; fall was discernible because wild geese and ducks appeared and the acorns ripened; and winter was recognized because of the rainfall.[111] In pre-mission days, women made no pottery but crafted baskets so tightly woven that they could be used to boil water for cooking. They continued their basketry work at the missions.

Missionization disrupted indigenous survival patterns and transformed some aspects of gender roles. At the missions, the acorn was no longer a mainstay of the indigenous diet, although the failure of agricultural efforts in the early mission years provided some Indians with opportunities to supplement their mission diet with wild foods. As food production at the missions became more efficient and changed the ecological patterns of the land, some of the priests restricted the opportunities for neophytes to engage in their pre-mission patterns of food gathering, hunting, and fishing.[112] The shift in patterns of food production may have affected female status as the acorn shifted to a less prominent place on the menu than it had held in pre-mission days.

Indigenous women at the missions nonetheless continued to be involved in aspects of childbearing and child rearing, food production, cooking, basket making, clothing production, and retrieval of water and wood, albeit on a greater scale and in a more systematic and controlled way than before.[113] The women no longer controlled their own labor but were directed by others and subject to punishment if they did not comply.

Men, who had previously engaged in hunting, fishing, and the gathering of some plants, now provided the missions with labor for agriculture, ranching, weaving, construction, and artisanry. At the San Francisco mission in 1827, Duhaut-Cilly observed more than two hundred Indians of both sexes at work. He noted that the women and children carded and spun the wool while the men "planned and wove blankets."[114] The new male roles in sustained agricultural labor apparently "generated disaffection and contributed to a general psychological disorientation" among the neophyte population.[115] Men's roles at the missions showed greater variation from pre-mission patterns than did those of females.

Just as priests cited the natives' inequitable gender roles and mistreatment of women in order to justify bringing indigenous women to the missions, so gender ideologies guided their enclosure of women in the monjeríos. The institution of the monjerío responded in part to Spanish ideas about gender and honor. Confinement of female neophytes was purported to assist the priests' efforts to regulate sexual relations between male and female Indians and to protect the women from abuse by Spanish-Mexican soldiers. Guadalupe Vallejo recalled that the young girls and widows at the San José mission lived in a "large adobe building, with a yard behind it, enclosed by high adobe walls."[116] The architectural arrangement at the missions, according to Vallejo, emerged from Mexican courtship customs meant to inhibit relations between the sexes. Separated from the men by these walls, the women could be courted only from below through the upper windows of the monjerío. The windows, cut into the thick adobe walls, measured about two feet square by three feet deep and were spanned with iron bars. Such buildings, reminiscent of Spanish convents, complemented a strict social code of conduct that was designed to protect female virginity as the basis of family honor. Vallejo observed that the rules for the Indians were no stricter than those prevailing for much "higher classes" throughout

Spanish America. One California *ranchero* noted that the boys on his ranch slept outside, and the girls in a locked room, to which the parents held the key.[117]

The walls of the monjerío, like the walls of other mission structures, were virtually impenetrable blocks of silence that hid the experiences of female neophytes. Church codes of silence converged with another code of silence on the part of the Indians, who were seldom in a position to reveal the abuse they experienced at the hands of the mission system. Lack of faith in the justice system of the Spanish priests, along with linguistic, cultural, and gender barriers, encouraged such reticence.

In this chapter I have tried to show how, within the confines of the mission system, female experiences varied by ethnicity, religion, age, and civil status. Gender ideologies provided the justifications for bringing women to the missions and the blueprint for their roles once they got there. Christianized Hispanic women worked to support the administration and functioning of the mission system and to cultivate European habits of hygiene and industry among the indigenous population. Soldiers, priests, and Indian men brought indigenous women to the missions by force. Sometimes women came of their own free will. Once at the missions, Christianized Indian women tutored newcomers in the ways of Hispanics. They were punished, they punished others, and they sometimes resisted missionization. Indigenous women suffered greater risks than men in their susceptibility to illness and death, due to their role in childbirth. Female confinement in the monjeríos made women more vulnerable than men to diseases and disrupted gender relations. Indigenous women were at risk both at the missions and away from them as Spanish soldiers sought to gratify their desires for violence, power, and sex.

6

Sexuality and Marriage

Spanish church authorities saw the transformation of indigenous patterns of marriage and sexuality as vital to the conquest of Alta California in general and to the success of the missions in particular. Like religious, cultural, and political conversion, this transformation was predicated upon the Franciscans' belief in the absolute superiority of Spanish Catholic civilization. Catholic codes of sexual behavior included chastity, restraint, monogamy, and the elimination of sexual activity outside of the sacrament of marriage. Franciscan discourse criticized the sexual "vices" of the Indians as measured against these Judeo-Christian norms.

In the previous chapter, I analyzed how a discourse critical of pre-mission indigenous gender roles provided an ideological justification for conquest. In this chapter, I argue that a discourse critical of indigenous gender relations and sexuality functioned similarly. The transformation of indigenous sexual behavior and marriage practices legitimated the evangelization project. The implicit, if not explicit, argument in favor of imposing Hispanic Catholic values centered on a critique of indigenous sexual practices, including polygamy and divorce. The Franciscans used this critique to advance an argument that the Indians, especially the women, were better off at the missions than they had been in indigenous society.

The Franciscans represented indigenous sexual practices as being at odds with the Christian notion of the family. When asked to respond to a government questionnaire in 1812 about which vices were dominant among the neophytes and in which sex,[1] the prelates almost unanimously listed licentiousness, and more than two-thirds of the respondents named debauchery as the prevailing vice among the Indians at their mission.[2] Ecclesiastic authorities decried the incontinence, the unfaithfulness, and the polygamous practices of the Indians and the willingness of Californian Indian husbands to barter or gamble away their wives. The depiction of the Indians as heathens who were sexually loose, unfaithful spouses, and polygamists made the California conquest a moral crusade.

The friars saw control of native sexuality as fundamental to their mission. Missionary priests Luis Antonio Martínez and Antonio Rodríguez from San Luis Obispo observed that idleness, and the inevitable lust to which it gave rise, had the potential to undermine the conquest itself. They observed, "The Indians are naturally given to vice, since from their infancy they have no occupation whatsoever and they survive on whatever the day provides for them. They live in idleness and thus they are full of vice, the chief one being lust, which soon finishes off the men as well as the women. If something is not done to remedy these results, the conquest will soon come to an end."[3] Father José Señán from San Buenaventura mission also linked idleness with unchasteness. The three main vices, he wrote, were idleness, incontinence, and the tendency to steal.[4] Many friars saw promiscuity as reflecting a lack of industry, whereas sexual restraint was believed to encourage "rational," productive behavior. Finding a way to reduce licentiousness would purportedly also make the Indians more industrious.

The priests maintained that the evangelization effort in California depended on changing the sexual patterns of their new flock, particularly as the proliferation of venereal diseases contributed to a dramatic population decline. At San Gabriel mission, one of the oldest missions, Father Luis Gil and Father José María de Zalvidea lamented that promiscuity had "penetrated" the Indians "to the very marrow with venereal diseases," such that many newborns showed "immediate evidence of the only patrimony their parents gave them."[5] The chief disease among the Indians at virtually all of the Alta California missions was venereal disease, which was, the missionary fathers at San Miguel mission wrote, "carrying them to the grave rapidly."[6] The San Antonio fathers attributed such deaths to indigenous lustfulness.[7]

Medical reports of the time likewise blamed the Indians for contracting venereal diseases. In his report on medical conditions in California in 1805, José Vicuña Muro charged that indigenous illnesses, particularly syphilis, were due to "unavoidable or voluntarily sought causes."[8] The "unavoidable" factors he listed tended to be climatic and environmental—cold weather, scanty clothing, bad water, the lack of vegetables, and badly prepared meat. On the other hand, the "voluntarily sought" factors that perpetuated their diseases were related to the character and lifestyle of the Indians themselves—their nakedness, their mixing with others who were infected, their "carnal disorders," and their "natural abandon." These factors were aggravated, according to Vicuña Muro, by the Indians' rejection of European "rational" medicine. Vicuña Muro effectively absolved the Spaniards of responsibility for the onset or spread of the diseases. A poor diet was hardly unavoidable, and the Indians, even those who chose to be at the missions, did not voluntarily seek the overcrowded conditions they sometimes endured.

In the context of a power struggle between the settlers of the Los Angeles pueblo, established in 1781, and the San Gabriel missionaries, the latter broke with the pattern of blaming the Indians for the venereal diseases they had contracted and pointed to the settlers as the culprits.[9] When Sergeant Xavier Alvarado, commissioner for the town of Los Angeles, charged that Fathers José Miguel and José María Zalvidea, the missionaries of San Gabriel, had twice refused to answer sick calls from settlers in Los Angeles, the priests wrote a scathing response. They noted that "a putrid and contagious malady" had begun to show itself at the San Gabriel mission following Anza's first exploratory excursion in 1774.[10] The disease had "spread among the Indians here to such an extent that as soon as a child is born it already has in itself this contagion."[11] As a result, the missionary priests were too busy attending the sick and dying of the mission to be available for the pueblos and presidios.[12]

This unusual example notwithstanding, the Franciscans' discourse and practices often found fault with indigenous sexuality patterns, and their policies centered on changing indigenous sexual relations. Control over intimate relations would reinforce the power of the conquerors on a psychological level and, on a more pragmatic level, stabilize the population by slowing the death rate from venereal disease.

Christianization and Hispanicization converged in the institution of marriage, which, in the eyes of the friars and the Crown, provided the antidote to a "heathen" condition that permitted or encouraged un-chasteness, infidelity, and polygamy. Although the formation of Christian families demanded monogamous behavior, almost certainly the missionaries exaggerated the extent of polygamy among the indigenous masses. Polygamy, when it was practiced, appears to have been restricted to the leadership of many California tribes.[13] For the groups whose leaders did practice polygamy, there appears to have been an important sociopolitical function for the multitude of wives. H. D. Richardson, an early California pioneer, noted that the chiefs in the Yerba Buena region around today's San Francisco "possessed eleven wives, the subchiefs nine, and the warriors two wives or as many more as they were able to care for." Multiple wives were helpful in times of war, Richardson observed, because "while in an actual engagement with other tribes the women would always follow and assist in securing the wounded from off the field of battle as well as packing all of the provisions of the tribe in their arms while their papooses were slung upon their backs."[14] Hugo Reid wrote that in the Los Angeles area, chiefs had one, two, or three wives, "as their inclinations dictated," while other members of the community had only one.[15] Chiefs of the coastal Miwok to the north of San Francisco Bay often had two wives, but that practice appears to have ended by the late Mexican period. The Russian observer P. Kostromitonov noted that by the late 1830s the Miwoks no longer permitted men to have more than one wife, although "in earlier times the *toyons* used to have two wives."[16] His reluctant informants seem to have tailored their responses according to what they knew of Christian marriage practices. They were careful to assure Kostromitonov that even in earlier times, the bigamists "exposed themselves to ridicule" for their practices. "Nowadays," they told him, "this custom has vanished completely."

In addition to expressing Christian intolerance of polygamy, the Franciscans censured the separation or divorce of a married couple. Throughout Alta California, most indigenous spouses were able to leave a marriage at will. The friars observed that non-Christian Indian couples remained married only "as long as they desired, that is, as long as both were satisfied and lived in harmony or until the man found another woman who pleased him more."[17] The facility with which spouses broke their matrimonial bonds was a source of consternation for the priests. The missionaries at San Buenaventura were amazed at the facility with which the male Indians "take and divorce their wives."[18] What really astonished them, however, was that women divorced their husbands frequently, too. "Neither party," the priests wrote, "cares for nor understands the indissoluble bond." A Spanish visitor, José Bandini, observed in 1828 that divorce was common among the California Indians. According to Bandini, marriage was contracted with a young Indian girl's father, who demanded from the fiancé "a quantity of glass beads reflective of the merit the daughter is presumed to have."[19] Divorce was obtained upon the return of the gift to the husband.

Spousal abuse occurred among the Indians and was one reason given for separating spouses at the missions. Hugo Reid wrote that among the Gabrielino Indians of Los Angeles County, if a woman's husband "ill-used her, and continued to beat her in a cruel manner," she informed her relatives, who "collected together all the money which had been paid in at the marriage" and took it to the husband's hut, where they exchanged the money for his wife, literally purchasing her return.[20] The wife was then remarried to a new spouse.

Attitudes toward adultery varied among indigenous groups in California. Sanctions against women adulterers were harsh in theory but often more lenient in practice. Among the Gabrielinos, the exchange of wives was considered legal, and the wife had no recourse but to submit. In cases of female adultery, a Gabrielino Indian husband was technically permitted to kill or injure an offending wife, "without any intervention of chief or tribe."[21] More commonly, however, the wronged husband "informed the wife's paramour that *he was at liberty to keep her.*" The husband then "took possession of the lover's spouse and lived with her." Spousal swapping was thus accepted as a legitimate consequence of adultery.

Among the Chumash in the Channel Islands region near today's Santa Barbara, indigenous tradition and practice differed somewhat. According to Fernando Librado Kitsepawit, a Chumash Indian who was born in 1804 at the village of Swahil on Santa Cruz Island and soon thereafter taken to the mainland and baptized, there were three pestilences that obliterated nearly all of the Indians. The last of these was a civil war that began at Muwu "because in those ancient days the punishment for adultery was very severe."[22] Librado noted that his grandfather had told him that "if a woman was unfaithful, she was sentenced to be shot three times with arrows by an executioner. On such occasions they would seat the woman down before the people and execute her." However, at an unspecified point in time, apparently prior to the mission period, the Chumash considered the death penalty for adulterous women to be excessive and rebelled against this practice. When one of their leaders sought to enact the death penalty for an adulterous woman, civil war broke out among the people. Following the war, the victorious leader was "unanimously asked by the people to do away with capital punishment, which he did."[23] Librado's narrative reminds us of the variation over time and place with regard to attitudes toward sexuality and marriage.

Most of the missionaries rejected the legitimacy of indigenous marriage ceremonies. The missionaries at San Miguel wrote that in pre-mission times, "mere natural love in the single man and woman was sufficient to unite them and have themselves regarded as married."[24] The priests noted that "the more sensible ones have asked for their bride from the parents or relatives so that after baptism it has been necessary to have them renew their marriage consent."

Ironically, indigenous and Hispanic marriage practices shared some similarities. In theory and often in practice, marriage choices were made largely by men in the various societies. In colonial Latin America, marriage policies offered the government a convenient vehicle for controlling social change. They codified Spanish ideas about gender relations while also reflecting the shifting power relations of the time. In the late eighteenth century, legal norms became increasingly restrictive for Hispanic women as the Bourbon reforms strengthened the patriarchal family and the state at the expense of the church. The *Royal Pragmática* of 1776, which was extended to Spain's American colonies in 1778, embodied many of the Spanish attitudes of the time about race, class, and gender. It required parental consent for youths under the age of twenty-five to marry, and it upheld parents' right to oppose their children's choice of mate.[25] In the Americas, however, obtaining parental consent for a marriage was not always possible, either because it was not known who the parents were or because the parents were unavailable. Thus, parental consent was not required for "Mulatos, Negros, Coyotes and similar races," in the Americas, unless those individuals "were officials or distinguished themselves from the others by their reputation, good service, etc., and therefore were obliged to respect their parents."[26]

In publishing the Pragmática in California,[27] the Audiencia of Mexico cited a case in Guanajuato that had been particularly offensive and that illustrates the nature of Spanish gender ideologies of the time.[28] In that case, Juan Antonio López and Doña María Manuela de Aranda y Laris wished to marry, despite the objections of her father. The *alcalde mayor,* or judge, of Guanajuato ruled in favor of the father and counseled disinheritance, the recommended punishment for ignoring the parents' wishes in such cases.[29] The disappointed suitor appealed to higher authorities in the Audiencia and Justicia, who upheld the father's objections.[30] To circumvent her husband's objections, the mother proposed to leave her inheritance (and even to increase it to account for the loss of her husband's share) to both her daughter and her daughter's suitor. After broad consultations with the Council of the Indies and the Crown's attorneys,[31] the king determined that such an action constituted a dangerous "lack of subordination of the woman to her Husband." In order to "conserve family honor," and so that "women might recognize the authority of their consort as the head of the family," the king prohibited women from leaving their inheritance to children who contracted marriage against their father's will.[32] This decree aligned the Crown squarely with the husband when parents disagreed over their children's marriage choices, and it upheld a husband's authority to overrule his wife's support of their children's marriage choices.

Marriage policies allowed parents to control their children, husbands to control their wives, and mission priests to control the Indians. The Crown used the law and policies of incentives or disincentives to encourage or inhibit race mixture, as it saw fit. On the California frontier, it encouraged interethnic marriages, especially early on. As it had done in New Spain, the Spanish Crown promised land and other incentives to single Spanish soldiers who married Christianized Indian women. Granting these interethnic couples land to be worked, Spanish policymakers believed, would put more land under cultivation, would provide the Indians with further instruction in cultivating it, and would address the problem of food shortages on the frontier.[33]

This intermarriage program was never consistent and never achieved tremendous success, but the policies did find some qualified success early on in the Monterey region. The first marriages between Spanish soldiers and Indian neophytes took place at the San Carlos mission in 1773, when three Catalán soldiers married, respectively, Margarita Domínguez, María Seraphina, and María de Gracia, probably their Spanish baptismal names.[34] Father Junípero Serra reported that the couples had already begun to have children by the following year, as the authorities had desired. He pleaded to the viceroy on behalf of the Catalán soldiers for the furlough, two years' salary, and five years' rations that had been promised to the men if they married the Indian women. All three soldiers had assured Father Serra that without the promised incentives, they never would have done so. The women, forced to leave their homes, families, and crops, did not speak their husbands' language. Although church regulations prohibited forced marriages, protest would have been difficult to register under such circumstances. Serra lamented that "when, without tying them up, they can be made to follow (their husbands), it must be with great disgust on their part and on the part of their relatives."[35] Serra argued that the soldiers who married Indian women from the missions should not be expected to stay at the presidios but should be excused from military duty, move to the missions, and dedicate themselves to working the land and raising families.[36]

The Crown and the missionaries hoped that legitimating unions between the cultures would check the rapid spread of venereal disease, gain the trust of the natives, reduce the incidents of rape, defuse tensions between the two cultures, and create kinship ties that would ensure the Indians' loyalty.[37] Indian women who married Spanish men gained for their husbands, and sometimes for themselves, legitimate title to Spanish mission land. Spanish men gained access to the labor of their wives' community, which often ensured the production of foodstuffs for the soldier and his cohorts. The women might have seen the marriages as avenues for protecting their future. They might have believed the Spaniards were powerful shamans, or they might have made political calculations based on the Spaniards' superior force of arms. Such marriages provided them with an opportunity to leave the mission compound and thereby escape the watchful scrutiny of the Franciscan missionaries and the llaveras.

Spain's promotion of intermarriage fluctuated in relation to its ability to attract Hispanic families and marriage prospects to Alta California. Antonia Castañeda's research has shown that rates for intermarriage between Spanish soldiers and settlers, on one hand, and Christianized Amerindian women, on the other, were high in the initial period, when Hispanic women on the frontier were relatively scarce. From 1773 to 1778, such intermarriages accounted for some 37 percent of all of the marriages contracted in the Monterey area.[38] Sixteen of the forty-three marriages recorded in Monterey between 1773 and 1778 were between Spanish, mestizo, black, or other *casta* (mixed background) men and indigenous women.[39]

Between 1790 and 1795, as Spanish policymakers planned new colonization ventures, the Crown reversed its land incentive programs and stopped entitling Hispanic settlers to receive mission lands when they married neophyte women.[40] Although government authorities did not actively oppose interethnic marriages (recall that in 1797, Viceroy Branciforte had given his approval for marriages between the Cataluña soldiers and Christianized Amerindian women), intermarriage rates declined dramatically in the absence of land incentives.[41] After 1798, no intermarriages were recorded in the Monterey region.[42] By 1800, some 24 marriages (most of these at San Carlos mission) had been recorded between neophyte women and Spanish soldiers in all of Alta California.[43] In addition to the lack of incentives, the strong bonds between neophyte women and their families and the poor quality of the prospective husbands (according to the friars) also seem to have inhibited greater intermarriage.[44]

Pre-mission customs among most California tribes gave young indigenous women little choice regarding their marriage partners. Parents contracted marriages for their children, although the latter's wishes were not usually ignored.[45] According to the friars' accounts, marriages among the "pagan" Indians usually occurred when the groom or his representative (either his father or a brother) went to the house of the bride or her closest relative and asked for her hand. The groom then offered a gift to the girl or her parents, which, if accepted, sealed the marriage contract. Variations arose in terms of who did the asking (the groom himself, the father, a brother, any relative); who granted the request (parents of the bride, the bride, or both); who received the gift (father of the bride, female relations, or both); and when the couple was considered to be married (after verbal consent was given, after the gifts were accepted, or after the pair lived together).

The practice of purchasing brides appears to have been common throughout California. The practice and its meaning differed by group, however. Among northwestern tribes, it was a "definite commercial and negotiated transaction, the absence of which constituted a serious injury to the girl's family."[46] Hugo Reid described the marriage customs of the Gabrielino Indians who lived in what is today Los Angeles County. He wrote of a commodity exchange in which the husband-to-be decided on the woman he wished to purchase, publicized his decision, and had it confirmed by the community. The bride and her family played an apparently minor role in the transaction. Reid noted,

> When a person wished to marry, and had selected a suitable part-
> ner, he advertised the same to all his relations, even to the *nine-
> teenth cousin*. On a day appointed, the male portion of the lodge,
> and male relations living at other lodges, brought in a collection of
> money beads. The amount of each one's contribution was about
> twenty-five cents. . . . [The males] proceeded in a body to the
> residence of the bride, to whom timely notice had been given. All
> of the bride's female relations had been assembled, and the money
> was equally divided among them; the bride receiving nothing, as
> it was a sort of purchase.[47]

In many cases, the woman seemed to have little say in the matter. Fathers Marcelino Marquínez and Jayme Escudé documented what they considered to be a relatively unceremonious exchange of goods in which the husband purchased the wife from her father. They observed that when a nonmission Indian at Santa Cruz mission wished to marry, he went to the girl's house and sat beside her. They observed, "He sighs without saying a word. Then he throws before the father of the girl some colored beads which we call *caracolillos* or small pieces of sea shell held together by a thread. They go forth then and without any further ceremony or rite are considered married."[48]

Among neophytes at the missions, the sequence of events involved in the marriage contract appears to have generally followed the same format. Fathers Estevan Tapis and Francisco Xavier Uría recounted that the male Indian at Santa Inés mission indicated which woman he wanted to marry, and the marriage was enacted following the verified acceptability by the parents of the bride and groom, and the consent of the couple. They noted: "When an Indian desires to get married he presents himself to the missionary father indicating the girl of his choice with whom he intends to live in the married state. The missionary father inquires if the proposed marriage is acceptable to the parents of both bride and groom. When these latter and the parents consent and no canonical impediment bars the marriage, the Indian partners then marry according to all the prescriptions of the Church."[49]

Similarly, Fathers Marcelino Marquínez and Jayme Escudé described how marriage petitions were made at the Santa Cruz mission. Their documentation serves as a reminder of the linguistic barriers that made communication between the priests and their subjects difficult. They wrote:

> The Catholic Indian, without indicating generally the nature of his petition, comes into the presence of the missionary, kneels down and blesses himself. This is the sign indicating he desires to get married. Consequently the missionary asks him: 'Whom do you wish to marry?' On learning the identity of the woman the missionary inquires from her if she desires to marry the petitioner. Then when the missionary determines that there is no impediment to the marriage the sacrament is administered according to the rite of our Holy Mother the Church.[50]

Of particular note was the required acceptability of the marriage choice to the couple's parents and the priests' formal review to be sure there were no "canonical impediments" barring the marriage. Such impediments included degrees of consaguinity as well as validation that neither party was entering into the marriage under protest. The Catholic marriage contract historically relied heavily on the concept of individual freedom. Approval by each of the participating spouses was central to the validity of the contract, although following the issuance of the *Royal Pragmática* in 1776, the church showed itself to be as or more interested in protecting the interests of the family and the state than in respecting the individual desires of the couple.[51]

Despite the patriarchism of the Spanish-Mexican institution of marriage, some Indian girls appear to have had increased opportunities for marriage choice at the missions. The Spanish soldier Inocente García related that when an Indian girl at San Miguel mission liked an Indian and wanted to marry him, she simply advised one of the priests, and he arranged the marriage. García told the story of Cashuco, a short Indian cowboy who had ten women lined up to ask for his hand. García wrote that the women "drew lots and they agreed among themselves that the lucky one should marry him."[52] This done, Cashuco "agreed to the bargain and the marriage was arranged."[53]

Guadalupe Vallejo, the nephew of General Mariano Guadalupe Vallejo, who was the commander of the Mexican Army in California, wrote that in the Sonoma region as well it was the woman's prerogative to inform the priests of her marriage choice. Although the woman was generally responding to the man's proposal, Catholic doctrine emphasizing free will at least theoretically provided the woman with the grounds on which to reject a suitor. Vallejo observed that "after an Indian, in his hours of freedom from toil, had declared his affection by a sufficiently long attendance upon a certain window [*sic*], it was the duty of the woman to tell the father missionary and to declare her decision. If this was favorable, the young man was asked if he was willing to contract marriage with the young woman who had confessed her preference."[54]

Bartolomea Comicrabit appears to have been the one to choose her spouse. She lived at her family's ranchería until she turned six, when she went to live at the monjerío as a neophyte of the San Gabriel mission. Apparently upon the recommendation of Eulalia Pérez, the Spanish-Mexican "housemother," thirteen-year-old Bartolomea asked to marry Pablo María, an elder of the nearby Yutucubit ranchería.[55] After the death of her first husband, Bartolomea married the Scotsman Hugo Reid and changed her name to Victoria Reid. In the 1830s, she received from the Mexican government a land grant of 128 acres.[56]

At some missions, when a male gentile was brought in to be married, the priest would give the couple variations of the same name.[57] Thus, many couples had similar names—Pabla and Pablo, Francisca and Francisco, María and Mario, Dionisia and Dionisio, Juana and Juan, and so on. This made it easier for the priests to keep track of the couples.

At the missions, Indian women were expected to monitor their family's behavior and to control their husband's actions in accordance with the new Catholic code of social behavior and religious teachings. Through Christian marriage, the friars hoped, Indian women, like their Hispanic counterparts, would become the guarantors of stable families and contribute to Alta California's population. Ironically, the potentially repressive aspects of an institution that counseled the subordination of wives to their husbands also provided indigenous women with a new external authority vis-à-vis their spouses and children.

The testimony of Isidora Filomena de Solano is marked by these inherent contradictions. In 1874, Henry Cerruti, a thirty-seven-year-old immigrant from Italy hired by Hubert H. Bancroft to interview early California settlers and collect documents for Bancroft's growing collection of Californiana, interviewed Solano, the ninety-year-old widow of Chief Francisco Solano. Isidora Filomena was the Christian name she was given by Father Lorenzo de la Concepción Quijas, the missionary priest at San Francisco Solano mission. Her real name, Chowi, meant "red bird."[58] In Hispanic tradition, her added surname, "de Solano," indicated that she was later married to Chief Solano. Cerruti described the "ex-Princess" as a woman who, "given the many services which her husband has loaned to the cause of civilization, is owed many considerations."[59] At the time of the interview, Isidora was living in a hut near Lachryma Montis, the residence of General Mariano Guadalupe Vallejo, who, wrote Cerruti, "in remuneration to [Chief] Solano for all the services he rendered him, takes care of his wife in her old age" (p. 7). Chief Solano (also known as Samyetoy) had enabled Vallejo to conquer and subjugate many of the local Indian groups, putting down a par-

ticularly threatening revolt against Mexican rule by the rival Pomos and
Patwin that lasted from 1836 until the early 1840s.[60]

Born near Cache Creek (Woodland) in 1784, Isidora Filomena stood
tall at 5 feet 8 inches, although she disclosed that she was one of the
shorter women from the "Chiuructos" (Churuptos) tribe to which she
belonged. Her tribe was part of the Wintun nation of Ohlone tribes that
dwelled in the area from Monterey to the northern part of San Francisco Bay. At the time of her interview, Cerruti noted that Isidora wore
women's boots on her tiny feet and had small hands. Her skin was of a
dark complexion, typical of her tribe, and she had a snub nose, a small
mouth, and heavy white teeth.

Probably aware of Christian taboos regarding polygamy, Isidora did
not mention that she had been one of Solano's eleven wives, although
she was the favored wife to whom he was joined in Christian marriage.[61] Nonetheless, Isidora's description of her relationship to her husband before she became a Christian suggests that her experience in the
pre-mission period was one of the sort in which women were seen as
commodities of exchange. She disclosed, "I belonged to Solano before
marrying him, and even before I was baptized. I do not belong to the
Suysons [Suisuns] like he does. I belong to the Chiuructus tribe. Solano
stole me in a trip he made to negotiate with my tribe. My father came
after him with many Satiyome, but could not overtake him."[62] Isidora's
narrative illustrates how well she had learned the precepts of Christianity. Father "Guias" had taught her "to be very charitable with the
poor, very docile with my husband and very compassionate with the
prisoners" (pp. 1–2). She noted in her interview: "Whenever my husband got angry, I did all I could to pacify him" (p. 1). She attributed her
efforts to appease her husband to the teachings of Father Lorenzo at San
Francisco Solano mission.

Here we see the crux of Christian matrimony as a means of social
control. Indian women were taught to take care of the poor and the
prisoners and to keep their spouse's temper under control. Isidora
underscored her influence on her husband's actions and her efforts to
encourage him to comply with "Christian" values. She noted that it was
her intervention that prevented her husband from killing several thousand Indians he had conquered. It was she, Isidora maintained, who

convinced her husband to release his prisoners to General Vallejo to work on his large ranch near the mission.

Isidora based her authority to tell her husband what to do on the external authority provided by the church representative, Father Lorenzo. The same church teachings that counseled women to be subservient to their husbands could be disregarded if the woman was seeking her spouse's submission to the new cultural order. She narrated that "when my husband at the head of eight thousand men defeated all his enemies, I kept him from killing them as they used to do by tying them to the trees and shooting them with arrows." She added, "I told him to release them to Vallejo, who would make them work the land, Father Guias also advised the same thing, and when Solano did what he had been advised to do, many poor people were saved" (p. 2).

The authority Isidora derived from the new Christian order was highly selective, and her story is marked by her loyalty to her husband and her defense of indigenous lifeways. Her husband was a close ally of the Spaniards in their fight against other Indians, but he was also a conqueror in his own right. He was, Isidora noted, "the great Solano, prince of the Suysunes, Topaytos, Yoloitos, Chuructas, and who made himself prince of the Topaitas after conquering them" (p. 1). She stressed the power her husband had wielded to terrify Spaniards and Indians alike. "During his life," Isidora told Cerruti and the men who accompanied him, "he made the Indian and white worlds, with the exception of his friend, General Guadalupe Vallejo, tremble" (p. 1).

Isidora testified to her and her husband's acculturation to the ways of the conquerors while concurrently informing Cerruti about and defending their pre-mission lifestyles. She underscored her husband's cultural conversion, as symbolized by his acquisition of European ways and clothing. She told how Solano wore feathers on his head in the beginning, but when he was leading all of the Indians he wore a hat and boots, dressed like the Spaniards, and carried good weapons (p. 3). Yet Isidora also defended indigenous nudity. The reason that Solano's warriors did not wear jackets, shirts, pants, or hats, she observed, was not that they were stupid but "because they didn't put anything on their bodies that the white man or other Indians could grasp" (p. 3). She described the Indians as healthier and happier before the coming of the white men. They were better fed, with no knowledge of liquor; they were able to heal themselves through astrologers and herbal medicines; they lived happily in houses made of tules; and they did not need to work very hard to eat. Isidora's affirmation of indigenous cultural values is characteristic of many Native American narrative strategies.[63]

Isidora's marriage to Chief Solano gave her the status to have her voice recorded for posterity, albeit in a distorted form.[64] Cerruti tried to undercut her critique of the new order by noting that she was intoxicated at the time of the interview. He wrote: "Unfortunately, if it had not been that she had allowed the vice of drink to dominate her, she could be considered a woman of great dignity" (p. 7). Yet it was Cerruti who brought her liquor in the first place to encourage her to speak to him. In his memoirs, "Ramblings in California," Cerruti revealed that after Major Salvador Vallejo (brother of Mariano Guadalupe Vallejo) "encouraged" Isidora to speak with Cerruti, Cerruti offered her a drink from a bottle of brandy, and "she laid aside her fears" and began to talk.[65] In her narrative, Isidora explicitly blamed the white man for her troubles and her drinking. "I drink a lot of liquor . . . because the white man robbed me of everything" (p. 2). She continued, "I am not ashamed to get drunk, because this is what reason teaches me."[66] Alcohol perhaps gave Isidora the courage to speak her truth, even as it provided Cerruti with the means of disputing its accuracy.

Supplied by Cerruti, the liquor came to have an even more nefarious purpose, for he used it to persuade Isidora to sell him her wedding gown. In his *Relación,* Cerruti noted simply in a postscript that, at the request of Major Don Salvador Vallejo, Isidora had agreed to sell him her wedding dress, which consisted of "a belt of shells—a string of bones that was used to wrap the top part of the body up to the neck and a penacho [cluster of feathers] that she wore on the forehead" (p. 7). Cerruti observed, "Isidora had many loving memories in connection with these things, as each time the strings to which the bones and shells were attached became rotten, she took new strings and retied them, and she had decided to be buried with these ornaments that she greatly esteemed as they were presents from Solano" (p. 6).

In his "Ramblings," however, Cerruti detailed how he managed to obtain Isidora's treasured wedding gown. He wrote that when he and his companions were about to leave, Princess Solano went into her room and came out carrying the various articles of adornment that constituted her wedding dress. Cerruti immediately offered to purchase them. "I laid a ten-dollar gold piece on the table, but she laughed at me and felt indignant at my presumption," wrote Cerruti.[67] "Nothing daunted, I offered her another drink," he continued.[68] Cerruti distracted her a bit, discussed the Princess's drinking habits with a thirty-year-old man named Bill, whom he later described as Isidora's son, offered Isidora yet another drink, and returned to the subject of her wedding dress. Finally, Cerruti got his way. He offered Isidora twenty-four dollars and the rest of the brandy contained in the bottle. According to Cerruti: "She accepted my offer, and I thus became the happy possessor of a sacred relic of days gone by."[69]

Isidora's wedding dress can be seen as a metaphor for indigenous syncretism and acculturation. The materials that constituted the gown, bones and shells, were prominent in indigenous cultures along the coastline of Alta California. She tied these native materials together to give shape to the garment she wore for the Christian sacrament of matrimony. Cerruti's somewhat romantic description of the care and beauty of the gown suggests Isidora's real or imagined pride in marrying Chief Solano, who had kidnapped her from her family, and participating in the marriage contract, a contract that had not existed in her own society. Cerruti's description of his subsequent dispossession of Isidora's wedding dress is a poignant reminder of how matrimony was an institution at the service of conquest. As a new generation of conquerors—the historians who inscribed earlier conquests—entered the picture, they too appropriated the symbols, relics, and anecdotes of "days gone by," transforming abduction into romance, resistance into cooperation, criticism into intoxication, and disease into promiscuity.

The Franciscans relied on a range of enticements to encourage procreation and Christian marriage. On the one hand, they tried to make marriage and family life attractive to the Indians. Food, clothing, and shelter improved dramatically for those who chose marriage. Lorenzo Asisara, the Christianized neophyte who sang in the Santa Cruz mission choir, noted that the Indians with families were given meat.[70] Once married, neophytes could keep chickens and their eggs.[71] Physical accommodations were qualitatively better for wedded pairs. The single men and women were confined to their respective dormitories until they contracted marriage, when they were permitted to move to separate homes in or near the mission compound. In some of the missions, such as San José, rows of whitewashed, tiled adobe huts with a "neat and comfortable appearance" were allowed only to "the married persons and the officers of the establishment."[72] Even so, wrote Beechey, it was not every hut that had "a white face to exhibit," because lime was given only to families who exhibited "industry and good conduct."[73] Often huts were built for couples "among the other Indian houses in the village near the Mission."[74]

Furthermore, the priests gave married couples greater freedom of movement than their unmarried neophyte counterparts. Marriage offered Indian girls the opportunity to escape confinement in the monjerío. At the San Francisco mission, female newlyweds left the supervision of the guards and moved to the ranchería, located "one hundred paces" from the mission buildings and consisting of eight long row houses.[75] The physician Georg Langsdorff described this situation at San Francisco mission. As soon as a girl marries, "she is free" and "lives with her husband in one of the villages of Indians belonging to the Mission . . . called *Las Rancherias*."[76] The friars hoped that allowing the married couple this bit of freedom would "bind their converts more closely to the establishment, and spread their religion more securely and extensively."[77]

Marriage also offered neophytes the possibility of companionship with members of the opposite sex. Such companionship was discouraged by the gender division of work, worship, and relaxation at the missions. Beechey wrote of how, during the day, the occupations of men and women "led to distinct places," which allowed the Indians of different sexes to "enjoy very little of each other's society," unless they formed a matrimonial alliance.[78]

Women who failed to respect the sanctity of marriage or to comply with their duty to procreate suffered severe punishments designed to ridicule them before the community at large. Miscarriages, abortions, sterility, concubinage, and neglect of one's child all warranted public sanction. At San Gabriel mission, Father José María Zalvidea, having discovered that the Gabrielino Indians were killing the "children born to the whites," believed that all miscarriages were intentional.[79] When a woman gave birth to a stillborn infant, she was punished. Her head was shaved, she was flogged for fifteen days, irons were put on her feet for three months, and she was forced "to appear every Sunday in church, on the steps leading up to the altar, with a hideous painted wooden child in her arms."[80] The public penance of carrying a wooden doll was a typical punishment for women whose pregnancies ended in miscarriage in some Christian communities in Europe as well.[81]

Women who engaged in relations with married men were also publicly condemned. Such a woman was "clipped like a horse, a doll was affixed to her breast and she was made to stand at the door of the church at the hour of mass every Sunday for a month, so that she might serve as an example," narrated the Spanish soldier José María Amador.[82] The men involved in these same crimes, on the other hand, were hidden from view in the penitentiary. Extramarital affairs were looked down upon and severely punished. According to Amador, any man who engaged in such a practice was "irremissibly sentenced to ten years in the penitentiary (presidio) in shackles."[83]

Guadalupe Vallejo noted that women charged with child neglect were similarly punished. In several cases where "an Indian woman was so slovenly and neglectful of her infant that it died," he recalled that the woman was forced "to carry in her arms in church, and at all meals and public assemblies, a log of wood about the size of a nine-months'-old child."[84] Vallejo wrote that public punishments of the women were extremely effective, "for the Indian women are naturally most affectionate creatures, and in every case they soon began to suffer greatly, and others with them."[85] Vallejo recalled one instance in which "a whole Indian village came to the girl's defense and begged the priest in charge to forgive the poor woman."[86]

Lorenzo Asisara related an anecdote that demonstrates the near obsession of some priests with women's fertility patterns.[87] Sometime after Padre Andrés Quintana's death in 1812, Asisara recalled, Father Ramón Olbés was put in charge of the Santa Cruz mission.[88] One day, Father Olbés noticed that two women's faces were scratched from fighting, and he took them aside to investigate. One of the women was sterile and the other had children. The priest asked the sterile one why she had no children. He then sent for her husband and asked him the same question. Her husband, an Indian who could not speak Spanish, "pointed to the sky, as though to signify that God alone knew the reason."[89] The priest then brought an interpreter and continued to interrogate the husband. He asked whether the couple slept together, and the husband replied affirmatively. Then, said Asisara, Father Olbés put the couple in a room "so they might perform the act of coition in his presence." The Indian refused but "was obliged by force to show his organ, so that it might be learned whether or not it was in good order." Here someone (probably Thomas Savage, the interviewer) crossed out the first version of the interview, which read that the Indian "was obliged by force to fornicate with his wife in the presence of witnesses." Although the intent of this manipulation of the text might have been to conceal the heinousness of Asisara's story, by leaving the text legible underneath, the writer actually succeeded in drawing the reader's attention to its obvious alteration.

After forcing the couple to have intercourse, the priest allegedly isolated the woman and "turned the husband over to the body guard in fetters." Through the interpreter, the padre asked why the woman's face was scratched, and she said that another woman "had done it through jealousy." Upon further inquiry, she informed the priest that her husband had been intimate with the other woman. Padre Olbés asked her whether her husband slept with her, and she replied that he did. The priest continued to interrogate her about why she did not bear children, and she maintained that she did not know. Olbés then made the woman "go into another room in order that he might examine her 'private parts.'" When the woman resisted and grabbed the cord around the priest's waist, a lengthy struggle resulted "between the two who were alone there in the room." The woman tried to bite the priest's arm, causing the priest to yell. Upon hearing Padre Olbés scream, the interpreter and the alcalde went in to help him. Olbés ordered them to tie the woman up by the hands and to give her fifty lashes. After she was beaten, she was put in shackles and locked in the monjerío. Padre Olbés then ordered that a wooden doll be made "in the likeness of a newly-born child." He gave it to the woman and commanded her to "treat that doll as though it were a child and to carry it in the presence of everyone for nine days."

Asisara related that the woman did so and stood at the church with the wooden doll. The woman's husband, on the other hand, was forced to wear "a set of cow horns fastened with leather thongs." He was kept thus fettered and brought daily "from his prison to the Mass," where the other Indians mocked him. The reactions of the Indians, according to Asisara, differed by sex. The women who were sterile "became greatly alarmed," but the men mocked the husband.

The extreme behavior of Father Olbés in Asisara's narrative underscores the importance the conquerors placed on procreation. Efforts to colonize California and protect it from other imperial powers depended on an increased loyal population in the territory. Venereal disease was steadily eroding the indigenous population both at the missions and at nonmission villages, making birth rates an ever-greater cause of concern. The punishments the missionaries inflicted on both male and female neophytes were designed to humiliate and make examples of couples who failed to produce children.

Asisara's observation that the Indian women who were sterile were alarmed underscores the exceptional vulnerability of the female neophytes, which contributed to a qualitatively different experience of missionization for males and females. The female reaction to the woman's plight also stands in vivid contrast to the apparent scorn the Indians displayed for the woman's husband. Although Ohlone culture valued monogamy and fidelity in marriage, Ohlone men were sometimes allowed to have a second wife in another village if the first wife failed to bear children.[90] We do not know whether the men's reactions mark a shift in attitudes toward this tradition.

Asisara's narrative demonstrates the ultimate failure of mission practices to control or transform indigenous sexual lifestyles. Despite all of the Franciscans' efforts to restrict sexual behavior, the Indian husband was apparently involved with a woman other than his wife anyway, showing that the Indians found opportunities to defy the strict standards of fidelity imposed by the priests. The priests' efforts to impose Christian marriage may have achieved little more than nominal acceptance of the rite, particularly when the couple was childless. The reports of the friars themselves testify to their failure to control indigenous desires. San Carlos missionaries observed that when Christianized Indian couples without children had a fight, it took considerable effort to reconcile them, and if they got involved with other partners, there was virtually nothing the priests could do to get them back together.[91]

Visitors to the missions commented on the priests' inability to control indigenous sexuality. Despite "severe corporal punishment . . . with a whip," the mission Indians sometimes endeavored "to evade the vigilance of their keepers, and are locked up with the opposite sex," according to Beechey.[92] In a criminal case against three neophytes accused of murder, Lieutenant José María Estudillo argued that the wild Indians thought nothing of stealing women and that even in Christianity they were accustomed to trading women or bribing their wives with beads or other knickknacks to "go with" other Indians.[93] In their defense, Estudillo argued that the Indians, apprentice Christians for "only six years," still had not learned Christian ways with regard to gender relations.

In their responses to a government questionnaire shortly after 1810, California missionary priests confirmed that the mission Indians exchanged women among themselves. "They are quick to lend each other money, beads, seeds . . . and their own women," wrote the San Fernando mission fathers.[94] Father Antonio Jayme, of Soledad mission, noted that although the southern Ohlone Indians liked their own women, they preferred to share them with others.[95] At the San Carlos mission, Father Amorós lamented that after the Indians married, they got bored with each other and separated, and their tendency to get involved with other partners was "an incurable evil."[96]

The mission Indians themselves provided the clearest evidence that the exchange of wives among neophytes and gentiles alike continued to occur well into the mission period.[97] Following a failed uprising in 1824 by the Chumash Indians at La Purísima, Santa Inés, and Santa Barbara missions,[98] Commandant José de la Guerra y Noriega ordered Ensign José Joaquín Maitorena to interrogate some of the mission Indians.[99] Among the questions put to them was one regarding the behavior of married men toward their wives. The testimony of five Indian neophytes so questioned confirmed that the missionaries had been unsuccessful in changing indigenous sexual practices and that "immorality" was being practiced by married and unmarried, Christian and non-Christian Indians alike. Zeñón of La Purísima mission testified that "the married and single men lived all mixed together and did whatever they wished with all the women, married and single alike" (7:144). Pelagio of San Fernando mission likewise reported that "the married and single men, Christians and heathen, were living intermingled and were doing whatever they wished" (7:145). Alberto of San Gabriel reported that "when the Christians got to the valley they exchanged their women with those of the heathen without distinction of married or unmarried for they were all mixed up with one another" (7:146). Leopoldo of Santa Barbara mission observed that the Christians exchanged their women (both married and unmarried) with the non-Christians, and vice versa (7:147). Fernando Huilidiaset, also of Santa Barbara mission, reported that he "noticed the married couples exchanged women with one another, but no one knew who was married and who was single for they were all mixed up" (7:150). Father Antonio Ripoll praised the neophyte Andrés for intervening when some of the Indians did not stay with their wives. "He [Andrés] separated the exchanged wives and returned them to their proper husbands," Ripoll wrote.[100]

Asisara's narrative also suggests that the priests believed the Indian women were controlling their own sexuality—that is, choosing not to give birth by deliberately inducing abortions and miscarriages. The priests viewed such female agency as intolerable and believed the behavior could be mitigated through harsh punishments. Although venereal diseases and other epidemics, aggravated by close living conditions at the missions, played a part in declining birth rates, missionaries asserted that an undetermined, but significant, number of Indian women were choosing abortion over mission life for their children. The historian Bancroft noted that many Indian women sought to prevent childbirth "by the use of the thorn-apple."[101] In their responses to the 1812 questionnaire, the missionaries at both the Santa Clara and San José missions decried the practice of abortion as the dominant vice among the Costanoan women. The friars from San José wrote that adherence to the practice of abortion by the female neophytes at their mission was the main reason for low birth rates.[102] In 1810, Father Mariano Payeras reported that at La Purísima mission farther south, nearly all of the

Indian mothers "gave birth to dead infants."[103] The priests at La Purísima mission expressed dismay and bewilderment at their inability to
control the number of stillbirths (some two to three a week) among the
Chumash women. Father Payeras noted that the large number of miscarriages had "exercised our patience in this year, and has grieved us
deeply."[104] Initially, he observed, the priests had believed that the large
number of stillbirths were due to the difficulties of childbearing, but
they were unable to "discover the origin and motive of such deplorable
happenings."[105] According to Payeras, neither instruction, preaching,
nor punishment could dissuade the women from begetting stillborn
infants. The anthropologist James Sandos argued that in the case of the
Chumash, abortions and infanticide represented a continuation of pre-
mission patterns in which Chumash women "routinely killed their first-
born in the belief that failure to do so would prevent them from having
further children."[106] Similar studies of pre-mission practices among
other groups are needed to facilitate interpretation of the meaning of the
practice in particular local contexts.

Some historians and contemporary observers attributed low birth
rates among Indian women not to abortion but to the nature of the
Indians themselves. In a report in 1791, the engineer Miguel Costansó
asserted that fertility rates were much greater among Spaniards and
those of mixed blood than among Indians. He suggested that Indian
woman procreated much less "when they are reduced to a civilized life
or a less wild existence."[107] Costansó noted that as progressive generations intermarried, the children would become "whiter" and would
lose their indigenous identities, "since they are reared among Spaniards
and their language, habits and customs no longer differ from ours."[108]
Hubert H. Bancroft contrasted the fertility of Hispanic women with
that of their native counterparts and found the latter to be lacking.
According to Bancroft, Hispanic women bore an average of ten children; California families of twenty or twenty-five children were not
uncommon.[109] In the decade from 1800 to 1810, an average of 680
marriages per year were performed among neophytes, and indigenous
families averaged just over one child per family.[110] Bancroft observed
that Indian women were "naturally not very fecund."[111]

In part, low birth rates at the missions may also have been related to

Christian practices that interrupted indigenous ceremonial life. The curtailment of traditional indigenous ceremonies thought by the priests to be idolatrous probably inhibited the transfer of information that was essential to pregnant women. The anthropologist Florence Shipek addressed this possibility in the autobiography she recorded for Delfina Cuero, an indigenous curandera, or medicine woman, from the San Diego area. She wrote that European efforts to eliminate indigenous religious ceremonies and customs led to the destruction of "the total educational, moral, and ethical system," which was often "completely integrated into the 'religious' ceremonies."[112]

Delfina Cuero emphasized the importance of ceremonies for indigenous survival. In her autobiography, she discussed indigenous taboos and rules for pregnant women—what they could and could not eat or look at, what activities were prohibited—and she contemplated how her grandmother's residency at the San Diego mission had interrupted the ceremonies for passing information about female culture from one generation to the next. Delfina believed she had lost her first baby because she had not been taught in initiation ceremonies how to "have good health and good babies."[113] She related:

> In the real old days, grandmothers taught these things about life at the time of a girl's initiation ceremony, when she was about to become a woman. Nobody just talked about these things ever. It was all in the songs and myths that belonged to the ceremony. All that a girl needed to know to be a good wife, and how to have babies and to take care of them was learned at the ceremony, at the time when a girl became a woman. We were taught about food and herbs and how to make things by our mothers and grandmothers all the time. But only at the ceremony for girls was the proper time to teach the special things women had to know. Nobody just talked about those things, it was all in the songs.[114]

The Crown issued explicit instructions that the Christian Indians were not to engage in their native ceremonies, although these instructions were not always followed. In California, such an order was issued in 1782, forbidding the Christian Indians from dancing.[115] Cultural codes defined the appropriate moments for conveying certain kinds of information. Without proper female ceremonies, "the special things women had to know" were not passed on. None of the elder Indian women with whom Cuero conversed had gone through the initiation ceremony, and many, like Delfina, had lost their first child.

Codes of silence among indigenous groups ensured that such information was not passed on to outsiders. Indigenous narratives do not address the extent to which Indian women consciously chose not to bear children within the confines of the missions. Shipek noted that many of the older Indians were reluctant to speak to her on topics related to childbirth. A Russian observer in the late Mexican period stressed the difficulties he had in obtaining information about indigenous marital practices. Kostromitonov wrote that the coastal Miwok and Pomo Indians of Bodega Bay "only grudgingly answered questions we asked them concerning these rites, and for this reason it was impossible to learn further details."[116] He lamented that the Indians were "completely taken with the delusion that they must necessarily die if they tell about their customs to a stranger."[117]

The reluctance of the women to speak about childbirth either to their daughters or to outsiders underscores the difficulty of evaluating the priests' charges that women were deliberately practicing abortion or choosing not to have children at the missions. Spanish discourse suggested that women were intentionally inducing miscarriages and thus were to blame for the dramatic population decline being experienced at the missions. Such charges deflected criticism away from the practice of cloistering the mission Indians in close quarters, the lack of adequate medical care on the frontier, and the role of the mission in interrupting traditional indigenous ceremonial life.

Finally, Asisara's narrative illustrates how conquest was tied to notions about sexuality and marriage and how the Franciscans used sexuality to reaffirm their power over a conquered population. Although it is not clear whether Father Olbés's physical abuse of the childless woman at Santa Cruz mission was also sexual, the fact that he isolated her in order to examine her private parts and that she fought him with such vehemence is suggestive. The priest's actions were at a minimum psychologically abusive to the woman, her husband, and the Costanoan community at and around the Santa Cruz mission. They served as a reminder of the Indians' utter powerlessness to challenge the conquerors' actions or to seek redress of any kind. Such violence against native women reinforced the power of the Spaniards by creating despair among the conquered and, as the anthropologist Douglas Monroy has written, by causing the vanquished to "internalize the power relations" of the conqueror and the conquered.[118] This gender-specific violence was veiled in secrecy, but it formed part of the fabric of the conquest of intimacy. It occurred both inside and outside of the mission compound, and although it caused concern among some Crown, ecclesiastical, and military authorities, efforts to stop it proved largely ineffective.

Neither the presence of Hispanic women nor legislative efforts to control the violence against women seem to have rectified the situation, and the political will to control such violence was negligible. In a dispute with Governor Felipe de Neve over Father Junípero Serra's right to dispense the sacrament of confirmation without formal papers from Rome, Serra complained that the governor "allows fornication among the soldiers, because—so I have heard him say from his own mouth—it is winked at in Rome and tolerated in Madrid."[119] In March 1785, José Antonio Rengel, one of the highest military authorities of the northern provinces, ordered de Neve's successor, Pedro Fages, to command the troops and officers to cease their "scandalous disorder" with the female Indians, with stiff penalties for noncompliance.[120] Four months later, Governor Fages, citing Rengel's instructions, ordered Diego González to circulate an edict that imposed severe penalties upon those who continued to exercise such "vicious license."[121] A decade later, the viceroy complained of the "excesses committed by various individuals of the companies with both Christian and gentile Indian women."[122] The Spanish soldier José Ramón Valdés recalled that despite an official prohibition against interaction with the Indians, such unauthorized interaction took place regularly. In his memoirs, Valdés recalled that although the soldiers in California "were not permitted to go to the Indian *rancherías*," they would go anyway, whenever they had the chance, "being careful that the corporal should not see" them.[123] He observed, "I have no doubt that some went to seek relations with the Indian women, but I myself had nothing to do with such things."[124]

The friars themselves were not exempt from abusing Indian women at the missions, but such "internal matters" rarely became public. Though incidents of missionary immorality were not unknown, Spanish colonial texts are silent on this topic, and female testimony is virtually nil. Foreign visitors who might have addressed this issue tended not to. Completely dependent on missionary hospitality for survival on the isolated frontier, they sometimes criticized the mission system, but rarely did they formulate specific, direct charges against their hosts.

Two indigenous narrators—Lorenzo Asisara and Fernando Librado Kitsepawit—broke the silence surrounding the abuse of female neophytes.[125] As we have seen in his narrative, Lorenzo Asisara was careful not to make any specific charges against Father Ramón Olbés. Elsewhere in the narrative, however, he described Olbés's predecessor at Santa Cruz mission, Father Gil y Taboada, whose "very amorous nature" led him "to embrace and kiss the Indian women."[126] José María Amador confirmed Asisara's statement that Father Gil y Taboada "had carnal contact with them until he contracted syphilis and developed buboes," and he added that he had treated the priest for venereal disease. Although Asisara noted Father Gil y Taboada's intercourse with the native women at the mission, he refrained from criticizing the priest's behavior and presented it as a natural occurrence. According to Asisara, Gil y Taboada's relations with the indigenous women did not diminish the Indians' warm feelings toward the priest. "Taboada," he wrote, "at length came to be greatly loved by all the Indians, especially by the Tulareños, whose language he understood to some extent." Despite Asisara's claim to speak for all of the Indians at the mission, however, his comments rendered virtually invisible the separate female experience of sexual vulnerability. His evaluation of Gil y Taboada may have been colored by the fact that it was Gil y Taboada who began teaching the prayers in indigenous languages to the young Indian boys, "so that they would understand them well." In his biographical dictionary of the Franciscans in Alta California, Maynard Geiger wrote that in 1826, charges were brought against Padre Gil y Taboada for "smuggling" and "occasional immorality."[127] However, most California historians, including Bancroft and Engelhardt, made light of such charges.[128]

Asisara's account suggests that the seeds of rebellion were nourished by Franciscan efforts to control indigenous sexuality. On October 12,

1812, neophytes at the Santa Cruz mission joined together to implement a plot to poison Father Andrés Quintana.[129] Publicly, Quintana's subsequent death was not initially attributed to malfeasance. The presidial officer noted that before witnesses, the cadet "examined the body and found on it no signs of a violent death."[130] Privately, Father Narciso Durán, president of the California missions, told a different story. In a letter penned nearly two years after the priest's death, Durán acknowledged that the priest had been cruelly tortured in the genitalia before being suffocated.[131]

Although witnesses at the time noted the removal of Father Quintana's testicles, Lorenzo Asisara, whose father was a participant in the assassination of Father Quintana, told a different story.[132] Asisara observed that "through modesty, they did not reveal the fact and buried the body with everyone convinced that the death had been due to natural causes."[133] Asisara related in graphic detail the premeditated plans to enact revenge upon the priest, first by poisoning him and then by the cutting off of his testicles. Scholars have debated the exact nature of what was done to Father Quintana before he was killed. Doyce Nunis recently criticized Edward Castillo for accepting as valid Asisara's description of a double castration of the priest, which Nunis believed to be "pure nonsense, totally without medical validity."[134] He concurred with the conclusions of Father Narciso Durán,[135] believing that Quintana was not castrated and that "his genitalia were severely manhandled but not sufficiently to leave any obvious wound, let alone such a severe one that would have been produced by double castration."[136]

Yet such debates, while important in establishing to the extent possible the nature of what happened, seem to lose track of a larger picture. Regardless of the accuracy of the details, Asisara's account speaks to a greater truth regarding indigenous interpretations of mission life. Symbolically, the assault on the priest's sexual organs mirrored indigenous feelings of violation. Poisoning, sexual mutilation, castration, and suffocation may be read as metaphorically appropriate responses to missionization. Each act mirrored the policies imposed upon the mission Indians. The Indians had been inculcated with values that "poisoned" their lifestyles. Their sexuality had been manipulated by orthodox teachings that severely regulated sexual intercourse among them and demanded the separation of women from men. The Indians had been castrated literally by disease and restriction and figuratively by their reduction to neutered beings who were denied full human agency. Finally, people who were used to living in and with the elements were housed under lock and key in stifling, disease-propagating mission structures.

The other indigenous narrator whose writings shed light on sexual relations at the mission was Kitsepawit, known to non-Indians as Fernando Librado. In a series of interviews conducted by the Smithsonian Institution's ethnographer John P. Harrington between 1912 and 1915, Librado included a few astonishingly candid anecdotes that had been passed down to him through oral traditions. The vehicle of storytelling and the interval of time that had passed following the incidents he described, as well as the shift toward more modern, twentieth-century mores, allowed Librado to speak with greater frankness than would have been acceptable in the earlier Victorian era. In addition, Librado softened the gravity of his accusations through his use of narrative strategies such as humor and hearsay that distanced him somewhat from the details of the priests' sexual escapades. His anecdotes illustrate the vulnerability of the neophyte girls to the priests' whims in a light and tragicomic way. Librado recalled telling a friend, "I was confirmed twice, baptized once, and the best of it is that Fr. Jimenez used to get on top of my godmother."[137] The priest at Santa Barbara, Father Jiménez [Antonio Jimeno], was said to have had sex right in the mission with a young married Indian woman named Barbara, who was a relative of Librado's godmother. Furthermore, Old Lucas, the Indian sacristan, told Librado that at Mission San Buenaventura, the priest regularly visited the monjerío for sexual favors. Librado recalled:

> They took all the best-looking girls, Lucas said, and they put them in the nunnery; the priest had an appointed hour to go there. When he got to the nunnery, all were in bed in the big dormitory. The priest would pass by the bed of the superior [*maestra*] and tap her on the shoulder, and she would commence singing. All of the girls would join in, which in the dormitory had the effect of drowning out any other sounds. While the singing was going on, the priest would have time to select the girl he wanted, carry out

his desires, and come back to where the superior was. Then the singing would stop. In this way the priest had sex with all of them, from the superior all the way down the line. It may be that it was some sort of game which had been concocted between the superior and the priest.

Though Librado made light of the incident by suggesting that the singing was just part of a game, his concluding comments betray an identification on the part of the mission Indians with the position of the women. When it came right down to it, Librado explained, "The priest's will was law. Indians would lie right down if the priest said so." The gender hierarchy that granted men power over women provided a paradigm for Spanish-Indian relations in the context of the mission system.

Ironically, the same literary devices that allowed Librado to address this delicate topic are the very characteristics that weaken the evidentiary character of his anecdotes. Librado was not a direct witness to the events he described, his anecdotes were based on hearsay, and he used the informal vehicle of storytelling to convey his knowledge of the incidents. Yet the nature of gender-specific violence is such that it often lacks witnesses and is thus difficult to prove. What is perhaps more important than the accuracy of the specific charges is that these accounts documented female indigenous vulnerability, implicitly proposed this vulnerability as a synecdoche for indigenous experiences at the missions, and passed on such incidents as part of the collective memory of mission life.

Only after the mission period ended do we find foreigners alluding to the irregular conduct of the mission priests. In the 1840s, Sir George Simpson, governor-in-chief of the Hudson's Bay Company's territories in North America, noted that "his present reverence of Santa Cruz . . . finds pleasant relaxation, to say nothing of his bottle, in a seraglio of native beauties."[138] Similarly, Bancroft described the philosophy of the "good man," Father Antonio Menéndez, an army chaplain at Santa Barbara, as "men's souls for heaven, but women for himself."[139] In the conquest of intimacy, the friars manipulated sexuality to serve their needs. They criticized indigenous premarital, marital, and extramarital sexual practices and sought to transform those practices as a means of controlling Indians at the missions. Their discourse on indigenous sexuality provided the ideological underpinnings for the friars' Hispanicizing project in the cloistering of women, the Christian marriage of Indian couples, and the regulation of indigenous sexuality. The extremely personal issues of marriage and reproduction provided the weft and web of the fabric of mission society. Woven into this fabric, yet invisible on the surface, were the threads of discontent. The loom of sexual control produced the fabric of resistance.

7

Resistance

Large-scale rebellions against the mission system in Alta California occurred occasionally, as did localized revolts. Women were sometimes involved in these revolts, directly or indirectly. The rape of the Indian chief's wife at the founding of San Gabriel mission brought together a united front of Indians from the coast and the sierra; their plan to attack the mission was thwarted by the arrival of military reinforcements.[1] Spanish abuse of Indian women in the San Diego region provided the backdrop for a major Indian revolt in 1775. Only months after Father Luis Jayme had warned of indigenous retaliation for the soldiers' abuse of Indian women in the San Diego mission region, eight hundred Indians from more than seventy rancherías, backed by thousands of others, burned the San Diego mission and killed Jayme, a blacksmith, and a carpenter.[2] Jayme's body was found naked, bruised, and disfigured at the bottom of a dry creek. Most accounts of this uprising neglect to analyze the immediate causes of the revolt or the context presented by Father Jayme's concerns. Bancroft noted that the incident appeared to have been sparked by some runaway neophytes who had been charged with stealing fish from an old woman.[3] Others attributed the revolt to the Indians' relative freedom of movement at San Diego. Because the mission there lacked sufficient water and arable land to support a resident neophyte population, a unique living arrangement allowed the neophytes to reside in their own villages and go to the mission only to work or for religious services.[4]

In 1785, Toypurina, a medicine woman from one of the rancherías near San Gabriel mission that had resisted missionization, and the

Christianized neophyte Nicolás spearheaded an unsuccessful attack on that mission by six Indian villages.[5] In a hearing held by military officials at the Santa Barbara mission, the twenty-four-year-old Toypurina testified through a Spanish interpreter that she sought to incite the mission Indians to revolt because "she was angry with the priests and with all those belonging to this Mission because we [the Spaniards] are living here on her land."[6] Following the hearing, the accused were duly punished. Toypurina was imprisoned for two years at San Gabriel and sent into permanent exile at the San Carlos de Borromeo mission in Monterey, where she married a presidial soldier on July 26, 1789.[7] She passed into legend as the model convert, and the native rebellion was transformed into a mission success story. One popular writer noted that he could think of "no more outstanding triumph of the Holy Cross than the conversion of Toypurina," nor any finer tribute to Padre Miguel Sánchez, "who led this sorceress from the darkness, evil, and rebellion of her heathen ways, into the Light of the Knowledge, Love, and Service of God."[8]

In 1797, military officials reported to Governor Diego de Borica that two gentile Indians were trying to stir up a revolt among the Christian Indians at San José mission, established less than a month earlier.[9] Reports accusing the nonmission Indians distracted attention from the involvement of mission neophytes in trying to resist the new social order. An investigation found that the vast majority of those deemed to be involved were neophytes who had escaped from the mission.[10] Eighty-three Christians and nine gentiles were arrested. Shortly thereafter, more than two hundred neophytes fled from the nearby San Francisco mission. Governor Borica's subsequent investigation found that the neophytes had fled the missions because of "excessive flogging, hunger and the death of relatives."[11] Lasuén, father president of the missions, denied the charges of mistreatment and claimed that an epidemic had caused the desertion.[12]

Often the missionaries defended those charged with attacking them, incredulous that such attacks could emanate from their flock. In 1801, three neophytes—Diego, Eleuterio, and Antonio—were imprisoned for their alleged involvement in a plot to poison Fathers Juan Martín and Baltasar Carnicer at San Miguel mission.[13] Martín, Carnicer, and their visitor, Father Marcelino Ciprés, were taken seriously ill with violent stomach pains, but they all recovered soon afterward. Lieutenant Colonel Pedro de Alberni, commander of the armed forces in California, wrote that although many Indians testified against the three neophytes, the suspects denied all charges. The following year, the priests at San Miguel mission requested that the military release the three neophytes; they had verified the Indians' innocence and recommended that the one year in prison already served was sufficient punishment.[14] Some months later, José Raymundo Carrillo, Alberni's successor, conveyed these wishes to the governor, adding his own recommendation that Diego, Eleuterio, and Antonio be whipped in front of their relatives "for their boastful pretense of having poisoned the Fathers."[15] None of the mission authorities appear to have believed that "their" Indians might have been complicit in an attack on the priests. Father Lasuén later noted that he believed the poisoning derived from drinking mescal from a copper container lined with tin.[16]

A third priest, Francisco Pujol, went to assist the priests at San Miguel and suffered a similar poisoning, which he did not survive. Bancroft noted, "There seems to have been no doubt in the minds of the people that his death was the result of poisoning by the Indians."[17] Other poisoning attempts and plots to kill priests and burn mission buildings were reported at the San Carlos and San Francisco missions in 1801 and at Santa Clara mission beginning in 1801 and again in 1805.[18] In 1812, Father José Pedro Panto apparently died from poisoning at San Diego mission.[19] Some months earlier, his cook, Nazario, had been arrested and admitted to having poisoned the priest's soup with powdered *cuchasquelaai* because of the priest's excessive floggings. Nazario had received four bouts of whippings ranging from twenty-four to fifty lashes each in the twenty-four hours prior to his retaliation.

Frequently, such resistance was portrayed as a conflict between different indigenous groups. Correspondence involving a plot among the mission Indians to assassinate the friar and burn Carmel mission (near Monterey) revealed a reluctance on the part of the Franciscans to believe that the Indians would rebel against them. According to the available documentation, the missionaries and other Spanish authorities accepted an informant's suggestion that intertribal hostilities were at the root of the conflict. Lieutenant Colonel Pedro de Alberni concurred that the neophyte who presented the charges "wanted revenge, implicating [those he denounced] with false accusations, out of hatred and because they were from enemy nations."[20]

The priests were generally inclined to give the mission Indians the benefit of the doubt. In January 1805, Father Pedro Cuevas requested that a military escort accompany him to visit the sick and hear confessions at a nearby Christian ranchería. A Christian neophyte who acted as a guide for Cuevas apparently led the group to a gentile ranchería, saying that it was a Christian one.[21] In the melée that ensued, the Indians killed Mayordomo Ignacio Higuera and two Indians from the San José mission and wounded the priest and his bodyguards. José Antonio Sánchez, one of the soldiers who accompanied the expedition, noted Father Cuevas's naive belief in the neophyte's innocence. According to Sánchez, Cuevas believed the neophyte had accidentally led them astray due to the heavy fog.[22] The priest, wrote Sánchez, was "recently arrived from Mexico" and ignored the advice of the more experienced and skeptical soldiers who accompanied him. Subsequent reports and correspondence downplayed the possible deception by the mission Indian and portrayed the attack on Father Cuevas first as the product of tensions between Christian and non-Christian Indians and later as an attack by nonmission Indians. Sergeant Luis Peralta attested that there was an "encounter between Christian and gentile Indians of the ranchería of the Asirines," during which Father Cuevas inadvertently "received injuries from a jar."[23] Two weeks later, the governor of California sent a letter to the viceroy describing the incident not as an encounter between indigenous groups but as an attack by gentiles on the priest.[24]

Later that year, the military ensign Luis Argüello wrote to the commander of the San Francisco presidio (which exercised oversight of the San José and Santa Clara missions) about a plan by one Christian Indian and "a great number of Gentiles" from two nearby rancherías to burn down the Santa Clara mission and kill the priests.[25] Military officers acknowledged that the plan included collaboration with mission Indians, but they described the nonmission Indians as the main actors. Five mission Indians were among those detained in the case; military

authorities recommended the prosecution of only the gentiles. Following the incident, at least two expeditions in search of fugitives were sent
out to the ranchería where Father Cuevas had been attacked, suggesting
that collaboration between mission and nonmission Indians continued
to occur despite efforts by the Spanish authorities to downplay it.[26]

In addition to armed resistance and assassination attempts, many
neophytes sought to escape the missions.[27] Beechey wrote that after the
Indians "became acquainted with the nature of the institution and felt
themselves under restraint," many took off, and he observed that despite the difficulty of escaping, desertions were "of frequent occurrence."[28] Hugo Reid, the Scotsman who wrote in the 1850s, described
the punishments for and consequences of attempting to flee the missions. He observed that deserters who fled to other missions were
"picked up immediately, flogged and put in irons until an opportunity
presented of returning them to undergo other flagellations."[29] If the
deserters fled to the rancherías, noted Reid, soldiers would generally
track them down on their monthly raids and severely punish those who
tried to conceal the refugees. The only alternative, suggested Reid, "was
to take to the mountains."[30] By 1831, nearly 3,500 of more than 81,000
Indians living at the missions had successfully escaped.[31]

Like attacks on the missionaries, escape attempts were sometimes
portrayed as a result of conflicts among Indians at the missions. On the
other hand, reports of indigenous flight were sometimes included in the
letters of religious to government authorities as evidence of the need for
additional military aid or reinforcements. In such letters, the priests
often attributed the Indians' desire to flee the missions to the nature
of the Indians rather than to the nature of the missions. Father President Lasuén noted that although the neophytes "know how greatly
improved is their condition as compared with that of the pagans,"
because of their "untrained nature, they recognize an affinity for the
mountains that more than offsets this obvious truth."[32] In 1804, Father
Tapis reported to the governor of California that forty neophytes had
escaped from San Gabriel, some two hundred from San Juan Bautista,
and an ample number from San Francisco.[33] In all of the other missions,
he noted, "there are always some inclined toward flight." As to the

reasons for these escapes, he observed, "We have not been able to discover any other reason for these flights than the inconstancy of the Indians themselves."

Women were among those who fled. María Solares, a Chumash Indian, noted that her grandmother was a "mission slave."[34] María recalled that her grandmother "had run away many, many times and had been recaptured and whipped till her buttocks crawled with maggots." Yet, she observed, her grandmother "had survived to hand down her memories of the golden age before white men came." Solares did not elaborate on her grandmother's motivations for fleeing the mission or give details of her grandmother's flight. Ironically, by the early twentieth century, the grandmother's descendants were all "very good Catholics."

The Spanish soldier Inocente García told of indigenous flight from the missions following a military campaign against one of the Indian villages in the sierras. In the campaign, recounted García, his men captured female prisoners whom they brought to the Carmel mission. García described how the chief of the raided village planned for the recapture of the women. The chief sent four men to the Carmel mission, where they instructed the female captives to escape at night and head toward Buenavista. The women did so, and under the leadership of a man named Domingo, they all managed to escape.[35]

Absenteeism from church or chores posed fewer risks than armed resistance or flight, although even this type of more discreet resistance was not without risk. In response to the problem of absenteeism, elaborate security and reporting mechanisms were set up at each mission, and Indians who failed to show up for their assigned duties or to attend mass could expect to be punished. The Spanish soldier José María Amador reported that at the Santa Cruz mission, Indians who failed to show up for the daily roll call at the church door were lashed. Every day, he observed, there were "up to ten such scourgings."[36] Following such a beating, he wrote, the Indian "got up happy and contented to set off for his work, for it is a fact that the Indians used to laugh at these punishments of short duration." The frequency of the offenses and the Indians' laughter suggest that the Indians did not accept mission regulations with docility but often sought to outwit the friars. Their flaunting of the regulations also served to remind the friars that there were limits to indigenous conformity. Humor played a subversive role in joining the mission Indians together in opposition to the friars.

In contrast to such flagrant resistance, the public record often depicted an indigenous population little inclined to resist the new order. Between December 31, 1813, and August 11, 1815, missionaries from eighteen of the nineteen existing California missions responded with varying degrees of candor and depth to a questionnaire from Ciriaco González Carvajal, secretary of Spain's Department of Overseas Colonies.[37] Although it would be inaccurate to presume the existence of a single "official" story, given the myriad interests of church, state, and military authorities, the responses nonetheless provide a record of the Franciscans' perceptions of the neophytes at a single moment in time. They allow us to analyze how the Franciscans viewed and represented the subjects of their discourse—the mission Indians—almost half a century after the founding of California's first Spanish missions and presidios in 1769. On the surface, these *respuestas,* or responses, almost uniformly show the mission Indians as docile subjects. They also reveal how the friars wished to portray themselves. California's eighteenth-century "enlightened" friars sought to avoid the debates that had taken place in the sixteenth century over the legitimacy of forced conversions.[38]

In the questionnaire, González asked the priests to describe the Indians' dominant virtues. (In the previous chapter I analyzed the vices, largely related to indigenous sexuality, that the priests reported in response to the same questionnaire.) In somewhat leading fashion, González inquired whether the Indians were charitable, generous, and compassionate, and he instructed the friars to differentiate by sex the Indians practicing such virtues.[39] Most of the friars characterized the mission Indians as a single collective unit that displayed a predictable range of behavior patterns considered to be positive in subject peoples, such as docility, obedience, and compassion. Eighty percent of the friars who responded to this question did not differentiate between the sexes but described the Indians at their missions collectively as charitable, generous with food, sympathetic, patient, docile, humble, timid, compassionate toward strangers, blindly obedient, respectful, hospitable, meek, submissive, indifferent toward material things, and patiently suffering.[40]

Only the missionaries at the Santa Barbara, San Miguel, San Diego, and San Antonio missions specified any difference between the virtues exhibited by males and females. In these cases, the responses reflected differences of degree rather than differences in the virtues themselves. At the Santa Barbara mission, Father Ramón Olbés noted that the Indian women were "more pious and inclined to virtue" than the men.[41] Fathers Juan Martín and Juan Cabot reported that the women at San Miguel mission surpassed the men in the practice of charity, sharing their food with anyone, "Indian or gente de razón," who came to their homes.[42] Friars Fernando Martín and José Sánchez wrote that they observed in the San Diego mission Indians, "especially in the women," the virtues of compassion, charity, and generosity.[43] At San Antonio mission, Fathers Juan Bautista Sancho and Pedro Cabot observed that although pity, "the most outstanding virtue of these Indians," was the source of charity among both men and women, compassion was "more natural to the feminine sex here as in other parts of the world."[44]

The depiction of a docile body of Indians was the cornerstone of a self-conscious mythology about the mission system and the role of the church in the Spanish conquest of the Americas. The friars' depiction of the Indians as docile, submissive subjects suggested that evangelization did not require force, and without the use of force, the friars could perpetuate an unambiguous glorification of their role in bringing civilization to the Indians. Likewise, missionaries and explorers in the service of the Spanish Crown wanted the latter to believe that the task of conversion could be easily carried out so that the Crown would continue to support their endeavors.

With independence wars of a decidedly anticlerical nature raging throughout Spain's American colonies in the first decades of the nineteenth century, the questionnaire was a useful way to evaluate the loyalty of the Crown's subjects—both Indians and friars—at the missions. Not surprisingly, the Spanish friars in Alta California, all fiercely loyal to the Crown, tended uniformly to justify their mission work and present it in the best possible light.

The Franciscans effectively recoded the behavior of the Indians by way of a discourse that emphasized the Indians' uniform docility to suit the purposes of the moment. In this political economy of images, the priests emphasized the benefits of the mission project by focusing on their successes in subduing the natives. Image was as important, or more important, than reality. An image of docile Indians who freely and willingly came to the missions and who required no coercion to keep them there was critical to the mission enterprise. The friars needed not only to inculcate and reinforce "docile" behavior among the mission Indians but also to promote an image of indigenous docility in order to give legitimacy to the mission project of a Crown under siege.

As colonial subjects, the Indians were therefore denied true autonomy. The priests ignored or minimized both indigenous collaboration and resistance and often depicted the Indians instead as a monolithic, powerless unit. When acknowledged at all, indigenous resistance to the missions was attributed to nonmission Indian provocation or to rivalries between Indian groups. According to the respuestas, the Indians harbored no animosity whatsoever toward the foreigners in their land. When asked about indigenous attitudes toward Europeans, virtually all of the friars replied that the California Indians exhibited only affection for the Europeans and Americans.[45] Only Fathers Escudé and Marquínez, from the Santa Cruz mission, suggested otherwise. They acknowledged that the fear of firearms might have inhibited the natives from expressing their true feelings.[46]

There was surely some truth to these images of docility, exaggerated as they were, which can be explained more accurately as a function of fear and indigenous coping strategies than as a function of inherent character traits. A Canadian study by the psychologists Susan Lee Painter and Don Dutton may have some relevance for understanding the manifestations of docility noted by the priests. The psychologists observed that in situations of perceived inequity, a "traumatic bond" is produced between a batterer and a victim similar to that between a captor and hostage, which virtually paralyzes the victim. Painter and Dutton wrote: "There are two common features of social structure in such apparently diverse relationships as battered spouse/battering spouse, hostage/captor, abused child/abusing parent, cult follower/leader or prisoner/guard. The first is the existence of a power imbalance wherein the maltreated person perceives herself or himself to be subjugated to or dominated by the other. The second is the intermittent nature of the abuse."[47]

They explained that a strong bond of loyalty and affection often develops under conditions where maltreatment is sporadic. Thus, if a pattern of paternal and beneficent treatment of the Indians were punctuated by the occasional use of force or harsh treatment against members of the mission population, a traumatic bonding might have occurred between the priests and their "captives" which manifested itself in behavior that appeared to be "docile." The "ripple effect"—by which I mean the repercussions on an entire community of a single violent act, whether it be the capture of an escaped neophyte, the whipping of an Indian who failed to show up for mass, or the punishment of someone who stole clothing from the mission—might in effect have held many indigenous inhabitants of the missions in a state of paralysis, if not terror.

I am not suggesting here that the use of force was the predominant mode of relating to the Indians or the only mechanism that kept them at the missions. I am suggesting, however, that coercion was an acceptable practice at the missions and an ever-present threat that encouraged indigenous "docility." I am arguing, furthermore, that the conscientious portrayal of the Indians as docile subjects clearly downplayed the coercive component of the mission project.

Given the likelihood of retribution against those who engaged in flagrant episodes of armed revolt, openly challenged the priests' authority, or fled from the missions, resistance more often expressed itself in much subtler forms, particularly within the realm of culture. Examples of such cultural resistance appear inadvertently in the very same texts that attest to the Indians' docility. The anthropologist James Scott has found that the records of colonizers are often infiltrated with "hidden transcripts" that depict the dissent and self-assertion of the subordinate groups.[48] Such subversion is clearly present in the respuestas. Contradictions occasionally disrupt the respuestas and inadvertently open a window onto experiences of cultural resistance that sometimes differed by gender.

Despite their assertions to the contrary, virtually all of the friars provided evidence that the mission Indians continued to hold "superstitious" practices or beliefs after coming to the missions. Fathers Marcelino Marquínez and Jayme Escudé wrote that there were no superstitions, "not even omens which are believed even by the gente de razón in other parts," among the Ohlones at Santa Cruz mission.[49] Nevertheless, the priests then described some "ill-intentioned old persons" who inspired fear of the devil in the others and sometimes gathered at night for "secret, nocturnal dances, and meetings with the devil."[50] Likewise, Father Juan Amorós denied that the indigenous groups at the San Carlos mission held many superstitions but then gave details of healing ceremonies, devil worship, and witchcraft conducted by old men and women.[51] The Ohlone Indians at the Santa Clara and San José missions were also said to engage in devil worship, healing ceremonies, and witchcraft and to hold "an undeterable belief in dreams."[52]

The inclusion of dreams as a form of superstitious practice appears odd at first glance, given the extremely private nature of dreams. Fathers Durán and Fortuny noted that above all else, the principal superstition of the Ohlone neophytes at San José was their "extremely obstinate belief in everything they dream about to such an extent that it is impossible to convince them of the unreality of their dream content."[53] Although the priests did not articulate the nature of indigenous dreams, they clearly felt threatened by them. In his bilingual manual written to assist San Buenaventura priests hearing Chumash confessions, Father José Señán included the translation of a question about dreams. "Do you believe in dreams?" the question read. "How many times have you believed in dreams?"[54] To believe in dreams was clearly seen by the priests as sinful.

In many California indigenous cultures (and Native American cultures in general), dreams and visions were signs of spiritual power that conveyed messages to the community at large and often conferred status upon the individual recipient of the vision.[55] Ethnographies and autobiographies of native Californians are full of "meticulous recountings of dreams and contacts with the spirit world" that are often inaccessible to the modern scholar.[56] Participants in late-nineteenth-century messianic movements in California, which have been better documented than movements during the earlier mission period, have emphasized the importance of dreams as a source of indigenous resistance, particularly in the context of the imposition of new religions. These later movements, noted the anthropologist Cora DuBois, were marked by the "appearance of local dreamers or prophets whenever an external impulse set a new religious form in motion."[57]

The role of women as dream visionaries was unremarked in the questionnaire responses by the friars, but other sources indicate that women were sometimes leaders of such resistance. In one account written sometime before 1831, Father Gerónimo Boscana reported that a female neophyte at the San Juan Capistrano mission claimed to have visionary powers and to have been to heaven, where the god Chinigchinich lived. In the woman's vision, Chinigchinich was surrounded by Indians who were dancing and playing games, activities that were prohibited at the missions.[58] A letter written by a priest at Santa Barbara mission to Governor José Joaquín Arrillaga of Alta California in 1805 told of another visionary rebel in greater detail. In his letter, Father Estevan Tapis described a female Chumash neophyte who had a dream experience that coalesced a community-wide antipathy for the missions. After a feigned paroxysm, the priest wrote, the woman said that Chupa (a goddess worshipped along the Santa Barbara Channel) had appeared to her and told her that the gentiles would die from an epidemic if they were baptized. Christianized Indians who did not offer tribute to Chupa or bathe their heads with a certain water would suffer a similar fate. Furthermore, Chupa had claimed that anyone who told the priests of these revelations would die immediately. Father Tapis wrote that word of the prophecies spread "throughout the rancherías of the Channel and the mountains," and almost all of the neophytes rushed to make offerings of beads and seeds and to attend the ceremony for the renunciation of Christianity at the visionary's home. Father Tapis was extremely concerned because the neophytes, including the *alcalde* leadership at the mission, managed to keep the entire sequence of events from the missionaries for three days.[59]

Tapis's letter provides a strong counterpoint to the respuestas. Whereas in the respuestas the friars denied the existence of "superstitious" practices and minimized the extent of cultural conflict at the missions, Tapis highlighted the extreme nature of this cultural warfare. He dramatized three elements of the dream vision: the goddess Chupa would kill any gentiles who were baptized, Chupa would kill any Christian who did not render her ceremonial honor, and Chupa would kill anyone who informed the priests of the matter.[60] Although Tapis undermined the legitimacy of female leadership (that of both the goddess Chupa and

the mere woman to whom she appeared), his letter shows nonetheless
how dream power and an alternative cultural project, notably embodied
in a female deity, was seized by one Chumash woman as a source of
leadership.

In his twentieth-century study of the Channel Chumash Indians who
inhabited the Santa Barbara mission region, the anthropologist John
Peabody Harrington wrote that Chumash shamans, or religious leaders, derived power from guardian spirits who appeared during trances
or visions and that the Chumash shaman was "invariably a man."[61]
Harrington's failure to note the existence of female shamans reflected
either the reluctance of his informants to discuss the issue, the move
underground of female shamanism during and following the mission
period, or Harrington's own gender biases. Although the extent of female spiritual resistance to the missions cannot be fully documented,
female leadership roles were certainly common among indigenous peoples throughout California.

In the northwestern part of present-day California, the Yurok and
some neighboring tribes allotted doctoring power to women, but in
other regions, anthropologists have reported that "the majority of the
doctors and the most powerful ones are men."[62] Nona Christiansen Willoughby noted that women predominated heavily over men as shamans
in northwestern California, with the reverse being true in the northeast.
James Culleton observed that women were shamans in Ohlone groups
in the area around Monterey Bay.[63] Willoughby noted that most of the
southern tribes had only male shamans, with the exception of some
Mono and Yokuts tribelets and Costanoan, Luiseño, Diegueño, Yuma,
Chemehuevi, and Mohave groups.[64] The Frenchman Duhaut-Cilly
noted that on his visit to the California missions in 1827–28, women
shamans and healers were customary in Alta California. He wrote that
"the Indians impute to some old women the art of sorcery, and then they
become objects of veneration and fear." Duhaut-Cilly's efforts to find out
more were rebuffed, however. "These old enchantresses stubbornly refuse to converse with strangers about their occult science," he observed.[65]

Traces of the worship of female deities remained among some Alta
California groups in the early nineteenth and twentieth centuries, as is
suggested by Father Tapis's references to Chupa, but it is impossible to
know to what extent a more widespread worship of female deities

might have been forced underground or provided a vehicle for indigenous resistance to new Catholic norms. Nor can we know to what
extent missionization affected the growth or decline of such practices.
Fathers Pedro Múñoz and Joaquín Pasqual Nuez observed that the
Indians at San Fernando mission, just north of today's Los Angeles,
worshipped five gods and one goddess, Manisar, a fertility goddess who
was said to provide corn and seeds to the Indians.[66] The anthropologist
Alfred Kroeber confirmed that Gabrielino Indians who occupied the
Los Angeles County area in the twentieth century continued to worship
a goddess named Manisar, as well as another goddess named Chukit.[67]
Among the Luiseño Indians, worship of the earth mother, Tomaiyowit
(or -wut), was common.[68] She was the founder who gave birth to the
earliest animals, people, and plants.[69] The extent to which worship
might have varied along gender lines has not yet been explored.

Cultural transformation in early Spanish–Native American relations
was often marked by a shift from indigenous female spirituality to a
Western patriarchal structure of religious beliefs. Ramón Gutiérrez articulated this shifting paradigm in the title of his study of Pueblo-
Spanish interactions in New Mexico, *When Jesus Came, the Corn Mothers
Went Away.* Similarly, Irene Silverblatt's study of Spanish-Andean relations, *Moon, Sun, and Witches,* highlighted the emergence in Peru of
feminine resistance to a Catholic belief system that excluded, alienated,
or delegitimated female spirituality or modes of worship. Both Riane
Eisler and Pamela Berger have studied similar phenomena on a more
global level.[70]

Some indigenous women, particularly older women, exerted leadership roles in agrarian rituals at the missions, much to the chagrin of the
priests. Father Amorós remarked that some old women in the Monterey
region claimed that they caused the fruits and seeds to grow. Should the
year be barren in produce, wrote Amorós, the old women pretended
that the harvests had failed because they were angry and unwilling to
produce.[71] Such women were consequently rewarded and honored in
good years and appeased during years of poor harvests. One cannot help
noting the apparent power and respect these elder women were accorded by the neophytes at San Carlos mission, as well as Amorós's
skepticism about their "productive" powers.

Other friars noted that the mission Indians revered certain sacred places. The priests from San Juan Bautista believed that Ohlone women maintained sacred places where sorceresses could communicate with the devil.[72] Fathers Luis Antonio Martínez and Antonio Rodríguez described the existence of such ceremonial sites at San Luis Obispo mission.[73] Father Señán, who, besides being president of the California missions, had served as a missionary since 1798 at San Buenaventura, some nine leagues south of the Santa Barbara mission, wrote in 1813 that the Indians gathered at nearby mountain plots "which were kept well cleared, swept and adorned with beautiful plumages fastened to poles."[74] He described in a tone of near veneration the ceremonies that took place at these sacred grounds, where one of the Chumash Indians would petition the "Invisible One" on behalf of all those gathered for rain, an abundance of acorns, seeds, wild fruits, fish, and deer, protection from bears and rattlesnakes, and good health. The Indians would then offer beads, acorns, and other seeds to "the Author and giver of rain, seeds, fruits and all other things."

Female participation was common in many indigenous ceremonies. At San Luis Rey, Fathers Francisco Suñer and Antonio Peyri described ceremonial dances in which Luiseño men and women both participated.[75] These forbidden dances were enveloped in secrecy. The San Luis Rey priests noted the reticence of the Luiseño Indians, despite the "most exacting of inquiries," to divulge the goals of these ceremonies.[76] Father Gerónimo Boscana, who relied largely on three older indigenous men at the San Juan Capistrano mission for his account, noted that the ceremonies were not meant to be understood by outsiders or even by uninitiated insiders. He noted, "A veil is cast over all their religious observances, and the mystery with which they are performed, seems to perpetuate respect for them, and preserve an ascendancy over the people."[77]

Often, the priests used age or time at the mission rather than gender as their unit of analysis. When asked, two-thirds of the respondents to the 1812 questionnaire indicated that superstitions were held primarily by the older generation. The inclusiveness of the Spanish language makes it difficult to determine whether the friars' remarks referred to women as well as men, and only rarely did the responses indicate explicitly the inclusion of both men and women. Fathers Estevan Tapis and

Francisco Xavier Uría specified that some of the older Chumash men and women at Santa Inés mission had "not yet been undeceived" concerning the "pagan superstitions" on which they had been brought up.[78]

The coexistence of indigenous traditions with Catholic practices was dependent upon discretion about the former, particularly after indigenous religious and cultural observances were forbidden at the missions. "It had become necessary to practice in secret those customs which they saw as indispensable to their culture," Victoria Brady wrote. "Even those who functioned in the white world often lived in a second private world of Indian ways and rituals."[79] Fathers Tapis and Uría wrote that the Chumash neophytes were "careful to do in secret what they formerly conducted in a public manner."[80] Likewise, Fathers Marquínez and Escudé noted that the Ohlone Indians at Santa Cruz mission always avoided "detection by the fathers."[81]

Even if outwardly accepting of Catholic practices, California Indians doggedly held on to their own religious beliefs.[82] One of anthropologist Carobeth Laird's informants, "the last traceable descendant of the tribe missionized at San Gabriel," told how her grandmother was simultaneously "very Catholic" and "an equally devout adherent of the Old Religion."[83] Laird wrote about the conversation she had with her informant, whom she called Doña Marta. Laird wrote that Doña Marta held her hands out, her "long, pale, brown forefingers extended, and moved first one and then the other ahead," as though they were "two animals running neck and neck, alternating in the lead position." The two run together, Doña Marta's grandmother had told Doña Marta, and "when one fails, the other helps."

The questionnaire responses revealed that some missionaries were engaged in a more polarized battle to wipe out native customs and beliefs, although the majority of the missionaries seemed uninterested in doing so. When asked what could be done to destroy indigenous superstitions, only one-third of the friars even responded. Some proposed exhortation. After describing Luiseño taboos regarding sexual intercourse (which was not allowed between new parents until their newborn child could walk) and eating (hunters and fisherman were not allowed to partake of their respective catches, and husbands were not to partake of certain foods following the birth of an infant), the San Luis

Rey priests noted, "The manner of destroying them is no other than 'Clama ne ceses [sic].' "[84] The priests at San José, Santa Clara, San Juan Bautista, and San Buenaventura missions stressed the importance of preaching, time, and patience as the remedies for superstitious beliefs. In two of the rare references in the respuestas to the priests' use of force, the priests of the San Diego and Santa Cruz missions stressed the need to punish those who engaged in superstitious feasts or ceremonial practices. The San Diego fathers wrote that they employed "trustworthy" Indians from the missions as lookouts to spy on the offenders and severely and publicly punished those who were caught.[85] The Santa Cruz fathers agreed that punishment, accompanied by persuasion, was the best way to turn the Indians away from their old ways. They noted that preaching and punishment had been used with good results to dissuade the older males from engaging in nocturnal ceremonies.[86]

Language was a vehicle for cultural resistance at the missions. Seemingly straightforward questions and answers about language challenge representations of the mission Indians as docile subjects and reveal invaluable information about indigenous responses to evangelization, as well as relations between the Crown and the Catholic missionaries on the California frontier.

After centuries of ambiguity and conflict over Spanish language policies in the New World, under Charles III (1759–88), the Bourbons called for the eradication of Amerindian languages and customs and the forced Hispanicization of the natives through obligatory education.[87] Like its other reforms, the Bourbon Crown's new language policy was meant to further unify and facilitate the administration of the Spanish colonies, to consolidate Crown control over the church, and to provide greater cohesion to the church's evangelization project. This new language policy was enacted in 1770, when King Charles III issued an order explicitly forbidding the speaking of any language other than Spanish in Spain's American colonies.[88] The king noted that the Crown's repeated decrees, laws, and instructions to the secular and religious authorities in the New World had "not managed to achieve their desired effect," and he lamented that after more than two and a half centuries, the Indians still maintained "many and different languages" and were "refusing to learn Spanish or to send their children to school."[89] The problem, wrote the king, was not that the natives did not understand Spanish but that they did "not wish to speak it." He largely blamed the priests for this state of affairs.

Despite the Bourbon Crown's repeated prohibitions, Indian languages thrived, in coexistence with the Spanish language, at all of the California missions. From the time the first missions were established, Father Serra had underscored the importance of the missionaries' learning the indigenous languages in order to be able to evangelize and to train local interpreters.[90] In response to the question regarding the use of the bishop-approved catechisms of Christian doctrine in indigenous languages in the 1812 questionnaire, the priests' replies indicated that all of the California missions had catechisms in the languages of the Indians, often several different versions at a single mission. None of the indigenous language catechisms had received official approval from the bishops, although they had been prescribed and approved by the superiors of the missions.[91] Most of the priests specified that they taught the texts in both Spanish and the native tongues. Father Antonio Jayme noted that Soledad mission had catechisms in four indigenous languages.[92] According to the respuestas, four native languages were spoken at San Gabriel mission, three at San Fernando, a "prodigious number" at San Buenaventura, fifteen at San Luis Obispo, four at San Miguel, two at San Antonio, two at San Carlos, "as many dialects as the number of the villages of their origin" at Santa Cruz, three at Santa Clara, and five at the San Francisco mission.[93]

The need for the Spaniards to learn the native tongues responded at least in part to the Indians' reluctance to learn the conquerors' language. Father Felipe Arroyo de la Cuesta expressed some frustration at the reluctance of the Ohlones at San Juan Bautista to use Spanish. He observed the difficulty he was having in making the Indians give up their native languages. Only "when the conquest is over and some generations have passed," he wrote, would the Indians be likely to speak Spanish.[94] Being Catalán, Father Arroyo de la Cuesta had special difficulty in teaching the Indians Spanish, because it was not his own native language. He learned the native languages at his San Juan Bautista mission and wrote a Mutsún grammar that could be used by other missionaries there.[95] Similarly, in an effort to systematize the learning of native tongues, Father Buenaventura Sitjar published a lexicon of the language of the Salinan Indians at San Antonio mission.[96] With the collaboration of native interpreters at La Purísima mission, Father Mariano Payeras produced catechism materials in Chumash, including a catechism with the Acts of Faith, Hope, and Charity and a complete confessional guide.[97] Father José Señán wrote a bilingual Chumash-Spanish manual for hearing confessions at San Buenaventura mission.[98]

The indigenous languages were often difficult for the priests to learn, as Father Lasuén noted in a letter in 1780 to the head of the College of San Fernando in Mexico.[99] In 1816, the Franciscan prefect Vicente Francisco de Sarria expressed concern that many priests in California seemed to have abandoned the use of indigenous languages as the vehicle for teaching catechism. Following a canonical visit to all of the California missions, he issued a circular letter encouraging the priests to teach in the indigenous languages.[100] In his memorandum, Sarria ignored more recent language policy directives from Spain that prohibited the speaking of indigenous languages; he drew selectively on earlier policies that encouraged the priests to teach the Indians in their native tongues. Sarria reminded the mission friars of the instructions of the Third Council of Lima, convoked by Archbishop Toribio in 1583, which decreed that the Indians should be taught in their native languages. Merely to give instructions in Spanish and say nothing in the language that the Indians could understand, advised Sarria, was insufficient. The Indians should be taught in their own tongues, even if it required employing interpreters.

Language training was one area in which indigenous experiences varied by gender at the California missions. Because the priests focused their efforts primarily on training the Indian boys, males had greater opportunities to learn Spanish than did females. As the first missions were being established, Father Serra had noted the importance of training boys to speak Spanish.[101] Fathers Estevan Tapis and Francisco Xavier Uría at Santa Inés mission mentioned that they had "selected several boys whom they were training to read the catechism."[102] In 1832, Father Antonio Peyri invited Agapito Amamix and Pablo Tac, two Luiseño neophytes from the largest of the California missions, San Luis Rey, to accompany him to the Franciscan Mission College of San

Fernando in Mexico, and then to Rome.[103] On September 23, 1834, at the age of twelve, Tac entered the Collegio Urbano di Propaganda Fede with his fourteen-year-old companion, Agapito Amamix. The latter died soon thereafter of smallpox. Tac spent seven years at the college studying grammar, rhetoric, and the humanities, until he died from influenza at nineteen. He left a remarkable manuscript—one of the few documents actually written by a Native American at this time—that included a treatise on indigenous customs and an unfinished lexicon of the little-known Luiseño language.[104]

The opportunity afforded Amamix and Tac would have been unavailable to Indian girls at the missions. Given the Crown directives that language education was to cease after girls reached the age of ten, they had little opportunity to obtain advanced tutoring or schooling, regardless of the aptitude they might have shown for the language.[105]

The priests were not necessarily opposed to female education, however. Father Luis Gil and José María de Zalvidea averred that there was a need for teachers in California who could provide language education to all of the young neophytes. They clearly favored separatist education—"male teachers in primary education for the boys and female teachers for the girls."[106] Their position followed Crown directives that for centuries had called for the establishment of schools and, where the numbers allowed it, a school for each sex.[107]

The priests were the primary, although not the only, Spanish speakers with whom the Indians regularly interacted. The priests' orders to limit their contact with females at the missions gave males something of an advantage in learning to speak Spanish.[108] Fathers Luis Antonio Martínez and Antonio Rodríguez noted that the Chumash men at San Luis Obispo mission were more inclined than the women to learn Spanish, "for no other reason than that they needed to communicate with the Priest, and the few gente de razón."[109]

Male Indians had greater incentives to learn Spanish than did females. The priests rewarded linguistic abilities, which they saw as evidence of indigenous loyalty, with positions of power in the mission system. The Indians' failure to learn Spanish was the single greatest obstacle to achieving such positions. Pablo Tac observed that the friar, knowing "that it would be very difficult for him to be able to rule by himself," appointed male neophytes as alcaldes. But males could be alcaldes, he noted, only if they "knew how to speak Spanish more than the others and were better than the others in their [the friars'] customs."[110] Tac's description of the role of the alcaldes at San Luis Rey further emphasized the linguistic requisites for advancement in the mission system. Each of the alcaldes needed to be able to communicate well in his own language in order to relay messages from the missionaries to the Indian villages, secure a work force as it was needed, and oversee the fields. This is not to say that Indian women had no opportunities or incentives to learn Spanish, but such opportunities were the exception and not the rule, and neither Crown nor Church policy articulated roles or rewards for women on the basis of their linguistic abilities.

A difference between male and female linguistic abilities was noted in 10 percent of the respuestas. At San Luis Obispo mission, Fathers Luis Antonio Martínez and Antonio Rodríguez described the facility with which the male Chumash Indians, in contrast to the females, adopted the new language. Although the neophytes there were from fifteen different villages where fifteen different languages were spoken, the priests noted that the natives used a single language among themselves, and the parents "preserve their native idioms in which they have been raised."[111] Martínez and Rodríguez noted that few of the Chumash Indians, "and particularly not the women," could understand Spanish.[112] Likewise, at San Luis Rey mission, Fathers Francisco Suñer and Antonio Peyri noted the relative reluctance of the Luiseño women to use Spanish. The priests observed on two occasions that the men showed greater linguistic promise than the women. Many of the Christians, "especially the men," spoke and understood Spanish, they wrote, and most of the Luiseño neophytes, "especially the men," used both Spanish and their native tongue.[113]

The extent of female resistance to learning Spanish was even greater than that reported in the questionnaire responses. Although the priests at La Purísima mission failed in their questionnaire response to differentiate between the language practices of men and women, in a private letter to Father President Estevan Tapis, the third of the mission presidents, Father Mariano Payeras noted that the Chumash men at the mission showed a greater willingness to learn the new language than the women. He observed that he and his colleagues had taught nearly all of the men a large catechism, and the elder men had learned a smaller version. They had had less luck with the Chumash women, Father Payeras reported, because "after all they are women."[114] Payeras's letter offers proof that the respuestas underreported female resistance to learning Spanish in at least one mission. His private letter, written at about the same time as the respuestas, suggests that because the priests did not expect females to excel in learning languages, they might not have thought to report their failure to do so. This same reasoning might account for the failure of priests at other missions to discern gender-based patterns of response toward language learning.

Although Father Payeras and other priests attributed the women's reluctance to learn Spanish to their female nature, it is clear that women had relatively little to gain by learning Spanish and perhaps stood to lose status within their own communities if they did. Such was the case in colonial Peru, where indigenous male cooperation with Spanish religious authorities often cost the males legitimacy among their own indigenous communities. Andean *kurakas* struggled to maintain their status among their local communities and before the conquering Spaniards.[115] The resulting power vacuum sometimes created leadership possibilities for indigenous females who were marginalized from the new colonial religious order.[116] Given the tradition of female leadership roles among some California groups, notably the Chumash, such paradigms may help to explain why indigenous women might have resisted adopting some Hispanic ways at the California missions.

Although linguistic resistance appears not to have been confined solely to Indian women, female neophytes as a group seem to have resisted learning Spanish to a greater degree than the men. The friars appear to have had varying degrees of success in their efforts to teach the natives Spanish, and their reports indicate that adoption of the Spanish language varied widely from mission to mission. Fathers Fernando Martín and José Sánchez expressed bewilderment that the Indians at San Diego mission were reluctant to speak Spanish. "We do not know what reasons keep them from using Spanish," they wrote.[117] Despite threats and punishment, particularly of the youths, the priests were unable to elicit compliance.

The priests' professed incomprehension of indigenous reluctance to use Spanish is yet another manifestation of imperial discourse. Here again we see the underpinnings of an imperial mythology that reformulated indigenous or female opposition to its policies to suit its own needs. Indigenous reluctance to conform to linguistic directives, like female diffidence, was rarely portrayed as resistance to missionization. Instead, it was a sign of indigenous inferiority, stupidity, or just plain stubbornness. Fathers Narciso Durán and Buenaventura Fortuny conjectured that the reason the Ohlone Indians at San José mission refused to speak Spanish was probably "their extreme and well-known crudity and their great repugnance to give up their own tongue."[118]

Indigenous acceptance of the Spanish language, when in fact it happened, did not necessarily translate into support for the Spanish missions. The apparent willingness of some of the neophytes to learn Spanish was a response to a variety of factors, not the least of which may have been that Spanish provided a potential base for communication between members of distinct linguistic entities within a single mission, as well as opportunities for cultural survival.

Cultural resistance to the mission project was apparent in the maintenance not only of indigenous religious and linguistic practices but also of other daily habits and attitudes of the mission Indians.[119] We saw in the previous chapter how Indians resisted Franciscan efforts to transform patterns of sexuality. In the respuestas, we find as well that responses to seemingly neutral questions about daily routines at the missions, such as how much it cost to feed each neophyte and queries about agricultural practices, contain a subtext which shows that as a whole, neophytes at the California missions often thwarted the missionary fathers' efforts to transform indigenous eating habits, dress patterns, and attitudes toward land and land use.

The priests' efforts to establish a strict dietary regime of three meals a day and a restricted menu at the mission were related in part to their desire to restructure indigenous notions of time. The Western model called for people to follow a daily schedule of worship, work, and rest, punctuated by meals. Fathers Juan Martín and Juan Cabot's description of daily mission life suggests that such an "ideal" routine was in place at the San Miguel mission. There, neophytes rose at sunrise for a breakfast of *atole* (a boiled mush of ground corn or barley), followed by mass, where they recited the catechism in their own language. After mass, they returned home for their tools and worked until half past ten in the morning. They lunched on wheat, Indian corn, and peas or cooked beans, rested until two o'clock (in summer until three), and then returned to work until an hour before sunset. After another meal of atole, they assembled in the church to recite the catechism and sing the *Alabado* or the *Salve* or *Adórate, Santa Cruz.* Following the church services, they returned home.[120]

This idyllic portrayal of life at San Miguel contrasts sharply with descriptions of other missions, where neophytes continually challenged the mission fathers' efforts to impose a regular schedule of sleep, meals, and labor. Many of the friars reported not only that the Indians ate at all hours of the day and night but that they supplemented the mission diet of *atole* and meat with the foods they ate before coming to the missions—acorns, pine nuts, seeds, sage, and meat from deer, rabbits, squirrels, and rats.[121] Many of the priests seemed unconcerned, however, about this deviation from mission diet and meal routines. Intermittent resource scarcity, particularly in the early mission days, may have caused some of the friars to allow or even encourage the Indians to supplement the mission food supply by hunting and gathering. Patterns varied by mission and over time, and consideration of changes in female roles and status at the missions must take into account such variations.

Many of the friars had a hard time calculating the amount of food consumed by the neophytes. Fathers Pedro Múñoz and Joaquín Pasqual Nuez at San Fernando mission reported that they could not say how many times a day the neophytes ate, because the Fernandeños ate "whenever they felt like it, and more so at night than in the daytime."[122] Likewise, at San Buenaventura mission, Father Señán found it difficult to estimate how much the Chumash neophytes were eating. He observed: "Owing to the variety of eatables which they keep in their homes and being children who eat at all hours it is not easy to compute the amount they daily consume."[123] Father Juan Amorós observed that before the Ohlones at San Carlos mission became Christians, they ate "whenever they desired," but as Christians they were given three meals a day.[124] Nonetheless, it was impossible to stop them from eating day and night, he lamented, or to force them to exercise moderation.

The questionnaire responses also reveal a clash of values with respect to landownership. Although the mission economy was one in which the Indians lived in community and primarily worked communal lands, the friars tried to instill in them a respect for individual private property by granting the neophytes private plots of land for gardening, but with the priests retaining oversight of the harvest. Father José Señán explained that the priests at San Buenaventura mission encouraged the Chumash neophytes to plant private gardens of pumpkins, watermelons, melons, corn, and other grains "in order to have them grow fond of an industrious life."[125] The Santa Clara priests Magín Catalá and José Viader encouraged a relationship toward the land that appears to have mixed the tenets of private property with a tolerance for indigenous communal practices. These missionaries encouraged individualism through the provision of resources—oxen, seeds, and leisure time.[126] The Ohlone Indians at San Juan Bautista mission appear to have taken little interest in cultivating their own plots of land, and the missionary fathers there took care of planting and harvesting. When the priests' efforts were insufficient, Father Arroyo de la Cuesta wrote, the neophytes simply returned to the countryside to search for wild seeds, notably a female endeavor among the Ohlones. Arroyo noted that although they liked to eat watermelons, sugar melons, pumpkins, spices, and Indian corn, the mission Indians still preferred "to live in idleness and on what the countryside supplies them without any efforts on their part."[127]

Despite the efforts and enticements of the priests, the women seem to have been particularly reluctant to cooperate with the friars. Not only were women reluctant to adopt new patterns of land use, but they also sometimes sabotaged the friars' plans. Father Juan Amorós expressed some frustration at the failure of the priests to induce "rational" behavior among the Ohlone Indians at San Carlos mission. Despite the Indians having each been given a small parcel of land, Amorós noted, the women often uprooted the shoots of corn and squash "in a fit of anger," and their husbands generally followed suit. Such signs of anger or protest were attributed to their infantile nature. "In these matters," noted Amorós, "they behave like children of eight or nine years who as yet have not acquired a constant or steady disposition."[128] Amorós did not entertain the possibility that the Ohlones might have resented the imposition of more sedentary agricultural practices than those to which

Figure 9. "A California Woman Habited in the Skin of a Deer," unsigned, 1780.
(Courtesy of the California State Library)

they were accustomed. The contentious attitude sometimes displayed by
the Ohlones at San Carlos might have reflected their discomfort with
new gender roles or resentment at an erosion of female status occa-
sioned by the new changes in diet and patterns of land tenure.

Clothing was another arena in which indigenous and European practices clashed (figs. 9–11). Indigenous acceptance of European dress varied among the missions. Priests reported that the Ohlones at San José

Figure 10. "Costume de la Haute Californie" and "Dame de Monterey," from Abel du Petit-Thouars, *Voyage autour du monde sur la frégate la Vénus, pendant les années 1836–1839: Atlas pittoresque,* 1841. (Courtesy of the Bancroft Library)

mission were enthusiastic about adopting the vestments of Hispanic society. There, Fathers Narciso Durán and Buenaventura Fortuny found that nudity did not exist and that the Ohlones were "quite interested in going about clothed."[129] In all of the other missions, however, some resistance to adopting Spanish patterns of dress was noted. At Santa Barbara, this resistance was marked among the elder generation of Chumash neophytes. Father Olbés noted that the priests often had to resort to threats to make the older Chumash men and women wear clothes "for the sake of modesty and decency."[130] Father Juan Amorós noted that there was a general lack of interest in clothing at San Carlos mission, despite the importance that the mission priests placed on changing indigenous dress patterns. He wrote, "If all valued wearing apparel much more would be given to them and in a short time we would have them going about as civilized beings."[131]

The San Francisco mission priests, too, highlighted the relationship they saw between wearing clothing and being civilized. To the priests, nudity signified idleness and a lack of industry. According to Fathers Ramón Abella and Juan Sainz de Lucio, the Ohlone Indians at the San

Figure 11. Masselot, "Costume of Upper California: Native Woman" and "Costume of Upper California: Native Man," from Petit-Thouars, *Voyage*. (Courtesy of the Bancroft Library)

Francisco mission disdained clothing. This rejection of clothing was seen as a sign of their lack of civility. The priests noted that the only way nudity could be reduced would be to change indigenous attitudes toward land and work, a difficult task given the Ohlones' "love for the beach and the open country."[132]

Mission friars used clothing as a reward for work and employed it to create hierarchies among the male neophytes. The Ohlones who looked after the property of the San Carlos mission were given the same clothing as that worn by the Europeans. Father Ramón Olbés noted that at Santa Barbara mission the priests gave Spanish clothing "to those who show more effort in some labor or service."[133] The priests at San Luis Obispo likewise rewarded service to the mission with European clothes. Fathers Luis Antonio Martínez and Antonio Rodríguez rewarded those of "irreprehensible conduct and Christianity" by giving them "pants of soft skin, a jacket of ordinary cloth."[134] Women enjoyed no such incentives related to clothing.

Although men and women alike led armed revolts, plotted assassinations, planned and executed escapes, and disrupted mission programs, on a daily basis Indians both adapted to and resisted new cultural norms in many less spectacular ways. Language, ceremonies, dreams, dances, dress, diet, land usage, and sexuality provided the spaces that allowed the Indians to confront the new social order without being confrontational and to resist without being perceived as resisting. Even in captivity, male and female Indians alike could and did assert themselves in their daily lives in such cultural realms. While the mission system restructured indigenous lifeways according to Western concepts of space and time, the Franciscans had less success in imposing new dietary patterns on the mission Indians. In some realms, gendered patterns of resistance may be discerned. Women sometimes offered greater resistance to learning Spanish and to adopting new patterns of land use than their male counterparts. In a new mission context that explicitly denied them religious leadership roles, female spirituality and dream visions provided women with alternative sources of power. Indigenous men and women alike, particularly those of the older generations, conducted healing ceremonies, dances, and agrarian rituals, sometimes in secret or in defiance of mission regulations. Some indigenous groups have continued to worship female deities since the pre-mission days. Unlike men, women also practiced abortion or infanticide at the missions, although generalizations about such practices must be analyzed within a given local context to determine to what extent this practice represented continuity or a break with the past.

Despite the record of such cultural resistance, imperial ideology that effectively denied autonomy to the mission Indians also denied their capacity or inclination to rebel. The Franciscans, even while providing details of the retention of certain cultural practices or open resistance to missionization, frequently recoded indigenous activities in ways that would reflect positively on the mission enterprise. Their failure to perceive or represent indigenous resistance as such meant that they frequently attributed tenacity in clinging to indigenous customs to old age, stupidity, or ignorance.

8

Partial Truths

Texts purporting to represent cultural and historical truths are systematically partial—that is, subjective, fragmentary, and exclusive. As the anthropologists James Clifford and George E. Marcus noted, "all constructed truths are made possible by powerful 'lies' of exclusion and rhetoric."[1] Even so, the texts of the Spanish colonial period provide a starting point for restoring women to the narratives of California history. Although their experiences were subordinated in the chronicles of conquest, colonization, and evangelization, women participated actively in that history. A close reading of the documents shows that both their absence and their presence shaped the encounters between the Old and New Worlds where they converged in Alta California. Conflicting gender ideologies likewise appear to have had a role in defining the nature of local encounters.

Female voices and information about gender roles and relations were often included in primary documents, only to be excluded in later historical narratives, extracts, or indices of these early documents. Petitions to Spanish authorities provide some of the few instances in which female voices were recorded, yet indices such as Herbert Bolton's eminent *Guide to Materials* often give no indication of the existence of such materials.[2] Undoubtedly, many such petitions and letters remain to be uncovered by future researchers.

Nor is Bolton alone in his dismissal of female experiences as marginal to the writing of history. In his five-volume index to the Archives of the Archdiocese of San Francisco, Alexander Taylor indexed the rape of two young girls, one of whom was killed, as a "report on some misconduct at Mission San Carlos."[3] Hubert Bancroft's index of California pioneers did not even list the women settlers.[4]

Beyond the exclusion and reductionism found inevitably in even the most valiant efforts to systematize data through indexing and cataloguing, historical narratives are also dependent on the data and documentation available. Much of the original correspondence between Spanish and Mexican authorities in California and those in Mexico City and Spain was destroyed in San Francisco's 1906 earthquake and fire. The transcripts and summaries of these originals made in the 1870s at the request of Hubert Howe Bancroft are extant in the Bancroft Library's sixty-three-volume *Archives of California,* but they are painfully fragmentary. Extracts of the "Libros de Misión" made by Bancroft's staff show painstaking notes on the first and last appearance of a particular priest officiating at a baptism, marriage, or funeral ceremony, but they customarily omit the names of the people who were actually baptized, married, or died.

My comparison of the texts of the responses to the government questionnaire of 1812 extant in the Santa Barbara Mission Archives and the transcripts and extracts of those documents in the Bancroft Library reveals how fragmentary records can distort our understanding of reality.[5] In an age before the photocopy machine, every document was copied by hand. In what were probably efforts to save time and energy or to eliminate redundancies, the scribes consistently failed to copy large sections of the respuestas. The repetition was important, however, and in distilling that information, Bancroft's scribes in effect minimized widespread patterns of cultural resistance occurring at the missions.

Cultural codes, spoken and unspoken, written and unwritten, have mediated whose stories were heard then and whose stories are heard now. Attentiveness to these institutional and cultural patterns of discourse reveals codes of silence regarding female experiences and gender ideologies. Female experiences have remained imbedded in a labyrinth of taboos related to the use of force at the missions, gender relations, indigenous dreams and ceremonies, and questions related to sexuality. Piercing these codes of silence inadvertently reveals other silences about a variety of groups, especially indigenous peoples. Mistreatment of the Indians and the use of force at the missions were highly sensitive areas that were intentionally protected from public scrutiny. Although the codes of silence were sometimes broken, discussion of the use of force at the missions was proscribed within the church, between the church and the Crown, and between missionaries and non-Spanish foreigners.

In examining the nature and epistemology of historical "truths," it becomes evident that some "truths" have been excluded, both intentionally and inadvertently, from historical narratives. The partiality of the historical record cannot be blamed only on chroniclers and subsequent historians, or even on church guidelines for discretion. Many cultures employ conscious strategies of discretion when dealing with outsiders. This point was brought home to me on a visit to Tucson, Arizona. A museum there featured an extensive display of indigenous historical artifacts and dioramas of religious rituals with a notable absence of female participants. The docent boasted of the mutual cooperation and extensive consultations in which the museum had engaged with local indigenous descendants. When asked about the lack of women in the display, the docent noted that the Tarahumara descendants had considered their female rituals too sacred to be put on display.

Chroniclers of history are limited by such codes of silence, as well as by their conceptions of what was and is important. The nature of my topic makes impartiality particularly problematical. The context for my examination of gender—the Spanish conquest of Alta California—was peopled with so-called winners and losers, all of whom had a stake in explaining their particular viewpoint. Following the Spanish conquest, during which the dominant Spanish culture was imposed upon indigenous peoples, another layer of history intervened. With the Mexican-American War, United States troops defeated the descendants of the Spanish conquerors and Anglo culture displaced the dominant Hispanic culture. The politics of these ethnocultural shifts inevitably contributed to the partiality of eighteenth- and nineteenth-century records and writings, as each generation sought to justify its own position in history or to correct previous histories. Sensitive records have undoubtedly been destroyed or remain hidden from public view.

Language and geography have been powerful mediators of discursive partiality. Dominant languages and forms of cultural preservation have changed in the shifting political landscape of California. Written conventions have replaced oral traditions. The Spanish language first displaced a multitude of native tongues as the dominant language and then was itself displaced by English. This has made the transmission of alternative interpretations of history particularly difficult. Ironically, many of the primary sources, particularly the journals from the Anza expedition, are more readily available in English translation than in Spanish.[6]

The indigenous sources that are extant regarding cultural resistance at the missions come largely from Indians who were raised or whose families were raised at the missions. The analysis of particular, sparsely documented revolts at the missions may misconstrue the broader resistance that kept many Indians from coming to the missions in the first place. Likewise, documents of indigenous practices during the mission period may not reflect pre-mission indigenous practices.

Spanish colonial California was largely an illiterate society, and Spanish texts were generally produced by scribes who accompanied expeditions, transcribers of court proceedings, mission priests, or researchers gathering information for a particular historical project. Misspellings of names were common, and each person who recorded it might spell a single name differently. Legibility of handwriting varied widely, making some documents more accessible to researchers than others. Such seemingly inconsequential factors come into play in the production of history, as scholars select the materials they will weave together to form a historical narrative. Narrative, by its very nature, gives priority to coherence. History and the production of historical narrative are highly selective processes in which one makes a "radical selection from the immensely rich swirl of past human activity" in order to transform the general past into the "significant past."[7] This significance is dependent in part upon the audience to which the narrative is being presented, whether it is Spanish regal or ecclesiastic authorities or individuals such as Hubert H. Bancroft.

If female experience (or that of any social grouping) is or was considered irrelevant by the chroniclers of history, then the reconstruction of a definitive history becomes impossible. One cannot assume that all of the documentary evidence needed to reconstruct the past was even produced, much less preserved. The priests who responded to the 1812 questionnaire were not particularly discerning in their appreciation of gender differences, and they tended to generalize for the mission Indians as a whole. Furthermore, it is clear that the Indians withheld from the priests vast arenas of information relating not only to female experience but also to sexuality, dreams, dances, ceremonies, and sacred places.

The relationship between silence and knowledge sometimes responds to questions of power and resistance. Female discourse has been classified as standing "nearer the absence, silence and death of words" and as embodying through its absence "the very lack of discourse."[8] This characterization may pertain to any group that does not hold power. When asked about indigenous sexual practices, native informants deliberately ignored the question, digressed, refused to answer, or constructed answers in keeping with what they knew to be acceptable to the dominant Christian practices of the time, or to their interviewers. The Stanford-trained anthropologist Greg Sarris, who was raised by a renowned Cache Creek Pomo medicine woman in Santa Rosa, California, has addressed the uses of silence in indigenous cultures in his collection of essays *Keeping Slug Woman Alive*. There, he grappled with epistemological questions related to being an insider or an outsider. "Silence," he quoted an aunt of his as saying, was "the Indian's best weapon."[9] His aunt equated being an Indian with being silent and counseled him to "be an Indian." She advised, "Cut yourself off with silence any way you can. Don't talk. Don't give yourself away."[10]

Even beyond the silences that protect cultural difference or announce power inequities are differences in operational modes for the transmission of knowledge. In his ethnographic study of one of Suriname's six Maroon tribes, the anthropologist Richard Price related a Saramaka folktale from that Afro-American tribe, the moral of which was that knowledge is power and one must "never reveal all of what one knows."[11]

My study of women, gender ideologies, and conquest has, perhaps inevitably, led to questions about partiality and the production of history. My focus has brought into relief some hidden arenas of female experience and highlighted the ways in which ethnicity and gender relate to these silent abysses of history. I have found that gender ideology played a role in the establishment, consolidation, expansion, decline, and mythology of the Spanish mission system in California. Furthermore, I have drawn conclusions about how women's presence or absence shaped conquest and how conflicting gender ideologies provided a justification for conquest, beginning with the myths about Queen Calafia and continuing into and beyond the mission period. I found that underlying ideas about gender and colonization shifted between the Spanish period and the early Mexican period and that Hispanic and indigenous women both carried out and resisted their assigned roles in colonization and at the missions. Far from being a definitive account, my account of women and gender at the missions is limited by the partial nature of data about women, by multiple codes of silence about female experiences, sexuality, ceremonies, and the use of force, and by the tremendous diversity of the indigenous groups in Alta California.

Abbreviations

Journals

AEA	*Anuario de estudios americanos*
AHR	*American Historical Review*
AIQ	*American Indian Quarterly*
AQ	*American Quarterly*
BIIH	*Boletín del Instituto de Investigaciones Históricas*
CH	*California History*
CHSQ	*California Historical Society Quarterly*
CLAHR	*Colonial Latin American Historical Review*
CLAR	*Colonial Latin American Review*
HAHR	*Hispanic American Historical Review*
HSSCQ	*Historical Society of Southern California Quarterly*
IJWS	*International Journal of Women's Studies*
JAF	*Journal of American Folklore*
JAH	*Journal of Arizona History*
JCA	*Journal of California Anthropology*
JCGBA	*Journal of California and Great Basin Anthropology*
JFH	*Journal of Family History*
JHG	*Journal of Historical Geography*
JLAS	*Journal of Latin American Studies*
JSDH	*Journal of San Diego History*
JSH	*Journal of Social History*

JW	Journal of the West
LARR	Latin American Research Review
LATR	Latin American Theatre Review
Masterkey	Masterkey for Indian Lore and History
NMHR	New Mexico Historical Review
PHR	Pacific Historical Review
PNQ	Pacific Northwest Quarterly
RHA	Revista de Historia de América
RIS	Revista Internacional de Sociología
RLA	Romance Languages Annual
SCQ	Southern California Quarterly
Signs	Signs: Journal of Women and Culture
UCPAAE	University of California Publications in American Archaeology and Ethnology
WHQ	Western Historical Quarterly

Archives and Libraries

AGI	Archivo General de las Indias (Seville, Spain)
AGN	Archivo General de la Nación (Mexico City)
AMSB	Archivo de la Misión de Santa Barbara
BL	Bancroft Library
BN	Biblioteca Nacional (Madrid)
FF	Fondo Franciscano (Mexico City)
INHA	Instituto Nacional de Historia e Antropología (Mexico City)
NAA	National Anthropological Archives (Washington, D.C.)
SBMA	Santa Barbara Mission Archives (Santa Barbara, California)
SI	Smithsonian Institution (Washington, D.C.)

Collections

Arch. de las Misiones	Archivos de las Misiones
Arch. of Calif.	Archives of California
Aud.	Audiencia
Calif.	Californias
CMD	California Mission Documents
Corr. Virr.	Correspondencia de Virreyes
Esp. y Cam.	Espediciones y Caminatas
HHBC	Hubert Howe Bancroft Collection
Ind.	Indiferente
Inf. y Corr.	Informes y Correspondencia
JSC	Junípero Serra Collection
Pap. Misc.	Papeles Misceláneos
Prov. Int.	Provincias Internas
Prov. Rec.	Provincial Records
Prov. St. Pap.	Provincial State Papers
R.C.	Reales Cédulas
RCD	Reales Cédulas Duplicados
RJE	Ramo Justicia: Eclesiástica
St. Pap.	State Papers
WA	Western Americana (Yale University Beinecke Library)

Notes

Introduction

1. Other works that use discourse analysis as a vehicle for studying colonial encounters in Latin America include Mary Louise Pratt, *Imperial Eyes: Travel Writing and Transculturation* (New York: Routledge, 1992); Peter Hulme, *Colonial Encounters: Europe and the Native Caribbean, 1492–1797* (London; New York: Methuen, 1986); George L. Scheper, "Re-Reading the 'Conquest of Mexico': Whose Story?" *Semiotics 1990* (New York: University Press of America, 1993), 195–210; and Tzvetan Todorov, *The Conquest of America* (New York: HarperPerennial, 1984).

2. See Francisco Javier Cevallos-Candau, Jeffrey A. Cole, Nina M. Scott, and Nicomedes Suárez-Araúz, *Coded Encounters: Writing, Gender, and Ethnicity in Colonial Latin America* (Amherst: University of Massachusetts Press, 1994); Jack J. Himelblau, ed., *The Indian in Spanish America: Centuries of Removal, Survival, and Integration; A Critical Anthology*, 2 vols. (Lancaster, Calif.: Labyrinthos, 1994); Kenneth Mills and William B. Taylor, eds., *Colonial Spanish America: A Documentary History* (Wilmington, Del.: Scholarly Resources, 1998); Electa Arenal and Stacey Schlau, *Untold Sisters: Hispanic Nuns in Their Own Works* (Albuquerque: University of New Mexico Press, 1989); and Beatriz González Stephan and Lúcia Helena Costigan, eds., *Crítica y descolonización: El sujeto colonial en la cultura latinoamericana* (Caracas: Universidad de Simón Bolívar and Ohio State University, 1992).

3. For bibliographies on these topics, see Karen Spalding, "The Colonial Indian: Past and Present Research Perspectives," *LARR* 7:1 (1972): 47–75; Frederick Bowser, "The African in Colonial Spanish America: Reflections on Research Achievements and Priorities," *LARR* 7:1 (1972): 77–94; James Lockhart, "The Social History of Colonial Spanish America: Evolution and Potential," *LARR* 7:1 (1972): 6–46; Eric Van Young, "Mexican Rural History since Chevalier: The Historiography of the Colonial Hacienda," *LARR* 18:3 (1983): 5–61; Lynne Phillips, "Rural Women in Latin America: Directions for Future Research," *LARR* 25:3 (1992): 89–107; Kathleen A. Myers, "Broader Canon, Interdisciplinary Approaches: Recent Works in Colonial Latin American Literary Studies," *LARR* 33:2 (1998): 258–70; and Matthew

Restall, "Central Issues: Social History and the Recent Study of Colonial Central America," *LARR* 33:2 (1998): 207–20. For an overview of the evolution of such scholarship in the United States, see Benjamin Keen, "Main Currents in United States Writings on Colonial Spanish America, 1884–1984," *HAHR* 65:4 (Nov. 1985): 658–82; Howard F. Cline, ed., *Latin American History: Essays on Its Study and Teaching, 1898–1965,* 2 vols. (Austin: University of Texas Press, 1967); and K. Lynn Stoner, *Latinas of the Americas: A Source Book* (New York: Garland, 1989).

4. See James Lockhart, *Postconquest Central Mexican History and Philology* (Stanford: Stanford University Press, 1991); Lockhart, *The Nahuas after the Conquest: A Social and Cultural History of the Indians of Central Mexico, Sixteenth through Eighteenth Centuries* (Stanford: Stanford University Press, 1992); and Juan de Betanzos, *Narrative of the Incas* (Austin: University of Texas Press, 1996).

5. See Rebecca Horn, *Postconquest Coyoacán: Nahua-Spanish Relations in Central Mexico, 1519–1650* (Stanford: Stanford University Press, 1997); Grant D. Jones, *The Conquest of the Last Maya Kingdom* (Stanford: Stanford University Press, 1998); Susan Elizabeth Ramírez, *The World Upside Down: Cross-Cultural Contact and Conflict in Sixteenth-Century Peru* (Stanford: Stanford University Press, 1996); Matthew Restall, *The Maya World: Yucatec Culture and Society, 1550–1850* (Stanford: Stanford University Press, 1997); Lawrence H. Feldman, *Indian Payment in Kind: The Sixteenth-Century Encomiendas of Guatemala* (Lancaster, Calif.: Labyrinthos, 1992); Kenneth Andrien and Rolena Adorno, *Transatlantic Encounters: Europeans and Andeans in the Sixteenth Century* (Berkeley: University of California Press, 1991); Robert Patch, *Maya and Spaniard in Yucatán, 1648–1812* (Stanford: Stanford University Press, 1993); Matthew Restall, *Maya Conquistador: Yucatec Perceptions of the Spanish Conquest* (Boston: Beacon, 1998); and John E. Kicza, *The Indian in Latin American History: Resistance, Resilience, and Acculturation* (Wilmington, Del.: Scholarly Resources, 1993).

6. See, for example, Washington Irving, *The History of the Life and Voyages of Christopher Columbus* (New York: G. P. Putnam's Sons, 1895–97); William H. Prescott, *History of the Conquest of Mexico, with a Preliminary View of the Ancient Mexican Civilization, and the Life of the Conquerer, Hernando Cortes,* 2 vols. (London: Routledge, Warre, and Routledge, 1865); Albert Gallatin, "Notes on the Semi-Civilized Nations of Mexico, Yucatan, and Central America," *Transactions of the American Ethnological Society,* 3 vols. (1845–53), 1:1–352; Hubert H. Bancroft, *History of Mexico,* 6 vols. (San Francisco: Bancroft, 1883–89); James Lockhart, *The Men of Cajamarca: A Social and Biographical Study of the First Conquerors of Peru* (Austin: University of Texas, 1972); William B. Taylor, *Magistrates of the Sacred: Parish Priests and Indian Parishioners in Eighteenth-Century Mexico* (Stanford: Stanford University Press, 1996); Robert Himmerich y Valencia, *The Encomenderos of New Spain, 1521–1555* (Austin: University of Texas Press, 1991); and Rafael Varón Gabai, *Francisco Pizarro and His Brothers: The Illusion of Power in Sixteenth-Century Peru* (Norman: University of Oklahoma Press, 1997).

7. See Ricardo Herren, *La conquista erótica de las Indias* (Barcelona: Planeta, 1991);

Marvin Goldwert, *Machismo and Conquest: The Case of Mexico* (Lanham, Md.: University Press of America, 1983); and Lisbeth Haas, *Conquest and Historical Identities in California, 1769–1936* (Berkeley: University of California Press, 1995).

8. Pat Caplan, *The Cultural Construction of Sexuality* (New York: Tavistock, 1987), 1.

9. See Jean R. Brink, Maryanne C. Horowitz, and Allison P. Coudert, eds., *Playing with Gender: A Renaissance Pursuit* (Chicago: University of Illinois Press, 1991).

10. Inga Clendinnen, "Yucatec Maya Women and the Spanish Conquest: Role and Ritual in Historical Reconstruction," *JSH* 15 (1982): 427.

11. See Sonya Michel and Robyn Muncy, eds., *Engendering America: A Documentary History, 1865 to the Present* (New York: McGraw-Hill College, 1999); Joan Wallach Scott, *Gender and the Politics of History* (New York: Columbia University Press, 1988); Elaine Showalter, *Speaking of Gender* (New York: Routledge, 1989); Constance Jordan, *Renaissance Feminism: Literary Texts and Political Models* (Ithaca, N.Y.: Cornell University Press, 1990); Kristin Hoganson, *Fighting for American Manhood: How Gender Politics Provoked the Spanish-American and Philippine-American Wars* (New Haven: Yale University Press, 1998); Judith Papachristou, "American Women and Foreign Policy, 1898–1905: Exploring Gender in Diplomatic History," *Diplomatic History* 14 (Fall 1990): 493–509; and Ana María Alonso, *Thread of Blood: Colonialism, Revolution, and Gender on Mexico's Northern Frontier* (Tucson: University of Arizona Press, 1995).

12. See June Nash, "Aztec Women: The Transition from Status to Class in Empire and Colony," in Mona Etienne and Eleanor Leacock, eds., *Women and Colonization* (New York: Praeger, 1980), 134–48; Irene Silverblatt, " 'The Universe has turned inside out. . . . There is no justice for us here': Andean Women under Spanish Rule," in Etienne and Leacock, *Women and Colonization,* 149–85; Inga Clendinnen, *Ambivalent Conquest: Mayan and Spanish in Yucatan, 1517–1570* (Oxford: Oxford University Press, 1987); Nancy Farriss, *Mayan Society under Colonial Rule: The Collective Enterprise of Survival* (Princeton: Princeton University Press, 1984); Susan Schroeder, Stephanie Wood, and Robert Haskett, *Indian Women of Early Mexico* (Norman: University of Oklahoma Press, 1997); Susan Kellogg, *Law and the Transformation of Aztec Culture, 1500–1700* (Norman: University of Oklahoma Press, 1995); and Elinor Burkett, "Indian Women and White Society: The Case of Sixteenth-Century Peru," in Asunción Lavrin, ed., *Latin American Women: Historical Perspectives* (Westport, Conn.: 1978), 101–28.

13. Irene Silverblatt, *Moon, Sun, and Witches: Gender Ideologies and Class in Inca and Colonial Peru* (Princeton: Princeton University Press, 1987).

14. See Julia Tuñón Pablos, *Women in Mexico: A Past Unveiled,* trans. Alan Hynds (Austin: University of Texas Press, 1999); and various essays in Schroeder, Wood, and Haskett, *Indian Women of Early Mexico.*

15. See Charles R. Boxer, *Mary and Misogyny: Women in Iberian Expansion Overseas, 1415–1815* (London: Duckworth, 1975); Maria Beatriz Nizza da Silva, ed.,

Families in the Expansion of Europe, 1500–1800 (Brookfield, Vt: Ashgate, 1998); Nancy O'Sullivan-Beare, *Las mujeres de los conquistadores: La mujer española en los comienzos de la colonización americana* (Madrid: Compañía Bibliográfica Española, [1956]); Juan Francisco Maura, "Esclavas españolas en el Nuevo Mundo: Una nota histórica," *CLAHR* 2 (Spring 1993): 185–94; Maura, *Women in the Conquest of the Americas* (New York: Peter Lang, 1997); José Torre Revello, "Esclavas blancas en las Indias occidentales," *BIIH* 6 (1927–28): 263–71; Vicenta Cortés Alonso, "Los esclavos domésticos en América," *AEA* 24 (1967): 955–83; Richard Konetzke, "La emigración de mujeres españolas a América durante la época colonial," *RIS* 9 (Jan.–Mar. 1945): 123–50; and María Teresa Villafane, "La mujer española en la conquista y colonización de América," *Cuadernos Hispanoamericanos* 59 (1964): 125–42.

16. See Maura, *Women in the Conquest of the Americas,* and Luis Martín, *Daughters of the Conquistadores: Women of the Viceroyalty of Peru* (Albuquerque: University of New Mexico Press, 1983).

17. For a sample of the kinds of work being done, see Kevin Gosner and Deborah E. Kanter, eds., "Special Issue: Women, Power, and Resistance in Colonial Meso-america," *Ethnohistory* 42:4 (Fall 1995); Ann Zulawski, "Social Differentiation, Gender, and Ethnicity: Urban Indian Women in Colonial Bolivia, 1640–1725," *LARR,* 25:2 (1990): 93–113; and Elizabeth Kuznesof, "The Construction of Gender in Colonial Latin America," *CLAR* 1, nos. 1–2 (1992): 253–70, 268.

18. See Lyman Johnson and Sonya Lipsett-Rivera, *The Faces of Honor: Sex, Shame, and Violence in Colonial Latin America* (Albuquerque: University of New Mexico Press, 1998); Steve J. Stern, *The Secret History of Gender: Women, Men, and Power in Late Colonial Mexico* (Chapel Hill: University of North Carolina Press, 1995); Asunción Lavrín, ed., *Sexuality and Marriage in Colonial Latin America* (Lincoln: University of Nebraska Press, 1989); Sylvia Arrom, *The Women of Mexico City, 1790–1857* (Stanford: Stanford University Press, 1985); Verena Martínez-Alier, *Marriage, Class and Colour in Nineteenth-Century Cuba: A Study of Racial Attitudes and Sexual Values in a Slave Society* (Ann Arbor: University of Michigan Press, 1974); Patricia Seed, *To Love, Honor, and Obey in Colonial Mexico: Conflicts over Marriage Choice, 1574–1821* (Stanford: Stanford University Press, 1988); Daisy Ripodas Ardanaz, *El matrimonio en Indias: Realidad social regulación jurídica* (Buenos Aires: Fundación para la Educación, la Ciencia, y la Cultura, 1977); Eni de Mesquita Samara and Dora Isabel Paiva da Costa, "Family, Patriarchalism, and Social Change in Brazil," *LARR* 32:1 (1997): 212–25; Richard Boyer, *Lives of the Bigamists: Marriage, Family, and Community in Colonial Mexico* (Albuquerque: University of New Mexico Press, 1995); Antonia Castañeda, "Marriage: The Spanish Borderlands," *Encyclopedia of North American Colonies,* 3 vols. (New York: Scribner's Sons, 1993), 2:727–38.

19. Carol Devens, *Countering Colonization: Native American Women and Great Lakes Missions, 1630–1900* (Berkeley: University of California Press, 1992). See also Carol Devens, "Separate Confrontations: Gender as a Factor in Indian Adaptation to European Colonization in New France," *AQ* 38 (1986): 461–80; Eleanor Burke Lea-

cock, ed., *Myths of Male Dominance: Collected Articles on Women Cross-Culturally* (New York: Monthly Review Press, 1981); and Leacock, "Montagnais Women and the Jesuit Program for Colonization," in Etienne and Leacock, *Women and Colonization*, 25–42.

20. See Nancy Shoemaker, ed., *Negotiators of Change: Historical Perspectives on Native American Women* (New York: Routledge, 1995); Frances E. Karttunen, *Between Worlds: Interpreters, Guides, and Survivors* (Rutgers, N.J.: Rutgers University Press, 1994); Laura F. Klein and Lillian A. Ackerman, eds., *Women and Power in Native North America* (Norman: University of Oklahoma Press, 1995); and Beatrice Medicine and Patricia Albers, eds., *The Hidden Half: Studies of Plains Indian Women* (Lanham, Md.: University Press of America, 1983).

21. Clara Sue Kidwell, "Indian Women as Cultural Mediators," *Ethnohistory* 39 (Spring 1992): 98.

22. See Jacqueline Peterson and Jennifer Brown, eds., *The New Peoples: Being and Becoming Métis in North America* (Lincoln: University of Nebraska Press, 1985); Jennifer S. H. Brown, "Women as Centre and Symbol in the Emergence of Métis Communities," *Canadian Journal of Native Studies* 3 (1983): 39–46; Jacqueline Peterson, "The People in Between: Indian-White Marriage and the Genesis of a Métis Society and Culture in the Great Lakes Region, 1680–1830" (Ph.D. diss., University of Illinois, Chicago, 1981); Peterson, "Women Dreaming: The Religiopsychology of Indian-White Marriages and the Rise of a Métis Culture," in Lillian Schlissel, Vicki L. Ruiz, and Janice Monk, eds., *Western Women: Their Land, Their Lives* (Albuquerque: University of New Mexico Press, 1988): 49–68.

23. Jennifer S. H. Brown, *Strangers in Blood: Fur Trade Company Families in Indian Country* (Vancouver: University of British Columbia Press, 1980); Sylvia Van Kirk, *Many Tender Ties: Women in Fur-Trade Society in Western Canada, 1670–1870* (Norman: University of Oklahoma Press, 1980); Walter O'Meara, *Daughters of the Country: The Women of the Fur Traders and Mountain Men* (New York: Harcourt, Brace and World, 1968).

24. John Mack Faragher, "The Custom of the Country: Cross-Cultural Marriage in the Far Western Fur Trade," in Schlissel, Ruiz, and Monk, *Western Women*, 200.

25. Robert Steven Grumet documented such intermediary roles among the middle Atlantic coastal Algonkians. See Robert Steven Grumet, "Sunksquaws, Shamans, and Tradeswomen: Middle Atlantic Coastal Algonkian Women during the Seventeenth and Eighteenth Centuries," in Etienne and Leacock, *Women and Colonization*, 43–62. See also Lucy Eldersveld Murphy, "Autonomy and the Economic Roles of Indian Women of the Fox-Wisconsin Riverway Region, 1763–1832," in Shoemaker, ed., *Negotiators of Change*, 72–89.

26. See Julie Roy Jeffrey, *Frontier Women: The Trans-Mississippi West, 1840–1880* (New York: Hill and Wang, 1979); Schlissel, Ruiz, and Monk, *Western Women*; Joan M. Jensen and Darlis A. Miller, "The Gentle Tamers Revisited: New Approaches to the History of Women in the American West," *PHR* 49 (May 1980): 173–214; Joan

Jensen and Gloria Ricci Lothrop, *California Women: A History* (San Francisco: Boyd and Fraser, 1987); Ruth Moynihan, Susan Armitage, and Christiane Fischer Dichamp, *So Much to Be Done: Women Settlers on the Mining and Ranching Frontier* (Lincoln: University of Nebraska Press, 1990); Sandra Myres, *Westering Women and the Frontier Experience, 1880–1915* (Albuquerque: University of New Mexico Press, 1982); Lillian Schlissel, *Women's Diaries of the Westward Journey* (New York: Schocken Books, 1982); Arlene Scadron, ed., *On Their Own: Widows and Widowhood in the American Southwest, 1848–1939* (Urbana: University of Illinois Press, 1988); Joanna L. Stratton, *Pioneer Women: Voices from the Kansas Frontier* (New York: Simon and Schuster, 1981); and Glenda Riley, *The Female Frontier: A Comparative View of Women on the Prairie and the Plains* (Lawrence: University Press of Kansas, 1988).

27. See Ray Allen Billington, *America's Frontier Heritage* (New York: Holt, Rinehart and Winston, 1966); Frederick Jackson Turner, *The Frontier in American History* (New York: H. Holt and Company, 1920); and Elizabeth Kuznesof and Robert Oppenheimer, "The Family and Society in Nineteenth-Century Latin America: An Historiographical Introduction," *JFH* 10:3 (Fall 1985): 215–35.

28. Classic studies in mission historiography include John Francis Bannon, "The Mission as a Frontier Institution: Sixty Years of Interest and Research," *WHQ* 10 (July 1979): 302–22; Herbert E. Bolton, "The Mission as a Frontier Institution in the Spanish-American Colonies," *AHR* 23:1 (Oct. 1917): 42–61; Zephyrin Engelhardt, *Missions and Missionaries of California*, 2 vols., 2d ed. (Santa Barbara: Santa Barbara Mission Archive-Library, 1930); Felix Almaraz, Jr., *The San Antonio Missions and Their System of Land Tenure* (Austin: University of Texas Press, 1989); and Erick D. Langer and Robert H. Jackson, eds., *The New Latin American Mission History* (Lincoln: University of Nebraska Press, 1995).

29. For literature on the presidios, see Max L. Moorhead, *The Presidio: Bastion of the Spanish Borderlands* (Norman: University of Oklahoma Press, 1975); Leon Campbell, "The First Californios: Presidial Society in Spanish California, 1769–1822," *JW* 11 (Oct. 1972): 582–95; J. Phillip Langellier and Daniel Bernard Rosen, *A History under Spain and Mexico, 1776–1846* (Denver: National Park Service, 1992); and Richard S. Whitehead, *Citadel on the Channel: The Royal Presidio of Santa Barbara, Its Founding and Construction, 1782–1798* (Spokane, Wash.: Arthur H. Clark, 1996).

30. Antonia I. Castañeda, "Presidiarias y Pobladoras: Spanish-Mexican Women in Frontier Monterey, Alta California, 1770–1821" (Ph.D. diss., Stanford University, 1990); Castañeda, "Gender, Race, and Culture: Spanish-Mexican Women in the Historiography of Frontier California," *Frontiers* 11 (1990): 8–20; Castañeda, "Engendering the History of Alta California, 1769–1848: Gender, Sexuality, and the Family," *CH* 76:2–3 (Summer–Fall 1997): 230–59.

31. Salomé Hernández, "No Settlement without Women: Three Spanish California Settlement Schemes, 1790–1800," *SCQ* 72 (Fall 1990): 203–78; Victoria Brady, Sarah Crome, and Lyn Reese, "Resist! Survival Tactics of Indian Women," *CH*

63 (Spring 1984): 141–51; Douglas Monroy, "They Didn't Call Them 'Padre' for Nothing: Patriarchy in Hispanic California," in Adelaida R. Del Castillo, ed., *Between Borders: Essays on Mexicana/Chicana History* (Encino, Calif.: Floricanto Press, 1990), 433–46; Monroy, *Thrown among Strangers: The Making of Mexican Culture in Frontier California* (Berkeley: University of California Press, 1990).

32. Ramón Gutiérrez, *When Jesus Came, the Corn Mothers Went Away: Marriage, Sexuality, and Power in New Mexico, 1500–1846* (Stanford: Stanford University Press, 1991); Deena González, "Spanish-Mexican Women of Santa Fe: Patterns of Their Resistance and Accommodation, 1820–1880" (Ph.D. diss., University of California, Berkeley, 1985); González, *Refusing the Favor: The Spanish-Mexican Women of Santa Fe, 1820–1880* (New York: Oxford University Press, 1999); González, "The Widowed Women of Santa Fe: Assessments on the Lives of an Unmarried Population, 1850–1889," in Scadron, *On Their Own,* 65–90.

33. See Janet Lecompte, "The Independent Women of Hispanic New Mexico, 1821–1846," *WHQ* 12 (Jan. 1981): 17–35; Rebecca McDowell Craver, *The Impact of Intimacy: Mexican-Anglo Intermarriage in New Mexico, 1821–1846* (University of Texas at El Paso: Texas Western Press, 1982); Darlis A. Miller, "Cross-Cultural Marriages in the Southwest: The New Mexico Experience, 1846–1900," *NMHR* 57 (Oct. 1982): 335–59; and Cheryl J. Foote, *Women of the New Mexico Frontier, 1846–1912* (Niwot, Colo.: University Press of Colorado, 1990).

34. See Georgellen Burnett, *We Just Toughed It Out: Women in the Llano Estacado* (University of Texas at El Paso: Texas Western Press, 1990); Jo Ella Powell Exley, *Texas Tears and Texas Sunshine: Voices of Frontier Women* (College Station: Texas A&M University Press, 1984); Ann Patton Malone, *Women on the Texas Frontier: A Cross-Cultural Perspective* (University of Texas at El Paso: Texas Western Press, 1983); Jane Dysart, "Mexican Women in San Antonio, 1830–1860: The Assimilation Process," *WHQ* 7 (Oct. 1976): 365–75; and Jane Downs and Nancy Baker Jones, *Women and Texas History: Selected Essays* (Austin: Texas State Historical Association, 1993).

35. See Sarah Deutsch, "Women and Intercultural Relations: The Case of Hispanic New Mexico and Colorado," *Signs* 12, no. 4 (Summer 1987): 719–39; and Deutsch, *No Separate Refuge: Culture, Class, and Gender on an Anglo-Hispanic Frontier, 1880–1940* (New York: Oxford University Press, 1987).

36. See Mary Aickin Rothschild and Pamela Claire Hronek, *Doing What the Day Brought: An Oral History of Arizona Women* (Tucson: University of Arizona Press, 1992).

37. Ramón A. Gutiérrez, "Contested Eden: An Introduction," *CH* 76: 2–3 (Summer–Fall 1997): 4.

38. Gutiérrez, *When Jesus Came;* Robert H. Jackson and Edward Castillo, *Indians, Franciscans, and Spanish Colonization: The Impact of the Mission System on California Indians* (Albuquerque: University of New Mexico Press, 1995).

39. Jackson and Castillo, *Indians,* 8–9, 38–39.

40. Monroy, "They Didn't Call Them 'Padre' for Nothing," 435.

41. Alonso, *Thread of Blood.*

42. Albert L. Hurtado, *Intimate Frontiers: Sex, Gender, and Culture in Old California* (Albuquerque: University of New Mexico Press, 1999).

43. In order to appreciate the relatively complex system of checks and balances and the intentionally ambiguous lines of authority and jurisdiction that the Spanish Crown imposed on its New World colonies, see John Leddy Phelan, "Authority and Flexibility in the Spanish Imperial Bureaucracy," *Administrative Science Quarterly* 5 (1960): 47–65.

44. These positions are put forth in Sherburne F. Cook, *The Conflict between the California Indian and White Civilization* (1943; reprint, Berkeley: University of California Press, 1963); Francis F. Guest, "An Examination of the Thesis of S. F. Cook on the Forced Conversion of Indians in the California Missions," *SCQ* 61 (Spring 1979): 1–78; and Edward D. Castillo and Doyce Nunis, Jr., "California Mission Indians: Two Perspectives," *CH* 70 (Summer 1991): 206–15, 236–38.

Chapter 1. Mythic Beginnings

1. For background on the exploratory voyages leading up to the sighting of California, see Harry Kelsey, "Mapping the California Coast: The Voyages of Discovery, 1533–1543," *Arizona and the West* 26 (Winter 1984): 307–24. For background on Juan Rodríguez Cabrillo, see Harry Kelsey, *Juan Rodríguez Cabrillo* (San Marino, Calif.: Huntington Library, 1986); and Henry R. Wagner, *Juan Rodríguez Cabrillo: Discoverer of the Coast of California* (San Francisco: California Historical Society, 1941).

2. Seymour I. Schwartz and Ralph E. Ehrenberg, *The Mapping of America* (New York: Abrams, 1980); John Leighly, *California as an Island* (San Francisco: Book Club of California, 1972).

3. See James Lockhart and Stuart B. Schwartz, *Early Latin America: A History of Colonial Spanish America and Brazil* (New York: Cambridge University Press, 1983), esp. 302–3; James Lockhart, "Encomienda and Hacienda: The Evolution of the Great Estate in the Spanish Indies," *HAHR* 49:3 (Aug. 1969): 411–29; Robert G. Keith, "Encomienda, Hacienda, and Corregimiento in Spanish America: A Structural Analysis," *HAHR* 51:3 (Aug. 1971): 431–46; and Charles Gibson, *Spain in America* (New York: Harper and Row, 1966), 48–68.

4. In this regard, see Josine H. Blok, *The Early Amazons: Modern and Ancient Perspectives on a Persistent Myth* (New York: E. J. Brill, 1995).

5. Cristóbal Colón, *Los cuatro viajes. Testamento,* ed. Consuelo Varela (Madrid: Alianza Editorial, 1986), 165.

6. Ibid., 168.

7. The rumors may have referred to the female-dominated society of Tehuantepec. See Schroeder, Wood, and Haskett, *Indian Women,* 188, 228.

8. Quotations in this paragraph come from Hernán Cortés to Emperor Carlos V,

"Cuarta carta-relación," Tenuxtitlán, October 15, 1524, in Mario Hernández Sánchez-Barba, ed., *Cartas de relación* (Madrid: Historia 16, 1985), 302.

9. The following quotations are from "The relation of Nunno di Gusman written to Charles the fifth Emperour," July 8, 1530, in Samuel Purchas, *Hakluytus Posthumus, or Purchas his Pilgrimes: Contayning a History of the World in Sea Voyages and Lande Travells by Englishmen and Others,* 20 vols. (Glasgow: J. MacLehose and Sons, 1905–7), 18:59–60.

10. In Brazil as well, Gaspar de Carvajal would narrate Orellana's encounter with tall, white, muscular women who fought side by side with their men near the river he would name the "Amazon." Gaspar de Carvajal, *Relación del nuevo descubrimiento del famoso río grande de las Amazonas* (1541–42; Mexico: Fondo de Cultura Económica, 1955).

11. Alexander Taylor, *The First Voyage to the Coasts of California, made in the Years 1542 and 1543, by Juan Rodríguez Cabrillo and His Pilot Bartolomé Ferrelo* (San Francisco: Le Count and Strong, 1853), 7–9. See also Irving Leonard, "Conquerors and Amazons in Mexico," *HAHR* 24 (Nov. 1944): 561–79.

12. For theories on the etymological origins of "California," see Edward Everett Hale, *The Queen of California: The Origin of the Name of California with a Translation from the Sergas of Esplandián* (1862; reprint, San Francisco: Colt Press, 1945); Donald C. Cutter, "Sources of the Name 'California,'" *Arizona and the West* 3 (Autumn 1961): 233–43; and Ruth Putnam, "California: The Name," *University of California Publications in History* 4:4 (1917): 289–365.

13. Other authors, such as Feliciano de Silva and Pedro de Luján, continued the literary tradition of the Amazon in sequels of the *Amadís Cycle.* See Alison Taufer, "The Only Good Amazon Is a Converted Amazon: The Woman Warrior and Christianity in the *Amadís Cycle,*" in Jean R. Brink, Maryanne C. Horowitz, and Allison P. Coudert, eds., *Playing with Gender: A Renaissance Pursuit* (Urbana: University of Illinois, 1991), 35. For a history of the myths, see Enrique de Gandía, *Historia crítica de los mitos de la conquista americana* (Madrid: Sociedad General Española de Librería, 1929).

14. Taufer, "The Only Good Amazon."

15. Cortés's foot soldier Bernal Díaz del Castillo made numerous comparisons between the escapades and discoveries in which he was engaged and those of the knights of the chivalrous romances. See his *Historia verdadera de la conquista de la Nueva España* (Mexico: Porrúa, 1986), 159, 346.

16. The original of *Amadís de Gaula* was written by Vasco de Lobeira at the end of the fourteenth century or the opening of the fifteenth; it was translated by Garcí Ordóñez de Montalvo between 1492 and 1504. Charles E. Chapman, *History of California: The Spanish Period* (New York: Macmillan, 1921), 57.

17. W. Michael Mathes, *Vizcaíno and Spanish Expansion in the Pacific Ocean, 1580–1630* (San Francisco: California Historical Society, 1968), 4.

18. Irving Leonard, *Books of the Brave: Being an Account of Books and of Men in the*

Spanish Conquest and Settlement of the Sixteenth Century (Cambridge, Mass.: Harvard University Press, 1949), 96–98.

19. This and the following quotations are from Ordóñez, *Sergas,* 540.

20. Howard Mumford Jones, *Ideas in America* (Cambridge, Mass.: Harvard University Press, 1944), 54.

21. Leonard, *Books of the Brave,* 13–14.

22. José María Ots Capdequí, *Instituciones sociales de la América española en el período colonial* (La Plata, Argentina: Imprenta López, 1934), 205–6.

23. Malveena McKendrick, *Women and Society in the Spanish Drama of the Golden Age: A Study of the* Mujer Varonil (New York: Cambridge University Press, 1974), 177. McKendrick analyzed Lope de Vega's *Las justas de Tebas y reina de las amazonas* (1596), *Las grandezas de Alejandro* (1604–12), and *Las mujeres sin hombres* (1613–18); Tirso de Molina's *Las amazonas en las Indias* (1631); and Antonio de Solís's *Las amazonas de Escitia* (1681).

24. See Helen F. Grant, "The World Upside-Down," in R. O. Jones, ed., *Studies in Spanish Literature of the Golden Age Presented to Edward M. Wilson* (London: Tamesis, 1973), 103–35; and Nancy K. Mayberry, "The Role of the Warrior Women in *Amazonas en las Indias,*" *Bulletin of the Comediantes* 29 (Spring 1977): 38–44.

25. *Tomar tierra, tomar relación,* and *tomar posesión* were the expressions most commonly used. See Antonyo de Mendoça, "Instrucción que debía observar el capitán Hernando de Alarcón en la expedición a la California que iba a emprender de orden del virrey D. Antonio de Mendoza," May 31, 1541, Mexico, in Buckingham Smith, *Colección de varios documentos para la historia de la Florida y tierras adyacentes,* vol. 1 (London: Trubner y Compañía, 1857), 2; Wagner, *Cabrillo,* 47; and Sebastián Vizcaíno, "Carta," May 23, 1603, in Donald Cutter, *The California Coast: Documents from the Sutro Collection* (1891; reprint, Norman: University of Oklahoma Press, 1969), no. 15, p. 114.

26. Lois Rudnick's "Re-Naming the Land: Anglo Expatriate Women in the Southwest," in Vera Norwood and Janice Monk, eds., *The Desert Is No Lady: Southwestern Landscapes in Women's Writing and Art* (New Haven: Yale University Press, 1987), 10–26, deals primarily with nineteenth- and twentieth-century writings, but her analysis of how traditional Anglo male myths of the West depicted the land as an entity to be expropriated and exploited is valid for earlier generations of Hispanic conquerors as well. Patricia Seed, *To Love, Honor, and Obey,* finds that this is more an Anglo than an Iberian trait. Seed has also explored this theme in her provocative study *Ceremonies of Possession in Europe's Conquest of the New World, 1492–1640* (New York: Cambridge University Press, 1995). See also Annette Kolodny, *The Land Before Her: Fantasy and Experience of the American Frontiers, 1630–1860* (Chapel Hill: University of North Carolina, 1984).

27. Steve Wall, ed., *Wisdom's Daughters: Conversations with Women Elders of Native America* (New York: HarperCollins, 1993).

28. Several studies have analyzed the role of the Virgin, particularly the Virgin of

Guadalupe, who was instrumental in the development of a spirit of "creole patriotism" in Mexico and was a banner symbol in the "Grito de Dolores" that launched the wars for Mexico's independence from Spain at the beginning of the nineteenth century. Studies on the general role of Marianism in the earlier period of the Spanish conquest of America, however, are fewer. See David A. Brading, *The First America: The Spanish Monarchy, Creole Patriots, and the Liberal State 1492–1867* (New York: Cambridge University Press, 1991); Jacques Lafaye, *Quetzalcoatl y Guadalupe: La formación de la conciencia en México (1531–1813)* (Mexico: Fondo de Cultura Económica, 1983); Eric R. Wolf, "The Virgen de Guadalupe: A Mexican National Symbol," *JAF* 71 (Jan.–Mar. 1958): 34–39; William B. Taylor, "The Virgin of Guadalupe in New Spain: An Inquiry into the Social History of Marian Devotion," *American Ethnologist* 14 (1987): 9–33; Serge Gruzinski, *The Conquest of Mexico: The Incorporation of Indian Societies into the Western World, Sixteenth–Eighteenth Centuries* (Cambridge, UK: Polity Press, 1993); Ena Campbell, "The Virgin of Guadalupe and the Female Self-Image: A Mexican Case History," in James J. Preston, ed., *Mother Worship: Theme and Variations* (Chapel Hill: University of North Carolina Press, 1982), 5–24; and Tristan Platt, "Simón Bolívar, the Sun of Justice, and the Amerindian Virgin: Andean Conceptions of the *Patria* in Nineteenth-Century Potosí," *JLAS* 25 (Feb. 1993): 159–85.

29. See especially article 7 in Rafael Altamira, ed., "El texto de las leyes de Burgos de 1512," *RHA* 4 (1938): 5–79.

30. See William O. Christian, Jr., *Local Religion in Sixteenth-Century Spain* (Princeton, N.J.: Princeton University Press, 1981), 121, 155–57.

31. Cited in Donald Demarest and Coley Taylor, *The Dark Virgin: The Book of Our Lady of Guadalupe* (Freeport, Maine: Coley Taylor, 1956), 9.

32. Ibid., 224. Tales of this Mexican virgin are generally believed to have been recorded more than a century later, beginning with the 1648 publication of a treatise authored by Miguel Sánchez, *Imagen de la Virgen María Madre de Dios de Guadalupe, milagrosamente aparecida en la ciudad de México,* as part of a growing "creole consciousness" among the elites born and raised in New Spain. See the discussion on the emergence of creole consciousness in Brading, *First America,* 343–61, and on the central role of the Virgin of Guadalupe in Lafaye, *Quetzalcoatl y Guadalupe.*

33. Kelsey, *Cabrillo,* 155.

34. Herbert E. Bolton, trans. and ed., *Anza's California Expeditions,* 5 vols. (New York: Alfred A. Knopf, 1930–39), 1:232–33.

35. See Maura, "Esclavas españolas," 185–94; Torre Revello, "Esclavas blancas," 263–71; Cortés Alonso, "Esclavos domésticos," 955–83; Konetzke, "Emigración de mujeres," 123–50; Villafane, "Mujer española," 125–42; O'Sullivan-Beare, *Mujeres de conquistadores;* and Boxer, *Mary and Misogyny.*

36. Maura, "Esclavas españolas."

37. Torre Revello, "Esclavas blancas," 226.

38. Cortés Alonso, "Esclavos," 955–83.

39. Maura, "Esclavas españolas," 188–91.

40. Konetzke, "Emigración," 124.

41. Ibid., 123. See also Boyer, *Lives of the Bigamists.*

42. Gonzalo Fernández de Oviedo, *Historia general y natural de las Indias,* 4 vols. (Madrid: Ediciones Atlas, 1959), 1:88–89.

43. Konetzke, "Emigración," 129.

44. Cesáreo Fernández Duro, *La mujer española en Indias* (Madrid: Estab. tip. de la viuda e hijos de M. Tello, 1902), 23.

45. McKendrick, *Women and Society,* 44.

46. See Rima de Vallbona, ed., *Vida i sucesos de la monja alférez: Autobiografía atribuida a Doña Catalina de Erauso* (Tempe: Center for Latin American Studies, Arizona State University, 1992).

47. Isabel de Guevara to Regent Princess Juana, Asunción, July 2, 1556, in Ministerio de Fomento, *Cartas de Indias* (Madrid: Impresa de M. G. Hernández, 1877), part 2, p. 619.

48. Fernández Duro, *La mujer española en Indias,* 142.

49. McKendrick, *Women and Society,* 42–43.

50. See "Instrucción," in Smith, *Colección,* 1.

51. Henry R. Wagner, *Spanish Voyages to the Northwest Coast of America in the Sixteenth Century* (San Francisco: California Historical Society, 1929), 172. Chapman notes that some of the soldiers' wives participated in the expedition. Chapman, *History of California,* 126.

52. The original reads, "la gente casada y mas embarazosa." Vizcaíno, "Relación," 1597, in Cutter, *California Coast,* 70.

Chapter 2. Exploration

1. Taylor, *First Voyage,* 9.

2. For the debate over indigenous population figures prior to Spanish conquest, see Susan Migden Socolow, "La población de la América colonial," in Carmen Bernand, ed., *Descubrimiento, conquista y colonización de América a quinientos años* (México: Consejo Nacional para la Cultura y las Artes/Fondo de Cultura Económica, 1994), 218–48.

3. Sherburne F. Cook, *The Population of the California Indians, 1769–1970* (Berkeley: University of California Press, 1976), 1–43.

4. Malcolm Margolin, ed., *The Way We Lived: California Indian Reminiscences, Stories, and Songs* (Berkeley: Heyday Books, 1981), 4.

5. The term has been used to refer to both racial and cultural attributes. See Gloria Miranda, "Racial and Cultural Dimensions of *Gente de Razón* Status in Spanish and Mexican California," *SCQ* 70 (Fall 1988): 265–78.

6. Juan Rodríguez Cabrillo, "Relación, o diario, de la navegación que hizo Juan Rodríguez Cabrillo," in Smith, *Colección,* 173–89.

7. For a discussion of the controversies surrounding the exact location of Cabrillo's landing, see Hubert H. Bancroft, *History of California,* 7 vols. (San Francisco: History Company, 1890), 1:70.

8. In the early mission period, "California" referred only to the Baja California peninsula, and either local names, "Nuevos Establecimientos," or "California Septentrional" was used to refer to the northern section of *las Californias.* By 1804, the term Nueva California was being used to distinguish upper California from the lower peninsula. In 1824, Alta and Baja California were legally separated. Ibid., 1:139.

9. Stephen Schwartz, *From West to East: California and the Making of the American Mind* (New York: Free Press/Simon and Schuster, 1998), 10.

10. AGI, Justicia, leg. 1021, pieza 1, cited in George P. Hammond and Agapito Rey, *Narratives of the Coronado Expedition, 1540–1542* (Albuquerque: University of New Mexico Press, 1940), 364.

11. See "Instrucción a Comendador Frey Nicolás de Ovando, Gobernador de las Islas y Tierra Firme del Mar Océano," Granada, September 16, 1501, in Richard Konetzke, *Colección de documentos para la historia de la formación social de Hispanoamérica, 1493–1810,* 3 vols. in 5 (Madrid: Consejo Superior de Investigaciones Científicas, 1953), 1:4.

12. The instructions issued by Mendoza to Cabrillo have not been located but were probably similar to those given to López de Zúñiga the previous year. See Antonio de Mendoza and Pedro de Alvarado to Diego López de Zúñiga, April 29, 1541, *Relaciones históricas,* fols. 384v–85, 382–82v, quoted in Kelsey, *Cabrillo,* 108; and Wagner, *Spanish Voyages,* 72, 418, 422. Original in Real Biblioteca de San Lorenzo del Escorial, Relaciones Históricas, sig. 5-2-4, no. 64.

13. Information in this paragraph is from Kelsey, *Cabrillo,* 43, 68n205, 167.

14. Wagner, *Cabrillo,* 40, 46.

15. Smith, *Colección,* 1:173–89.

16. Antonio de Herrera, *Historia general de los hechos de los Castellanos,* 4 vols. (Madrid: En la Emplentarea, 1601–15), December 7, lib. 5, cap. 3–4.

17. Taylor, *First Voyage,* 10.

18. Bancroft, *History of California,* 1:70.

19. Chapman, *History of California,* 77–78.

20. Kelsey, *Cabrillo,* 144.

21. The anthropologist Eleanor Burke Leacock noted that among the Tor and the Iroquois, female allocation of food to strangers "set the stage for the reception of newcomers." Leacock, *Myths of Male Dominance,* 136, 159–60.

22. Smith, *Colección,* 1:183.

23. Herrera, *Historia general,* December 7, lib. 5, cap. 3–4.

24. Bancroft, *History of California,* 1:74.

25. Chapman, *History of California,* 78.

26. In fact, Wagner mistranscribed "podían" as "podrían," which might partially

account for his error. The facsimile version reads, "Por todo este camino no podían valerse de yndios cuales venían a vordo con agua y pescado y amostraban mucho amor." Wagner, *Spanish Voyages*, 458.

27. Ibid., 319; 335n97.

28. Admittedly, this study is based on available late-nineteenth-century and early-twentieth-century sources that may mask post-mission changes in gender roles. Nonetheless, it is likely that such changes favored a move toward greater similarity between Spanish and indigenous gender roles, rather than the reverse. See Nona Christiansen Willoughby, *Division of Labor among the Indians of California* (Berkeley: University of California Archaeological Survey, 1963), 29.

29. For further background on Vizcaíno and his explorations of the Pacific coast, see Mathes, *Vizcaíno and Spanish Expansion;* Cutter, *California Coast;* Juan de Torquemada, *The Voyage of Sebastián Vizcaíno to the Coast of California; Together with a map & Sebastián Vizcaíno's letter written at Monterey, December 28, 1602* (San Francisco: Book Club of California, 1933); José Porrúa Turanzas, ed., *Noticias y documentos acerca de las Californias, 1764–1795* (Madrid: Porrúa Turanzas, 1959); Francisco Carrasco y Guisasola, *Documentos referentes al reconocimiento de las costas de las Californias en los años 1584 a 1602* (Madrid: Dirección de Hidrografía, 1882); Alvaro del Portillo y Diez de Sollano, *Descubrimiento y exploración en las costas de California* (Madrid: Consejo Superior de Investigaciones Científicas, 1947), 141–57.

30. For a discussion of the various accounts of the expedition, see Wagner, *Spanish Voyages*, 378–92.

31. Cutter, *California Coast,* 113; Vizcaíno to Consejo de Indias, December 28, 1602, in Carrasco y Guisasola, *Documentos,* 57–58.

32. This and subsequent quotations in this paragraph are from Sebastián Vizcaíno, "Carta," Mexico, May 23, 1603, in Cutter, *California Coast,* 114.

33. Parallel portrayals may be found in Christopher Columbus's journal of his first voyage to the Indies and in Bartolomé de las Casas's *Brevísima relación de la destruyción de las Indias* (Seville: Sebastián Trugillo, 1553). See Cristóbal Colón, *Textos y documentos completos* (Madrid: Alianza, 1982); Edmundo O'Gorman, *La idea del descubrimiento de América: Historia de esa interpretación y crítica de sus fundamentos* (México: Centro de Estudios Filosóficos, Universidad Nacional Autónoma de México, 1951); Todorov, *Conquest of America;* Beatriz Pastor Bodmer, *Discursos narrativos de la conquista: Mitificación y emergencia* (Hanover, N.H.: Ediciones del Norte, 1988); and Beatriz Pastor Bodmer, *The Armature of Conquest: Spanish Accounts of the Discovery of America, 1492–1589* (Stanford: Stanford University Press, 1992).

34. Antonio de la Ascensión, "Relación de la Jornada que hizo el General Sevastián Vizcayno al Descubrimiento de las Californias el año de 1602." I have used the microfilm version at the BL of the original at the Newberry Library. Portions of this document have been translated and are available in "Father Antonio de la Ascensión's Account of the Voyage of Sebastián Vizcaíno," in Wagner, *Spanish Voyages,* 234–42.

35. Antonio de la Ascensión, "Relación breve en que se da noticia del descubrimiento que se hizo en la Nueva-España," Convent of San Sebastián, México, October 12, 1620 [1602–3?], in Joaquín Pacheco, Francisco de Cárdenas, and Luis Torres de Mendoza, eds., *Colección de documentos inéditos, relativos al descubrimiento, conquista y organización de las antiguas posesiones españolas de América y Oceania*, 42 vols. (Madrid: Imprenta de Fias y Compañía, Misericordia, 1867), 8:551. The original is in Madrid: BN, J. 89, fol. 21.

36. Ascensión, "Relación," 69.

37. Ibid., 61v, 62f.

38. Vizcaíno to Consejo de Indias, December 28, 1602, in Carrasco y Guisasola, *Documentos*, 57–58; Wagner, *Spanish Voyages*, 236. That men, women, and children came out to meet the strangers was later interpreted to mean that the Indians did not fear the Europeans. "Los gentiles de sus immediaciones avisados de nuestra venida salieron a recibirnos, tan aseguardos al parecer, y ciertos de nuestra amistad, que trageron a todas sus mujeres," wrote Miguel Costansó, a member of the Portolá expedition of 1769–70. Peter Browning, ed., *The Discovery of San Francisco Bay: The Portolá Expedition of 1769–1770. The Diary of Miguel Costansó in Spanish and English* (Lafayette, Calif.: Great West Books, 1992), 6; original is in AGN, Historia, vol. 396, exp. 2.

39. Ascensión, "Relación," 21, 21v, and 51.

40. Ibid., 71.

41. Ascensión, "Relación breve," 8:539–74.

42. Ibid., 555.

43. Ibid., 555.

44. Bancroft, *History of California*, 1:100; Chapman, *History of California*, 134.

45. This would have been December 1–3, 1602. No record of this council exists among the record of councils held on board the *San Diego*, 60-4-37, published in Carrasco y Guisasola, *Documentos*.

46. Ascensión, "Relación," 72.

47. Ascensión, "Relación breve," 8:555. Chapman suggested that the reasons were both the favorable winds and the impending winter. Chapman, *History of California*, 134.

48. Ascensión, "Relación," 94v–95.

49. Estimates range from 42 to 48 deaths. Vizcaíno reported that 42 men had died; Ascensión put the figure at 44. Vizcaíno, "Carta," May 23, 1603, in Cutter, *California Coast*, 116–17; Ascensión, "Relación breve," 8:542; Chapman, *History of California*, 138.

50. Ascensión, "Relación," 95v–96.

51. Ibid.

52. Ibid., 67.

53. "Son los yndios de buen cuerpo, blancos de rrostro [*sic*] y las mugeres algo menores y bien agestadas." Sebastián Vizcaíno, "Carta a S.M. de Sebastián Vizcaíno

fechada en Megico a 23 de mayo de 1603, participando su regreso del descubrimiento y demarcación de las costas de las Californias hasta los 42 grados de latitud norte," in Cutter, *California Coast,* 114–15.

54. Bancroft, *History of California,* 76; Wagner, *Spanish Voyages,* 74. Chapman and Culleton contend that Cabrillo passed Monterey Bay without seeing it. Chapman, *History of California,* 79; James Culleton, *Indians and Pioneers of Old Monterey: Being a Chronicle of the Religious History of Carmel Mission* (Fresno: Academy of California Church History, 1950), 3.

55. Culleton, *Indians and Pioneers,* 4; Chapman, *History of California,* 104; Bancroft, *History of California,* 94; Thomas Maynarde, *Sir Francis Drake His Voyage, 1595* (London: Hakluyt Society, 1849).

56. Culleton, *Indians and Pioneers,* 4; Bancroft, *History of California,* 1:94; Bancroft, *History of California,* 113–15.

57. Culleton, *Indians and Pioneers,* 4.

58. Ibid.; Sebastián Rodríguez Cermenho, *The Voyage to California of Sebastián Rodríguez Cermeño in 1595* (San Francisco: California Historical Society, 1924).

59. For a discussion of sixteenth-century attitudes toward race, see Eva Alexandra Uchmany, "El mestizaje en el siglo XVI novohispano," *Historia Mexicana* 37 (1987): 29–48; and Vicenta Cortés Alonso, "La imagen del otro: Indios, blancos y negros en el México del siglo XVI," *Revista de Indias* 51 (May–August 1991): 259–92.

60. Ascensión, "Relación breve," 8:564.

61. Ibid., 8:563.

Chapter 3. Evangelization

1. The only other voyage was a brief excursion by Gemelli Carreri recorded at the close of the seventeenth century. Bancroft, *History of California,* 1:69–109.

2. Ibid., 1:114.

3. See Herbert I. Priestley, *José de Gálvez, Visitor-General of New Spain, 1765–1771* (Berkeley: University of California Press, 1916).

4. Erick D. Langer and Robert H. Jackson, "Colonial and Republican Missions Compared: The Cases of Alta California and Southeastern Bolivia," *Society for Comparative Study of Society and History* (1988): 290.

5. Ibid.

6. For variations on this main pattern, see Willoughby, *Division of Labor,* 64–67.

7. Verger to Casafonda, June 30, 1771, and August 3, 1771, Museo Nacional, Trasuntos, fols. 127–28; quoted in Engelhardt, *Missions and Missionaries,* 2:654–55.

8. Notably, two of the three largest donors to the Pious Fund were women: Josefa Paula de Argüelles and María de Borja, Duchess of Gandia. Chapman, *History of California,* 182.

9. Engelhardt, *Missions and Missionaries,* 2:247 and 2:653–55.

10. Chapman, *History of California,* 359.

11. Campbell, "First Californios," 586.

12. Ibid.; Chapman, *History of California*, 389.

13. Joseph de Gálvez to Pedro Fages, "Instrucciones que ha de observar el Teniente de Infantería, Dn. Pedro Fages, como comandante de la Partida de veinte y cinco hombres," January 5, 1769, in BL, Arch. of Cal., vol. 1, Prov. St. Pap., vol. 1, p. 42.

14. Gálvez to Vila, "Instrucción que ha de observar Don Vicente Vila," January 5, 1769, Puerto de la Paz (Baja California), in Gálvez to Fages, "Instrucciones," vol. 1, p. 40.

15. Ibid.

16. Gálvez to Portolá, "Instrucción que deberá observar el Capitán de Dragones de España Don Gaspar de Portolá, Gobernador, y Comandante en Jefe de esta Península de Californias en la Expedición y viaje por tierra a los Puertos de San Diego y Monterrey," February 20, 1769, San Lucas, p. 3; typescript, SBMA, JSC, doc. 162.

17. Ibid.

18. Serra to Palou, July 3, 1769, San Diego, in Antonine Tibesar, ed., *Writings of Junípero Serra*, 4 vols. (Washington, D.C.: Academy of American Franciscan History, 1955–66), 1 (1956): 144.

19. Donald Smith and Frederick Teggart, eds., *Diary of Gaspar de Portolá during the California Expedition of 1769–1770* (Berkeley: University of California Press, 1909): 26; diary entry for August 21, 1769.

20. Ibid.

21. Miguel Costansó, "Diario Histórico de los Viages de Mar, y Tierra Hechos al Norte de la California," Mexico, October 24, 1770, BL, fols. 53–54.

22. Junípero Serra to Juan Andrés, July 3, 1769, San Diego, in Tibesar, *Writings*, 1:135.

23. Antonio Rodríguez and Luís Antonio Martínez to José Señán, February 20, 1814, San Luís Obispo mission, p. 2, SBMA.

24. Florence C. Shipek, "California Indian Reaction to the Franciscans," *Americas* 41:4 (1985): 491.

25. Francisco Palou, *Noticias de la Nueva California*, 4 vols. (San Francisco: California Historical Society Publications, 1874), 2:267.

26. Ibid., 2:269.

27. Gaspar de Portolá, "Notificación de toma de posesión: modelo o borrador," [1769?], BL, Portolá Papers (M-M 1811:1), n.p.; and Palou, *Noticias*, 2:269.

28. Pedro Fages, *Breve descripción histórica política y natural de la Alta California 1770–1774* (1775; Mexico: Fondo Pagliai, 1973), 78.

29. Ibid., 78–79.

30. Shipek, "California Indian Reaction," 491.

31. Ibid., 482.

32. Walter Goldschmidt, *Nomlaki Ethnography, UCPAAE* 42:4 (Berkeley: University of California Press, 1951): 311.

33. For more specifics on the deaths of members of the sacred expedition, see Junípero Serra, "Nota Previa," in San Diego mission, "Libros de Misión," extracts by Thomas Savage, BL, 1878.

34. Willoughby, *Division of Labor,* 57–61.

35. On the question of female modesty, see Francisco Palou, *Relación histórica de la vida y apostólicas tareas del venerable padre Fray Junípero Serra* (Mexico: Editorial Porrúa, 1970), 149 (hereafter *Vida*); and Tibesar, *Writings,* 1:135 and 1:144.

36. Will Roscoe, "Bibliography of Berdache and Alternative Gender Roles among North American Indians," *Journal of Homosexuality* 14:3–4 (1987): 81–171.

37. Charles Callender and Lee M. Kochems, "The North American Berdache," in David N. Suggs and Andrew W. Miracle, eds., *Culture and Human Sexuality: A Reader* (Pacific Grove, Calif.: Brooks/Cole Publishing Company, 1993), 368.

38. Lester B. Brown, ed., *Two Spirit People: American Indian Lesbian Women and Gay Men* (New York: Haworth, 1997), 10.

39. *Webster's Encyclopedic Unabridged Dictionary of the English Language* (New York: Gramercy Books, 1996), 196.

40. Fages, *Breve descripción,* 66.

41. Willoughby, *Division of Labor,* 57.

42. Costansó, "Diario Histórico," xxviii–xxix.

43. Fages, *Breve descripción,* 66.

44. Ibid.

45. Christopher Brian Weimer, "Sor Juana as Feminist Playwright: The *Gracioso's* Satiric Function in *Los empeños de una casa,*" *LATR* (1992): 91–98.

46. Catherine Larson, "New Clothes, New Roles: Disguise and the Subversion of Convention in Tirso and Sor Juana," *Romance Languages Annual* 1 (1989): 500–503.

47. Weimer, "Sor Juana."

48. Sandra Messinger Cypess, "Los géneros re/velados in *Los empeños de una casa* de Sor Juana Inés de la Cruz," *Hispamérica* (1993): 177–85; and Weimer, "Sor Juana."

49. See Boyer, *Lives;* and Mary E. Giles, *Women in the Inquisition: Spain and the New World* (Baltimore: Johns Hopkins University Press, 1999), 7.

50. Edith Wallace, "Sexual Status and Role Differences," in Robert F. Heizer, ed., *Handbook of North American Indians, 8: California* (Washington, D.C.: Smithsonian Institution Press, 1978), 685.

51. Costansó, "Diario Historico," xxviii–xxix.

52. Fages, *Breve descripción,* 42, 53, 83, 66.

53. Ibid., 95.

54. Serra, "Diario," June 30, 1769, in Tibesar, *Writings,* 1:118.

55. Smith and Teggart, *Diary of Gaspar de Portolá,* 18; diary entry for June 27, 1769.

56. Ibid.

57. Chapman, *History of California,* 133.

58. Jackson and Castillo, *Indians,* 74; Bancroft, *History of California,* 1:138.

59. Bancroft, *History of California*, 1:139. Chapman says that none was registered before 1771. Chapman, *History of California*, 245.

60. Chapman, *History of California*, 246.

61. Bancroft, *History of California*, 1:139.

62. Maynard Geiger, ed., *The Letter of Luis Jayme, O.F.M., San Diego, October 17, 1772* (Los Angeles: Glen Dawson, 1970).

63. Ibid., 58–59.

64. All quotations in this paragraph are from Geiger, *Letter*.

65. Pedro Fages to Marqués de Croix, July 17, 1771, San Diego, SBMA, JSC, transcript, doc. 263.

66. Mariano Carrillo, April 14, 1773, San Diego, AGN, Calif., vol. 2, part 1, exp. 8–9, fols. 244.

67. Ibid.

68. Pedro Fages to Antonio Bucareli y Orsúa, June 2, 1773, Presidio of San Carlos de Monte Rey, AGN, Calif., vol. 2, part 1, exp. 8–9, fols. 251–52. See especially marginalia by Areche.

69. Edicts for the apprehension of the fugitive were issued on October 20, 1775. Ibid., fol. 287.

70. Ibid.

71. Pedro Galindo Navarro to De Croix, August 28, 1778, Chihuahua, in Fages to Bucareli y Ursúa, fol. 291.

72. Serra to Bucareli, Mexico, March 13, 1773, in Tibesar, *Writings*, 1:305.

73. Ibid.

74. Ibid.

75. Viceroy Bucareli submitted Father Serra's petition on May 6, 1773, and shortly thereafter Serra was granted his request. Viceroy Bucareli and the Council of War and Treasury (Junta de Guerra y Real Hacienda), "Resolution of the Council," May 12, 1773, SBMA, JSC.

76. Bancroft, *History of California*, 1:179.

77. Serra to Bucareli, May 21, 1773, in Tibesar, *Writings*, 1:358.

78. Bancroft, *History of California*, 1:179; Palou, *Vida*, 129–30; Charles J. G. Piette, *Le secret de Junípero Serra: Fondateur de la Californie-Nouvelle, 1769–1784*, 2 vols. (Washington, D.C.: Academy of American Franciscan History, 1949), 1:324–25.

79. Palou, *Noticias*, 2:297–300.

80. Ibid., 1:478–9 and 2:299; Palou, *Vida*, 130–32.

81. Bancroft, *History of California*, 1:181.

82. Engelhardt, *Missions and Missionaries*, 2:92.

83. Serra to Rafael Verger, Monterey, August 8, 1772, in Tibesar, *Writings*, 1:256–58; original is in Mexico, BN, Letters of Junípero Serra, fols. 14–15.

84. Serra to Bucareli, Mexico, April 22, 1773, in Tibesar, *Writings*, 1:340.

85. Serra to Bucareli, Mexico, May 21, 1773, in Tibesar, *Writings*, 1:362.

86. Hugo Reid, "First Arrival of the Spaniards," no. 16, Los Angeles County

Indians: A Collection of Letters, Scrapbook, BL [n.d.]. Father Ascensión wrote of the Indians' respect for animals and their astonishment at seeing the Spaniards shoot and throw stones at the giant-size crows. Ascensión, "Relación," 237.

87. Reid, "First Arrival," n.p. For further information on Hugo Reid and his Indian wife, and for a printed edition of the newspaper clippings, see Susana Bryant Dakin, *A Scotch Paisano: Hugo Reid's Life in California, 1832–1852, Derived from His Correspondence* (Berkeley: University of California Press, 1939).

88. The remaining quotations in this paragraph are from Dakin, *Scotch Paisano.*

89. Engelhardt, *Missions and Missionaries,* vol. 2, part 1, p. 92.

90. Chapman, *History of California,* 250.

91. Dorothy Krell, *The California Missions: A Pictorial History* (Menlo Park, Calif.: Sunset Publishing, 1991), 127.

92. Pedro Font, "Diary," in Bolton, *Anza's California Expeditions,* 4:271.

93. Some historians have downplayed this incident. Culleton concluded that it was not a case of rape. Culleton, *Indians,* 243; Palou, *Vida,* 135; Bolton, *Anza's California Expeditions,* 4:313.

94. Serra to Verger, August 8, 1772, in Tibesar, *Writings,* 1:260.

95. Serra to Bucareli, May 21, 1773, in Tibesar, *Writings,* 1:356. In this letter, Serra refers to a letter from Father Cavaller (Father Jayme's predecessor) to Serra, October 12, 1772, San Luis Obispo, in which Serra was probably informed of the situation. I have been unable to locate Cavaller's letter.

96. Chapman, *History of California,* 246.

97. Ibid., 249. Engelhardt says the total miilitary personnel at that time numbered 131 officers and men. Engelhardt, *Missions and Missionaries,* 2:144–45.

98. Fages, *Breve descripción,* 78–79.

99. Antonia Castañeda develops this theme in her Ph.D. dissertation, "Presidarias y Pobladoras: Spanish-Mexican Women in Frontier Monterey, Alta California, 1770–1821."

100. Serra to Bucareli, Mexico, April 22, 1773, in Tibesar, *Writings,* 1:341.

101. Tibesar, *Writings,* 3:253, 3:199.

102. Serra to Bucareli, "Representación," Mexico City, March 13, 1773, in Tibesar, *Writings,* 1:325.

103. Serra to Bucareli, Mexico, March 13, 1773, in Tibesar, *Writings,* 1:308.

104. Ibid.; Serra to Bucareli, January 8, 1775, Monterey, in Tibesar, *Writings,* 2:202.

Chapter 4. Colonization

1. In early October 1772, Serra requested provisions for the families and unmarried Indians who had been brought from Baja California. Serra to Fages, October 2, 1772, San Diego; Serra to Bucareli, Mexico, March 13, 1773, in Tibesar, *Writings,* 1:283–85 and 1:310.

2. Ibid., 1:310.

3. San Gabriel mission, "Libro Primero en que se assientan las partidas de los Bautismos de los Gentiles qe se christianan en esta misión de San Gabriel Arcangel," 1771–95, entry 13, p. 3. SBMA photocopy.

4. Theodore Hittell, *History of California,* 4 vols. (San Francisco: N. J. Stone, 1885–97), 1:362.

5. San Gabriel mission, Book of Baptisms, April 7, 1776, entry 271. SBMA transcript, Thomas Workman Temple Collection, Chancery Archives, Los Angeles, vol. 5.

6. Palou, *Noticias,* 1:245.

7. Ibid., 1:246.

8. Tibesar, *Writings,* 1:311.

9. Ibid., 1:310.

10. For some reason, these individuals were not included in the roster Palou included in his July 20, 1773, letter to California governor Felipe de Barri. AGN, Calif., vol. 66, fols. 396–97.

11. These included Bernardo de Alcantara and his wife, Loreta; Joseph Bona and his wife, Rosa; Pablo Ojeda and his wife, Rosa; and the orphans Agustín Giménez and Juan Giménez. Palou to Barri, July 20, 1773, AGN, Calif., vol. 66, fol. 398.

12. Palou, *Noticias,* 1:250, says five boys; in his July 20, 1773, letter to Barri, he lists only four: the orphans Joseph, Saturnino, Gaspar, and Fabian. In addition, he notes the following family members from San Borja mission: Estevan María Bucareli, his wife, Clara María, and "her" daughter, Brigida; Joseph María Zeballos and his wife, Simphorosa María; Nicholas María Torres and his wife, Gertrudis María; Joseph María Bornino, his wife, Gertrudis María, and their son, Estevan; Antonio María Lisboa and his wife, María Salomé; Everardo María Mendoza and his wife, Petra María; and Torre María Mendoza and his wife, María Antonia. Palou to Barri, July 20, 1773, fols. 398–99.

13. Palou to Governor Phelipe Barry, July 20, 1773, Misión y Frontera de San Fernando de Vellicatá, AGN, Calif., vol. 66, fols. 396–99.

14. In Palou, *Noticias,* 1:240–70, Palou wrote that he took only six Indian families (three from Santa Gertrudis and three from Borja), but his details of the distribution of the families in Alta California suggest that ten families actually accompanied him. He confirms this in his letter to Barri, July 20, 1773, in which he names the members of seven families from San Borja and three from Santa Gertrudis, as well as ten single male orphans.

15. Palou, *Noticias,* 1:259–60. Hittell mistakenly dated their arrival on July 30, rather than August 30, and wrote that the families were all left at the San Luis Obispo mission. Hittell, *History of California,* 1:365.

16. Palou, *Noticias,* 1:261.

17. Again, Hittell was mistaken on this point. He stated that Palou left all six of the Baja California families at San Luis Obispo mission. Hittell, *History of California,* 1:365.

18. Here Palou mistakenly wrote San Javier mission, but from the context, the geography, and the missionaries who were there, he clearly meant San Gabriel mission. See Palou, *Noticias,* 1:262.

19. San Gabriel mission, Book of Baptisms, September 13, 1774, entry 86. SBMA copy from Chancery Archives, Los Angeles, Thomas Workman Temple Collection, vol. 5, book 1.

20. Palou, *Vida,* 101.

21. Francisco Hijosa and Josef Faustino Ruiz, "Lista de las familias que pasan a Monterrey en la Fragata de S.M. nombrada Santiago alias la nueva Galicia al mando del Alferez de Fragata dela Real Armada Don Juan Pérez," San Blas, January 23, 1774, and "Lista de los oficiales, Artilleros, Marineros," San Blas, January 22, 1774, AGN, Historia, vol. 61, n.p. Palou wrote that the ship left San Blas on January 24, 1774. See Palou, *Vida,* cap. 36, pp. 157–59, and Palou, *Noticias,* cap. 42, 147–48.

22. Bancroft, *History of California,* 1:224.

23. Castañeda, "Comparative Frontiers," 289. See also Palou, *Noticias,* 3:148.

24. Hijosa and Faustino Ruiz, "Lista," n.p.

25. Culleton, *Indians,* 65–66. None of these women appears in Marie Northrop, *Spanish-Mexican Families of Early California: 1769–1850,* 2 vols. (Burbank, Calif.: Southern California Genealogical Society, 1987).

26. Thomas Savage, comp., "Libros de la Misión de San Gabriel: Copias y extractos," MS, BL, 1877, p. 7. These extracts made by Savage include little information about the individuals being baptized, married, or buried; they focus more on matters such as the dates of the first and last baptism performed at San Gabriel mission, the date of the marriage or death, and the names of the officiating priests.

27. San Gabriel mission, Book of Baptisms, September 27, 1774, entry 82, SBMA transcript, Thomas Workman Temple Collection, Chancery Archives, Los Angeles, vol. 5, book 1.

28. Castañeda, "Comparative Frontiers," 289. Culleton, *Indians and Pioneers,* 62, says that six women remained in Monterey and one returned to San Diego.

29. Engelhardt, *Missions and Missionaries,* 2: Part 1: 133; see also Palou, *Noticias,* 3, cap. 43, pp. 150–51; Bucareli to Palou, May 25, 1774, MS, BL; Bucareli to Rivera, August 7, 1773, MS, BL.

30. Francisco Garcés, "Diario dela Expedición que practicó por tierra el año de 1774 el Capitán Dn Juan Baptista de Ansa desde Sonora a los nuevos Establecimientos de Californias y Diario llevado en ella por el P. fr. Francisco Garcés," AGN, Prov. Int., vol. 23, exp. 6, fol. 241.

31. Bucareli to Gálvez, Mexico, August 27, 1776, AGN, Corr. Virr. 2nd Series, Bucareli, 1776, vol. 65/82, doc. 2429; quoted in Bolton, *Anza's California Expeditions,* 5:352.

32. Antonio Bucareli y Ursúa, Decreto, November 28, 1774, SBMA, CMD.

33. Bucareli, December 15, 1774, SBMA, JSC.

34. Ibid., 1.

35. This belief was common throughout the colonization of the Americas. See "Ordenanzas Municipales," Tenochtitlán, March 1524, MS, cited in William H. Prescott, *History of the Conquest of Mexico and History of the Conquest of Peru* (New York: Modern Library [1900?]), 635; and Konetzke, "Emigración."

36. Ignaz Pfefferkorn, *Sonora: A Description of the Province* (Albuquerque: University of New Mexico Press, 1949).

37. Anza to Bucareli, Mexico, November 17, 1774, AGN, Calif., vol. 35, fol. 17v.

38. Pfefferkorn, *Sonora,* 290.

39. "Hoja de servicio de Juan Bautista de Anza," Tubac Presidio, September 1, 1767, in Donald Garate, "Notes on Anza," unpublished MS (Tumacácori National Historical Park: National Park Service, Nov. 15, 1994), p. 3.

40. Pfefferkorn, *Sonora,* 286.

41. Bancroft, *History of California,* 1:258.

42. Juan Josef de Echeveste, "Memorandum," Mexico, December 5, 1774 (copy by Melchor de Peramas, March 20, 1777), AGN, Calif., vol. 35, exp. 1, fols. 31–36.

43. Eduardo W. Villa, *Historia del Estado de Sonora,* 2d ed. (Hermosilla, Sonora: Editorial Sonora, 1951), 147–48.

44. Hubert H. Bancroft, *The Works of Hubert Howe Bancroft, vol. 34: California Pastoral, 1769–1848* (San Francisco: A. L. Bancroft, 1888), 611; Chapman, *History of California,* 233.

45. Pfefferkorn, *Sonora,* 284.

46. Chapman, *History of California,* 304; Manuel Servín, "California's Hispanic Heritage," in David Weber, ed., *New Spain's Far Northern Frontier* (Albuquerque: University of New Mexico Press, 1979), 117–33.

47. Bancroft, *California Pastoral,* 612.

48. Jack D. Forbes, "Black Pioneers: The Spanish-Speaking Afroamericans of the Southwest," in George E. Frakes and Curtis B. Solberg, eds., *Minorities in California* (New York: Random House, 1971), 23.

49. The first three recruits were Valerio Mesa, Felipe Tapia, and Ignacio Gutiérrez. AGN, Prov. Int., vol. 237, cited in Garate, "Notes on Anza," 27.

50. Juan Bautista de Anza, "Informe," October 20, 1775, cited in Garate, "Notes on Anza," 34.

51. María Eustaquia (Gutiérrez), daughter of Feliciana, was born a few days before the expedition left Horcasitas for Tubac. Garate, "Notes on Anza," 28.

52. Francis Weber, *Vignettes of California Catholicism* (Mission Hills, Calif.: Libra Press, 1988), 5.

53. Chapman, *History of California,* 304. Anza's breakdown of the roster is slightly different, although the total is the same. His list differs in the inclusion of 5 interpreters, 15 muleteers, 3 cowboys, and 7 servants.

54. Winston Elstob and Helen Shropshire, *Handbook for the Re-enactment of the Juan Bautista de Anza Expedition, 1775–1776* (Monterey: California Heritage Guides, 1975), 2. Garate compared the official military tally of the expedition three days

202 NOTES TO PAGES 61–63

before it left Tubac with Father Font's official count and found a total of 201 people, including 43 men, 39 women, and 119 children. Bancroft, *History of California,* 1:259, wrote that the delegation totaled 235 plus 8 infants born on the way. See discussion on numbers in Garate, "Notes on Anza," 26–30.

55. Those aged 40 and over were María Martina Botiller, 40; Gabriel Peralta, 40; Francisca Xaviera Ruelas, 40; María Carmen del Valle, 40; Juan Antonio Vasquez, 40; José Antonio Garcia, 42; Joaquín de Castro, 43; Pablo Pinto, 43; Felipa Neri, 45; Juan Salvio Pacheco, 46; and Sebastián Antonio López, 47. Juan Bautista de Anza, "Informe," October 20, 1775, cited in Garate, "Notes on Anza," 28–30.

56. AGN, Prov. Int., vol. 197, exp. 7, fols. 162–87.

57. Elstob and Shropshire, *Handbook,* 27–30.

58. Juan Bautista de Anza, "Diario de la Ruta, y Operaciones que Yo el Ynfraescripto Theniente Coronel, y Capitan del Rl. Presidio de tubac, en la Provincia, y Governación de Sonora, practicó segunda vez," Horcasitas, October 23, 1775–June 1, 1776, Mexico, AGN, Prov. Int., vol. 169, exp. 7, fols. 176–81v.

59. They were Ignacio de Higuera and Maria Micaela Bojorques; Tiburcio Vasquez and Maria Antonia Bojorques; and Gregorio Antonio Sandoval, a widower, and Maria Dolores Ontiveros. Janet Newton, *Las Positas: The Story of Robert and Josefa Livermore* (Livermore, Calif.: Janet Newton, 1969), following page 20.

60. Anza, "Diario," fols. 176–335.

61. Pedro Font, "Diario que forma el P. Fr. Pedro Font Pdor Apco del Colegio de la Sta Cruz de Queretaro, sacado del borrador que escrivio en el camino del viage que hizo à Monterey y Puerto de Sⁿ Francisco," Horcasitas, September 29, 1775–June 23, 1776, MS, Cowan Collection, BL, hereafter referred to as "Diario breve"; and Pedro Font, "Diario que formó el P. Pdo. Apco. Fr. Pedro Font Missionero . . . en el viage que hizo à Monterey," Horcasitas, September 29, 1775–Tubutama, May 11, 1777, original in John Carter Brown Library, Brown University, Providence, R.I., photocopy in BL, Bolton Papers, no. 137, carton 11, fol. 15, hereafter referred to as "Diario à Monterey."

62. Francisco Garcés, "Diario que ha formado el Padre Fray Francisco Garcés . . . en el viage hecho este año de 1775," October 1775–September 1776, AGN, Historia, vol. 24, exp. 1, fols. 1–54.

63. Thomas Eixarch, "Diario formado por el P. Fr. Thomas Eixarch, que él hizo en el Rio Colorado," December 4, 1775–May 11, 1776, in Font, "Diario à Monterey," fols. 271–311.

64. Anza, "Diario," October 23, 1775, 181v–82.

65. Font, "Diario à Monterey," fol. 15.

66. Anza, "Informe," October 20, 1775, cited in Garate, "Notes on Anza," 28.

67. Anza, "Diario," November 10, 1775, fol. 194v.

68. Ibid., fols. 194v–95.

69. Font, "Diario à Monterey," November 10, 1775, fol. 31.

70. Diego Pascual Gutiérrez was born on November 19, 1775. Ibid.

71. Font, "Diario à Monterey," fol. 35.

72. Ibid., November 24, 1775, fol. 38.

73. Anza to Bucareli, Laguna de Santa Olalla, December 8, 1775, AGN, Prov. Int., vol. 169, exp. 4, fols. 159–59v.

74. Zoeth Skinner Eldredge, ed., *History of California,* 5 vols. (New York: Century History, 1915), 1:391–92.

75. Anza, "Diario," May 14, 1776, fol. 323.

76. Ibid.

77. Ibid., December 7–10, 1775, fols. 213–15.

78. Ibid., 213–24.

79. Ibid., December 24, 1775, fols. 228–28v.

80. Font, "Diario à Monterey," December 24, 1775, fol. 85.

81. Ibid. The boy referred to here was Salvador Ygnacio Linares, son of Ygnacio and Gertrudis Rivas Linares.

82. Anza, "Diario," December 26, 1775, fols. 229–29v.

83. Ibid., fol. 230.

84. Ibid., December 27, 1775, fols. 230–32.

85. Ibid., January 4, 1776, fol. 236v.

86. Ibid., March 10, 1776, fols. 268–69v.

87. Font, "Diario à Monterey," April 13, 1776, fol. 239.

88. See Francisco Palou, "Noticias de Nueva California," 1776, translation available in Bolton, *Anza's California Expeditions,* vol. 3; and Josef de Moraga, "Carta del Thente. Dn. Josef de Moraga en que dà quenta [de la] ocupación del Puerto de S. Fran[cisco] Erección de una Misión, terreno reconocido, y demas Progresos," March 20, 1777, Mexico, AGN, Prov. Int., vol. 23, photocopy of MS in Bolton Collection, no. 133, carton 11, BL.

89. The figures vary. Bancroft says four officers and ten soldiers with their families (Bancroft, *History of California,* 1:259); Hittell cites Hermenegildo Sal's report of names, December 31, 1776 (Hittell, *History of California*); Palou notes alternatively ten soldiers versus one sergeant and sixteen soldiers (Bolton, *Anza's California Expedition,* 3:387; Palou, *Vida*).

90. Bancroft, *History of California,* 1:259, refers to eight infants being born on the journey. Antonia Castañeda found Bancroft's total to be in error. However, either Bancroft might have arrived at his total by counting the five miscarriages and three births on the journey to Monterey or there might have been five additional births on the journey from Monterey to San Francisco. Castañeda, "Comparative Frontiers," 300n39.

91. Bolton, *Anza's California Expedition,* 3:388.

92. Moraga, "Carta," 6.

93. Anza listed "Veinte, y nuebe Mugeres, pertenecientes à los Soldados" in his roster of participants. Anza, "Diario," 178.

94. Font, "Diario à Monterey," December 17, 1775, fols. 78–79.

95. Ibid.

96. Ibid., November 26, 1775, fol. 38.

97. There appear to be some discrepancies regarding their baptism and marriage, because ordinarily couples were baptized *before* the wedding ceremony. Their marriage was recorded as having taken place alternatively on March 6, 1776 (Northrop, *Spanish-Mexican Families,* 1:200) or on April 7, 1776 (handwritten note in SBMA, San Gabriel mission, Book of Baptisms, April 7, 1776, entry 271). The San Gabriel mission "Libros de Misión" in the Bancroft Library recorded the baptisms on September 15, 1776, of Juan Francisco López and his wife, María Arbayo, "españoles."

98. Northrop, *Spanish-Mexican Families,* 1:200.

99. SBMA, San Gabriel mission, Book of Baptisms, entry 297, Thomas Workman Temple Collection, Chancery Archives, Los Angeles, vol. 5.

100. Their children were Juan José López, baptized on December 27, 1786, at San Juan Capistrano, and María Juliana Josefa López, baptized on March 19, 1791, at San Diego mission. Ibid., 1:200–206, 1:263. On January 6, 1800, Juan Francisco died, and two months later, on March 10, 1800, Feliciana married Mariano Tenerio.

101. Serra to Bucareli, January 8, 1775, Monterey, in Tibesar, *Writings,* 2:202.

102. Font, "Diario à Monterey," February 6, 1776, fols. 124–26. For the petition for a military pension on behalf of Anza's widow, see Galindo Navarro to Commander General, March 29, 1783, Chihuahua, in Jacob N. Bowman and Robert F. Heizer, *Anza and the Northwest Frontier of New Spain* (Los Angeles: Southwest Museum, 1967), 97.

103. Font, "Diario à Monterey," February 6, 1776, fols. 124–26.

104. Chapman, *History of California,* 398.

105. "Ynstancia de Doña Eulalia Callis . . . sobre que se le oyga en Justicia, y redima de la opresion que padece," August 23, 1785, AGN, Prov. Int., vol. 120, exp. 4, fol. 70v.

106. Ibid., fols. 70–71. See also discussion of Callis in Castañeda, "Engendering History," 247–49.

107. María de León [to De Croix], Arispe, December 29, 1780, AGN, Prov. Int., vol. 197, exp. 7, fols. 181–83v; María de León [to De Croix, 1776], AGN, Calif., vol. 2, part 1, exp. 6, fols. 184–85. See also petition of Moraga to have his family come, AGN, Calif., vol. 2A, exp. 6, fols. 175–96.

108. AGN, Calif., vol. 2, part. 1, exp. 6, fol. 184.

109. León to De Croix, December 29, 1780, AGN, Prov. Int., vol. 197, exp. 7, fols. 181–83v.

110. Manuel Ramón de Goya to the Fiscal de Real Hacienda, Mexico, July 17, 1783, AGN, Calif., vol. 31, exp. 37, fols. 318–21v. All citations in this paragraph may be found therein.

111. Ibid., fol. 319v.

112. Beilharz, *Felipe de Neve,* 107.

113. Northrop, *Spanish-Mexican Families,* 1:xii.

114. For one of the few records by Spanish women of the times, see the account of María Montielo, widow of Ensign Santiago Islas, in Kieran McCarty, "The Colorado Massacre of 1781: María Montielo's Report," *JAH* 16 (Autumn 1975): 221–25. See also Robert L. Bee, *Crosscurrents along the Colorado: The Impact of Government Policy on the Quechan Indians* (Tucson: University of Arizona Press, 1981); Fages, *Breve descripción;* and Herbert I. Priestley, ed. and trans., *The Colorado River Campaign, 1781–1782: Diary of Pedro Fages* (Berkeley: University of California, 1913).

115. Eixarch, "Diario," December 5, 1776, fol. 271.

116. Ibid., December 7, 1776, fol. 272.

117. Font, "Diario à Monterey," December 7, 1775, fol. 60.

118. Ibid.

119. Eixarch, "Diario," February 25, 1776, fol. 300.

120. Ibid.

121. Ibid.

122. Font, "Diario à Monterey," May 15, 1776, fols. 316–17.

123. Robert F. Heizer and Albert B. Elsasser, *The Natural World of the California Indians* (Berkeley: University of Calfornia Press, 1980), 52–53.

124. For an illuminating account of the relationship between the Yuma people and the Spaniards, which nonetheless gives no consideration to gender issues, see Jack D. Forbes, *Warriors of the Colorado: The Yumas of the Quechan Nation and Their Neighbors* (Norman: University of Oklahoma Press, 1965).

125. Anza to Bucareli, "Instancia del Capitan De la Nación Yuma Salvador Palma sobre que se establescan Missiones en su territorio à las Margenes de los Rios Colorado y Gila donde habitan," Mexico, November 11, 1776, AGN, Prov. Int., vol. 23, exp. 21, fols. 436–39v. This letter was signed by Anza "Arruego del Capn Salvor Palma."

126. Ibid.

127. Eixarch, "Diario," February 25, 1776, fol. 300.

128. Forbes, *Warriors of the Colorado,* 175–220.

129. Chapman, *History of California,* 337–38.

130. Forbes, *Warriors of the Colorado,* 204.

131. Chapman, *History of California,* 348.

132. The term *coyote* referred to someone who was three-quarters Indian and one-fourth Caucasian.

133. Arch. of Calif., vol. 5, Prov. St. Pap., vol. 9, pp. 159–65.

134. Ibid.

135. Forbes, "Black Pioneers," 22.

136. Ibid. In a study of an earlier period, Douglas Cope found that more than 16 percent of the people in a Mexico City parish had changed their racial status during their adult lifetime. See Douglas Cope, *The Limits of Racial Domination: Plebeian Society in Colonial Mexico City, 1660–1720* (Madison: University of Wisconsin Press, 1994), 76–77.

137. Borica directive, Monterey, January 5, 1796, BL, Arch. of Calif., vol. 8, Prov. St. Pap., vol. 14, pp. 178–83.

138. Borica to Viceroy, 1797, quoted in Hittell, *History of California,* 1:581.

139. Salomé Hernández reviewed these programs in her excellent study "No Settlement without Women, 203–78.

140. See especially "Documentos relativos al traslado a Californias en calidad de colonos, de diversos reos sentenciados, 1800–1805," AGN, Prov. Int., vols. 15, 16, and 17, fols. 444–539.

141. See Hernández, "No Settlement without Women," 207–22.

142. Daniel Garr, "A Rare and Desolate Land: Population and Race in Hispanic California," *WHQ* 6 (Apr. 1975): 133.

143. Chapman, *History of California,* 348.

144. Governor Goycochea to Fiscal of the Royal Treasury, December 20, 1805, Arch. of Cal., vol. 12, Prov. St. Pap., vol. 19 (1805–15), pp. 14–17.

145. The idea of moving youths from the poor houses and orphanages to the colonies was adopted "no para una sola vez, sino para cuantas se proporcionasen." Ibid., 27.

146. Pablo Vicente Sola, "Informe General al Virey sobre Defensas de la California," [1807] Monterey, January 2, 1817, cited in Bancroft, *History of California,* 2:215.

147. Sola, "Observaciones," cited in Bancroft, *History of California,* 2:250.

148. The Mexican government had approved colonization laws in 1824 and 1828, and decrees in 1833 ordered the secularization of the missions. See Cecil Alan Hutchinson, *Frontier Settlement in Mexican California: The Híjar-Padrés Colony and Its Origins, 1769–1835* (New Haven: Yale University Press, 1969): 158–62; and Keld J. Reynolds, "The Reglamento for the Hijar y Padres Colony of 1834," *HSSCQ* 28:4 (Dec. 1946): 144.

149. In the original: "la perla mas preciosa de su collar." Antonio Coronel, "Cosas de California," BL, MS, 1877, p. 6.

150. Ibid.

151. Hutchinson, *Frontier Settlement,* 200.

152. Cecil Alan Hutchinson, "An Official List of the Members of the Híjar-Padrés Colony for Mexican California, 1834," *PHR* 42 (Aug. 1973): 407.

153. Lombardo, "Instructions," April 23, 1834, cited in José Figueroa, *Manifesto to the Mexican Republic,* trans. C. Alan Hutchinson (Berkeley: University of California Press, 1978): 24–25.

154. Ibid., 24–25.

155. Coronel, "Cosas de California," 6.

156. Reynolds, "Reglamento," 143–44.

157. At least twenty-nine of the overall participants were garment workers, and twenty-two were identified as teachers. Ibid., 348, 419–22.

158. Figueroa to Secretario de Estado, May 23, 1834, BL, Departmental State Papers, 3, cited in Hutchinson, *Frontier Settlement,* 323.

Chapter 5. The Missions

1. Krell, *California Missions*, 316.

2. Jackson and Castillo, *Indians*, p. 180, n. 16.

3. Francis F. Guest, "An Inquiry into the Role of the Discipline in California Mission Life," *SCQ* 71 (Spring 1989): 7.

4. Pedro Font, cited in Monroy, *Thrown among Strangers*, 62.

5. Finbar Kenneally, trans. and ed. *Writings of Fermín Francisco de Lasuén*, 2 vols. (Washington, D.C.: Academy of American Franciscan History, 1965), 2:198.

6. Frederick William Beechey, *Narrative of a Voyage to the Pacific and Beering's Strait . . . in the Years 1825, 26, 27, 28*, 2 vols. (London: H. Colburn and R. Bentley, 1831), 2:31.

7. George Vancouver, *A Voyage of Discovery to the North Pacific Ocean, and Round the World . . . under the command of Captain George Vancouver*, 3 vols. (London: Printed for G. G. and J. Robinson, Paternoster Row, and J. Edwards, Pall-Mall, 1798), 3:34–36.

8. Alice Eastwood, trans., "Menzies' California Journal," *CHSQ* 2 (Jan. 1924): 296.

9. Beechey, *Narrative*, 2:18–19.

10. Vancouver, *Voyage of Discovery*, 2:11.

11. Font, "Diario," January 5, 1774, cited in Engelhardt, *Missions and Missionaries*, 249.

12. Apolinaria Lorenzana, "Memorias de Doña Apolinaria Lorenzana 'La Beata' Vieja de unos setenta y cinco años," Santa Barbara, 1878, BL, HHBC, C-D 116, p. 8.

13. Eulalia Pérez, "Una vieja y sus recuerdos dictados a la edad avanzada de 139 años," dictated to Thomas Savage, San Gabriel, Calif., 1877, in *Three Memoirs of Mexican California* (Berkeley: Friends of the Bancroft Library, 1988), 100.

14. Rebecca R. Ord, "Recuerdos," as told by her mother, Angustias de la Guerra Ord (trans. Luis Moreno), December 31, 1880, Santa Barbara. Typescript, Santa Barbara Trust for Historic Preservation, 17. (Original at SBMA.)

15. Ibid., 18.

16. Guadalupe Vallejo, "Ranch and Mission Days in Alta California," *Century Magazine* 41 (Dec. 1890): 186.

17. In 1800, San Diego was the largest of the missions, with a population of 1,523 neophytes. Its population grew to some 1,611 in the first decade of the nineteenth century, dropped to 1,430 in 1817, and stood at 1,455 neophytes at the end of 1832. Bancroft, *History of California*, 2:107, 2:346; Robert H. Jackson, *Indian Population Decline: The Missions of Northwestern New Spain, 1687–1840* (Albuquerque: University of New Mexico Press, 1994), 120; Krell, *California Missions*, 316.

18. Lorenzana, "Memorias," 4–5.

19. Ibid., 6.

20. Pérez, "Una vieja," 90.

21. Regina Teresa Manocchio, "Tending Communities, Crossing Cultures: Mid-

wives in Nineteenth-Century California," (Master's thesis, Yale University School of Nursing, 1998), 23–24.

22. Juana Machado Alipaz de Ridington, "Times Gone By in Alta California: Recollections of Señora Doña Juana Machado Alipaz de Ridington (Wrightington)," *HSSCQ* (Sept. 1959): 195–240.

23. Manocchio, "Tending Communities," 46; Helen Lara-Cea, "Notes on the Use of Parish Registers in the Reconstruction of Chicana History in California prior to 1850," in Del Castillo, *Between Borders,* 139.

24. Pérez, "Una vieja," 96.

25. Ibid., 11.

26. Jacob N. Bowman, "Prominent Women of Provincial California," *HSSCQ* 39 (June 1957): 149–66.

27. Richard Griswold del Castillo, "Neither Activists nor Victims: Mexican Women's Historical Discourse—The Case of San Diego, 1820–1850," *CH* (Fall 1995): 235.

28. Pérez, "Una vieja," 77.

29. Jackson, *Indian Population Decline,* 87; Bancroft, *History of California,* 2:355; Krell, *California Missions,* 316.

30. Bancroft, *History of California,* 2:355; Krell, *California Missions,* 316.

31. Pérez, "Una vieja," 96.

32. Ibid., 97.

33. Reid, "First Missionary Proceedings," Los Angeles County Indians: A Collection of Letters, BL, Scrapbook, no. 18, n.d., n.p.

34. Pérez, "Una vieja," 90.

35. Dorotea Valdez, "Reminiscences," June 27, 1874, BL, HHBC, C-E 65:8, p. 1.

36. Vicente Francisco Sarria and Ramón Abella, "Libro de Patentes y de Inventario perteneciente a la Misión de San José en la Nueva California, año de 1806," *Patentes ù Ordenes,* 1807, MS, BL, C-C 42.

37. Vicente Francisco de Sarria, Circular letter, San Carlos de Monterey, January 25, 1817, SBMA, CMD, 1373, pp. 2–3.

38. See Shipek, "California Indian Reactions," 483–91; Robert H. Jackson, "Disease and Demographic Patterns at Santa Cruz Mission, Alta California," *JCGBA* 5:1–2 (1983): 33–57; Jackson, "Gentile Recruitment and Population Movements in the San Francisco Bay Area Missions," *JCGBA* 6 (Winter 1984): 225–39; Lowell J. Bean, "Social Organization in Native California," in Lowell J. Bean and T. F. King, eds., *Antap: California Indian Political and Economic Organization* (Menlo Park, Calif.: Ballena Press, 1974); Florence C. Shipek, "A Native American Adaptation to Drought: The Kumeyaay as Seen in the San Diego Mission Records, 1770–1798," *Ethnohistory* 28:4 (1981): 295–312; John Johnson, "The Chumash and the Missions," in David Hurst Thomas, ed., *Columbian Consequences, vol. 1: Archeological and Historical Perspectives on the Spanish Borderlands West* (Washington, D.C.: Smithsonian Institution Press, 1987); and Randall Milliken, "An Ethnohistory of the Indian People of the San Francisco Bay Area from 1770 to 1810" (Ph.D. diss., University of California, Berkeley, 1991).

39. Robert Archibald, "Indian Labor at the California Missions: Slavery or Salvation?" *JSDH* 24 (Spring 1978): 172–82; Rupert Costo and Jeannette Costo, eds., *The Missions of California: A Legacy of Genocide* (San Francisco: Indian Historian Press, 1987); Engelhardt, *Missions and Missionaries;* Guest, "Examination," 1–77; Guest, "Inquiry," 1–68; Clement Meighan, "Indians and California Missions," *SCQ* 49 (Fall 1987): 187–201; Cook, *Conflict.*

40. Lasuén, "Refutation of Charges," in Kenneally, *Writings* 2:216.

41. Lorenzo Asisara, "Narrative of a Mission Indian," in Edward S. Harrison, ed., *History of Santa Cruz County, California* (San Francisco: Pacific Press Publishing Company, 1892), 47.

42. Child captivity as a stratagem has also been explored as an issue in the Mexican conquest. See Richard Trexler, "From the Mouths of Babes: Christianization by Children in Sixteenth-Century New Spain," in John Davis, ed., *Religious Organization and Religious Experience* (New York: Academic Press, 1982), 115–35.

43. José de la Guerra to Governor Arrillaga, "Espedición contra Indios," extract, Monterey, January 29, 1804, BL, Arch. of Calif., vol. 16, Prov. St. Pap., Benicia, Military, vol. 34, p. 266.

44. Ibid., 266–67.

45. Chapman, *History of California,* 419.

46. Bancroft, *History of California,* 2:151.

47. Gutiérrez, *When Jesus Came,* 75–76.

48. Quotations in this paragraph are from Beechey, *Narrative,* 2:24 and 2:29.

49. Kirill Timofeevich Khlebnikov, "Memoirs of California," *PHR* 9 (Sept. 1940): 312.

50. Hugo Reid, "Conversion," Los Angeles County Indians: A Collection of Letters, BL, Scrapbook, no. 17, n.d., n.p.

51. Ibid.

52. Cook, *Conflict,* 11–12.

53. Pangua to Father President and others, February 8, 1775, WA, Beinecke Library, Yale University.

54. Georg H. von Langsdorff, *Voyages and Travels in Various Parts of the World, during the Years 1803, 1804, 1805,* 2 vols. (London: B. Clarke, 1813–14), 2:159.

55. Vancouver, *Voyage of Discovery,* 3:19.

56. Sarria and Abella, "Libro de Patentes," 7.

57. Ibid.

58. Malcolm Margolin, ed., *Monterey in 1786: The Journals of Jean François de la Perouse* (Berkeley: Heyday Books, 1989), 82.

59. Sarria and Abella, "Libro de Patentes," 3.

60. Governor [José Joaquín] Arrillaga, August 6, 1808, in BL, Arch. of Calif., vol. 26, Prov. Rec., vol. 12, p. 728.

61. Antonio de la Concepción to Viceroy, July 12, 1798, in BL, Arch. of Calif., vol. 10, Prov. St. Pap., vol. 17, pp. 50–53; Hermenegildo Sal to Governor, "Respuesta a las preguntas que se le dirijieron," December 14, 1798, Monterey, BL, Arch. of Calif.,

vol. 10, Prov. St. Pap., vol. 17, p. 63; Comandante José Darío Argüello to Borica, "Respuestas a las 15 preguntas dirigidas," December 11, 1798, BL, Arch. of Calif., vol. 10, Prov. St. Pap., vol. 17, pp. 58–59.

62. Horra, "Representacion al Virey contra los Misioneros de California," 1798, cited in Bancroft, *History of California*, 1:587.

63. Concepción to Viceroy, July 12, 1798, AGN, PI, vol. 216, exp. 1, fol. 8v.

64. Bancroft noted that "there was nothing in the document to indicate that the writer was of unsound mind, unless it was his closing request to be sent away because his life would be in danger if it were known that he had revealed prevalent abuses to the viceroy." Bancroft, *History of California*, 1:587.

65. Kenneally, *Writings*, 2:197.

66. Tapis and Cortés to Lasuén, October 30, 1800, AGN, PI, vol. 216, exp. 1.

67. Kenneally, *Writings*, 2:217.

68. Ibid.

69. Bancroft, *History of California*, 1:596–97, n33.

70. Altimira to Señán, July 10, 1823, MS, Archivos del Arzobispado, vol. 4, pt. 3, pp. 21–26; cited in Bancroft, *History of California*, 2:500.

71. Sarria, "Argumento contra el traslado de San Francisco, 1823," MS, quoted in Bancroft, *History of California*, 2:503.

72. Sarria to Argüello, September 12 and 30, 1823, cited in Bancroft, *History of California*, 2:504.

73. Bancroft, *History of California*, 1:160.

74. Irving B. Richman, *California under Spain and Mexico, 1535–1847* (Boston: Houghton Mifflin, 1911), 227. This figure masks great variation between the missions. See Jackson, *Indian Population Decline*, 83–116.

75. José Señán, "Contestación al Interrogatorio," in AMSB, Pap. Misc., vol. 7, 112–216, copied from the Santa Barbara Mission Archives for the Bancroft Library by E. G. Murray in 1877. Responses for San Diego mission are in BL, AMSB, *Inf. y Corr., 1802–1822*, vol. 3, pp. 27–37. (Note that I reserve the abbreviation AMSB [Archivo de la Misión de Santa Barbara] to refer to transcripts in the Bancroft Library of the original documents in the Santa Barbara Mission Archives [SBMA]).

76. Sherburne F. Cook, *Population Trends among the California Mission Indians, Ibero-Americana* 17 (1940): 16.

77. Cook, *Conflict*, 11–12.

78. Jackson, *Indian Population Decline*, 111.

79. M. Rollins, "Philological and Pathological Memoir on the Americans by M. Rollins, M.D., Surgeon Major of the Boussole Frigate," in *The Voyage of La Perouse round the World, in the Years 1785, 1786, 1787, and 1788, with the Nautical Tables*, vol. 2 (London: J. Stockdale, 1798), 271.

80. Cook, *Conflict*, 11–12.

81. See excerpts in AMSB, Esp. y Cam., 1806–21, MS, BL, 1876, vol. 4.

82. Beechey, *Narrative*, 2:26.

83. Ibid., 2:31.

84. For an English translation of the report by Auguste Bernard Duhaut-Cilly on his trip to the California missions during 1827–28, see Charles Franklin Carter, trans., "Duhaut-Cilly's Account of California in the Years 1827–1828," *CHSQ* 8 (June 1929): 130–66, *CHSQ* 8 (Sept. 1929): 214–50, and *CHSQ* 8 (Dec. 1929): 306–36.

85. Remaining quotations in this paragraph are from Carter, "Duhaut-Cilly's Account," 242.

86. Quotations in this paragraph are from Carter, "Duhaut-Cilly's Account," 149–50.

87. Margolin, *Monterey,* 82.

88. Vassilli Petrovitch Tarakanoff, *Statement of My Captivity among the Californians* (Los Angeles: Glen Dawson, 1953), 15–18.

89. Kenneally, *Writings,* 2:204.

90. See BL, "Padrón de 1826," San Francisco Solano mission, Folder 90, p. 102.

91. Inocente García, "Hechos Históricos de California, Relatados por Inocente García, Vecino de San Luis Obispo, 1878, Apuntados por Thomas Savage," San Luis Obispo, April 12–15, 1878, MS, HHBC, BL, p. 10.

92. Ibid., 10–11.

93. For essays on patriarchal structures in Latin America, see Soledad González Montes, ed., *Mujeres y relaciones de género en la antropología latinoamericana* (Mexico: Colegio de México, 1993); Eleanor Leacock and Richard Lee, eds., *Politics and History in Band Societies* (New York: Cambridge University Press, 1982); Etienne and Leacock, *Women and Colonization;* and Leacock, *Myths of Male Dominance.*

94. Sherburne Cook's translation of a portion of García's narrative includes a definitive comment that the women were being rounded up for conversion, but I would argue that the term *monjas,* with its religious overtones, suggests strongly that the women were escaped neophytes. Sherburne F. Cook, "Colonial Expeditions to the Interior of California, Central Valley, 1800–1820," *Anthropological Records* (Berkeley: University of California Press) 16:6 (1960): 281.

95. José María Amador, "Memorias sobre la historia de California," dictated to Thomas Savage, Whiskey Hill (San Luis Obispo), 1877, BL, HHBC, C-D 28, 40–41.

96. Ibid., 39.

97. For a discussion of the cooptation of the Indian leadership at the missions, see George Harwood Phillips, *The Alcaldes: Indian Leadership in the Spanish Missions of California,* Newberry Library Occasional Papers in Curriculum Series, no. 11 (Chicago: D'Arcy McNickle Center, 1989).

98. Serra to Neve, January 7, 1780, Monterey, in Tibesar, *Writings,* 3:415; copy is in SBMA, JSC, no. 278.

99. Quotations in this paragraph are from Beechey, *Narrative,* 2:23–24.

100. Kenneally, *Writings,* 2:113.

101. Asisara, "Narrative," 47.

102. Monroy, *Thrown among Strangers,* 26.

103. Gerónimo Boscana, *Chinigchinich: A Historical Account of the Origin, Customs, and Traditions of the Indians at the Missionary Establishment of St. Juan Capistrano, Alta California* (New York: Wiley and Putnam, 1846), 233.

104. Kenneally, *Writings,* 2:204.

105. Willoughby, *Division of Labor,* 40.

106. Boscana, *Chinigchinich,* 285.

107. Engelhardt, *Missions and Missionaries,* 232.

108. Narciso Durán and Buenaventura Fortuny, "Los infrascriptos Mintros. de esta Misión del Gloriosisimo Patriarca Sr. Sn. Jose en la N. California," November 7, 1814, San José mission, p. 2.

109. Juan Amorós, "Respuesta que dan al Interrogatorio Los P.P. Misioneros Apostólicos hijos del Colegio de S. Fernando de Mexico, Ministros de esta Misión de S. Carlos de Monterrey de la Alta California," February 3, 1814, San Carlos de Monterey mission, p. 3v.

110. Durán and Fortuny, "Infrascriptos," 2.

111. Ramón Abella and Juan Sainz de Lucio, "Respuesta de los R.R. P.P. Ministros dela Misión de N. de San Francisco," November 11, 1814, Dolores mission, San Francisco, pp. 5–6.

112. Stodder, *Mechanisms,* 33.

113. Castillo and Jackson, *Indians,* 38–39.

114. Carter, "Duhaut-Cilly's Account," 160.

115. Castillo and Jackson, *Indians,* 50.

116. Vallejo, "Ranch and Mission Days," 186–87.

117. José Carmen del Lugo, "Vida de un ranchero: Los Angeles," October 30, 1877, BL, HHBC, C-D 118, p. 22.

Chapter 6. Sexuality and Marriage

1. Ciriaco Gonzalez Carvajal [Secretario Interino de la Governación de Ultramar], "Ynterrogatorio," Cádiz, October 6, 1812, copy signed by Don Ignacio María Saludo, Culiacán, August 13, 1813, SBMA.

2. Señán, "Contestación al Interrogatorio." Responses for San Diego Mission are in BL, AMSB, Inf. y Corr., 1802–22, vol. 3, pp. 27–37.

3. Antonio Rodríguez and Luis Antonio Martínez to José Señán, February 20, 1814, San Luís Obispo mission, SBMA, p. 3.

4. Señan, "Contestación," 11.

5. Luís Gil and José María de Zalvidea, "Respuesta qe los Pes. Mntros. de la Misión del Arcangel S. Gabriel, dan al Ynterrogatorio," June 28, 1814, San Gabriel mission, p. 4.

6. Juan Martín and Juan Cabot to José Señán, April 5, 1814, San Miguel mission, p. 2, SBMA.

7. Juan Bautista Sancho and Pedro Cabot to José Señán, February 26, 1814, San Antonio de Padua mission, p. 4.

8. José Vicuña Muro to Viceroy, "Dictamen sobre clima y enfermedades en California," Mexico, May 10, 1805, in BL, Arch. of Calif., vol. 12, Prov. St. Pap., vol. 19, p. 62.

9. This incident is summarized in Zephyrin Engelhardt, *San Gabriel Mission and the Beginnings of Los Angeles* (San Gabriel, Calif.: Mission San Gabriel, 1927), 82.

10. Fathers José de Miguel and José María de Zalvidea to Esteban Tapis, March 17, 1810, SBMA.

11. Ibid.

12. Xavier Alvarado to Captain José Argüello, January 17, 1810, SBMA. See also Argüello to Governor José Joaquín de Arrillaga, February 22, 1810; Arrillaga to Fray Presidente Estevan Tapis, March 1, 1810; Tapis to Juan de Miguel and José María de Zalvidea, March 6, 1810; SBMA.

13. Wallace, "Sexual Status," 685.

14. Quotations in this paragraph are from H. D. Richardson, "History of the Foundation of the City of Vallejo," 1874, MS, Sketches of California Pioneers Series, BL, C-E 65:3, p. 10.

15. Hugo Reid, "Letters on the Los Angeles County Indians," *Los Angeles Star,* in Dakin, *Scotch Paisano, 232.*

16. Quotations in this paragraph are from P. Kostromitonov, "Notes on the Indians in Upper California," in *Ethnographic Observations on the Coast Miwok and Pomo by Contre-Admiral F. P. Von Wrangell and P. Kostromitonov of the Russian Colony Ross, 1839* (Berkeley: University of California, Department of Anthropology, 1974), 10.

17. Maynard Geiger and Clement Meighan, eds., *As the Padres Saw Them: California Indian Life and Customs as Reported by the Franciscan Missionaries, 1813–1815* (Santa Barbara: Santa Barbara Mission Archive Library, 1976), 65.

18. This and the following quotations are from Geiger and Meighan, *As the Padres Saw Them,* 66.

19. José Bandini, *Descrision de l'Alta California,* 1828, BL, Cowan Collection, p. 4.

20. Dakin, *Scotch Paisano,* 233.

21. Quotations in this paragraph are from Dakin, *Scotch Paisano,* 226.

22. John P. Harrington, *The Eye of the Flute: Chumash Traditional History and Ritual as Told by Fernando Librado Kitsepawit to John P. Harrington* (Banning, Calif.: Malki Museum Press, 1981): 11–17.

23. Ibid.

24. Quotations in this paragraph are from Geiger and Meighan, *As the Padres Saw Them,* 67.

25. A landmark study of the impact of the Royal Pragmatic in Mexico City is that by Seed, *To Love, Honor, and Obey.* A useful overview of such laws can be found in Edith Couturier, "Women and the Family in Eighteenth-Century Mexico: Law and Practice," *JFH* 8 (Fall 1985): 294–304.

26. De Croix to Felipe de Neve, "Sobre matrimonios de hijos de familias," abstract, Arispe (Sonora), December 29, 1779, MS, BL, Arch. of Calif., vol. 1, Prov. St.

Pap., vol. 2, 1778–80, p. 343. This manuscript abstract contains a full transcription of the *real cédula* of April 7, 1778, including the earlier *Pragmática* of March 23, 1776.

27. [Governor Antonio] Romeu, "Sobre Pragmática de Matrimonios," Monterey, January 20, 1790; published by Hermenegildo Sal, San Francisco, February 26, 1792; José Argüello, Monterey, 1792; Felipe de Goycoechea, Santa Barbara, August 8, 1792; Juan Pablo Grijalba, San Diego, August 14, 1792; José Joaquín de Arrillaga, Loreto, October 24, 1792, BL, Arch. of Calif., vol. 5, Prov. St. Pap., vol. 9, p. 248.

28. Neve to Fages, "Sobre una real cédula de 26 de Mayo del Cort. año, por la cual una madre no puede instituir por heredero al hijo o hija que haya contraido matrimonio contra la voluntad del padre," Arispe, November 18, 1783, extract, Arch. of Calif., vol. 2, Prov. St. Pap., vol. 4, p. 439.

29. *Pragmática Real,* March 23, 1776, in De Croix to Neve, "Sobre matrimonios," p. 338.

30. Neve to Fages, "Sobre una real cédula," p. 439.

31. Antonio Ventura de Taranco, auto, September 12, 1783, and Consejo de las Indias, February 27, 1783, cited in Antonio Ventura de Taranco, Aranjuez, May 26, 1783, Arch. of Calif., vol. 2, Prov. St. Pap., vol. 4, 1783–84, p. 439.

32. Neve to Fages, "Sobre una real cédula," p. 439.

33. "Virey Bucarely al Comandante de Monterey sobre casamiento de soldados voluntarios con Indias cristianas y mercedes de tierras," September 21, 1774, in BL, Arch. of Calif., vol. 1, Prov. St. Pap., 1:91.

34. Serra to Bucareli, "Report of the Spiritual and Material Status of the Five California Missions, Monterey, February 5, 1775," in Tibesar, *Writings,* 2:237.

35. Tibesar, *Writings,* 2:150–51.

36. Serra to Bucareli, March 13, 1773, in Tibesar, *Writings,* 1:325.

37. Kenneally, *Writings,* 2:212.

38. Antonia I. Castañeda, "Engendering the History of Alta California, 1769–1848: Gender, Sexuality, and the Family," in Ramón A. Gutiérrez and Richard J. Orsi, eds., *Contested Eden: California before the Gold Rush* (Berkeley: University of California Press, 1998), 241, 256n32.

39. Castañeda, "Presidarias y Pobladoras," 256.

40. Ibid.

41. Branciforte to Borica, June 4, 1797, AGN, Calif., vol. 74, exp. 61, fol. 166.

42. Castañeda, "Presidarias y Pobladoras," 256.

43. Kenneally, *Writings,* 2:212.

44. Borica to Viceroy, 1797, quoted in Hittel, *History of California,* 1:581.

45. Wallace, "Sexual Status," 684.

46. Ibid.

47. Dakin, *Scotch Paisano,* 232.

48. Geiger and Meighan, *As the Padres Saw Them,* 68.

49. Ibid., 66.

50. Ibid., 68.

51. For a discussion of the concept of free will and the changing role of the church, state, and family in marriage choices from the sixteenth to the eighteenth entury, see Seed, *To Love, Honor, and Obey.*

52. García, "Hechos historicos," 35.

53. Ibid.

54. Vallejo, "Ranch and Mission Days," 186.

55. Dakin, *Scotch Paisano,* 33–34.

56. Jacob Bowman, *Ranchos of California* (Fresno, Calif.: Academy Library Guild, 1956), 31.

57. Papers of John Peabody Harrington, SI, NAA, vol. 3, microfilm reel 50, frame 94.

58. Gloria Ricci Lothrop, "Reminiscences of a Princess, Isidora Solano," *The Californians* 11:3 (1994), 27.

59. Henry Cerruti, "Relación de la entrevista que tuve con Isidora viuda del Principe Solano," in *Pioneer Sketches,* no. 12, April 9, 1874, MS, BL, p. 6. For an English translation, see Isidora Solano, "My Years with Chief Solano," *Touring Topics* 22 (Feb. 1930): 39, 52. Page numbers in the text refer to Cerruti's "Relación."

60. Carl Waldman, *Who Was Who in Native American History: Indians and Non-Indians from Early Contacts through 1900* (New York: Facts on File, 1990), 333.

61. Richardson, "History," 65:3.

62. Cerruti, "Relación," 2.

63. Gretchen M. Bataille and Kathleen Mullen Sands, *American Indian Women: Telling Their Lives* (Lincoln: University of Nebraska, 1984).

64. See discussion of the interview context in Virginia M. Bouvier, "Women, Conquest, and the Production of History: Hispanic California, 1542–1840" (Ph.D. diss., University of California, Berkeley, 1995), pp. 343–56.

65. Henry Cerruti, "Ramblings in California," 1874, BL, 113.

66. "Yo no tener vergüenza emboracharme porque el razón enseña." Cerruti, "Relación," 6. Here Isidora is playing on the meaning of *gente de razón.* Both "reason" and people "of reason" (i.e., Christians) teach her to get drunk.

67. Cerruti, "Ramblings," 112–13.

68. Ibid., 113.

69. Ibid., 113–14.

70. Asisara, "Narrative," 47.

71. Robert Heizer, *The California Indians: A Source Book* (Berkeley: University of California Press, 1957): 131.

72. Beechey, *Narrative,* 2:16.

73. Ibid.

74. Vallejo, "Ranch and Mission Days," 186.

75. Langsdorff, *Voyages and Travels,* 2:160.

76. Ibid., 2:159.

77. Ibid., 2:159–60.

78. Beechey, *Narrative*, 2:21.

79. Hugo Reid, "New Era in Mission Affairs," no. 19, n.p., BL, Scrapbook. Reid noted elsewhere that every white child born among the Gabrielino Indians was "secretly strangled and buried!" Reid, "First Arrival of the Spaniards," in Dakin, *Scotch Paisano,* 262.

80. Reid, "New Era in Mission Affairs."

81. On this topic, see Richard C. Trexler, "Infanticide in Florence: New Sources and First Results," *History of Childhood Quarterly* 1 (Summer 1973): 108.

82. Amador, "Memorias," 190–91.

83. Ibid.

84. Vallejo, "Ranch and Mission Days," 186.

85. Ibid.

86. Ibid.

87. The existence of Asisara's testimony, buried within another interview done in the 1870s, is quite fortuitous. Bancroft's research assistant, Thomas Savage, was interviewing José María Amador, a Spanish-Mexican army officer, when Asisara came by and added his own commentary for the record. Asisara's account (hereafter, Asisara, "Memorias") can be found in Amador, "Memorias," 58–77 and 90–113.

88. In fact, Olbés served at Mission Santa Cruz from 1818 until November 1821. See Maynard J. Geiger, *Franciscan Missionaries in Hispanic California, 1769–1848: A Biographical Dictionary* (San Marino, Calif.: Huntington Library 1969), 167; and Bancroft, *History of California,* 2:387. The certificate of burial signed by Father Marquínez may be found in Santa Cruz mission, "Libro de misión," BL, MS, 36–37.

89. The following account comes from Asisara, "Memorias," 94–98.

90. Malcolm Margolin, *The Ohlone Way: Indian Life in the San Francisco-Monterey Bay Area* (Berkeley: Heyday Books, 1978), 83.

91. Juan Amorós, "Respuesta que dan al Interrogatorio Los P.P. Misioneros Apostólicos hijos del Colegio de S. Fernando de Mexico, Ministros de esta Misión de S. Carlos de Monterrey de la Alta California," February 3, 1814, San Carlos de Monterey mission, p. iv.

92. Beechey, *Narrative,* 2:21.

93. José María Estudillo, April 15, 1809, San Francisco, BL, Arch. of Calif., vol. 17, Prov. St. Pap., Benicia, Military, vol. 11, pp. 1, 4.

94. Pedro Múñoz and Joaquín Pasqual Nuez, "Respuesta que dan los Minsitros dela Misn. de Sn Fernando Rey dela Alta California," February 3, 1814, San Fernando mission, SBMA, p. 3.

95. Antonio Jayme, "Ynforme ó respuestas al interrogatorio," June 20, 1814, Soledad mission, SBMA, p. 1.

96. Amorós, "Respuesta," 3.

97. Maynard Geiger, "The 1824 Chumash Revolt," *SCQ* 7 (Dec. 1970): 345–64.

98. On the Chumash uprising, see AGN, RJE, vol. 31; Thomas Blackburn, ed., "The Chumash Revolt of 1824: A Native Account," *JCA* 2 (Winter 1975): 223–27;

Travis Hudson, "Chumash Canoes of Mission Santa Barbara: The Revolt of 1824," *JCA* 3 (Winter 1976): 5–15; Travis Hudson, ed., "The Chumash Revolt of 1824: Another Native Account from the Notes of John P. Harrington," *JCGBA* 2 (Summer 1980): 123–26; and James A. Sandos, "Levantamiento! The Chumash Uprising Reconsidered," *SCQ* 67 (Summer 1985): 109–33.

99. "Interrogatorio," Santa Barbara Presidio, June 1, 1824, *Documentos para la historia de California,* de la Guerra Collection, BL, 7:142–50.

100. Ripoll to Sarria, Santa Barbara, May 5, 1824, Taylor Collection, Archivo del Arzobispado de San Francisco, doc. 1599, quoted in Maynard Geiger, ed., "Fray Antonio Ripoll's Description of the Chumash Revolt at Santa Barbara in 1824," *SCQ* 52:3 (Dec. 1970): 354.

101. Bancroft, *California Pastoral,* 614. Hugo Reid recorded the Indians' medicinal use of the thorn apple but did not mention its use to induce abortion or prevent pregnancy. Hugo Reid, "Medicine and Diseases," no. 8, n.p., Scrapbook, BL, n.d.

102. Durán and Fortuny, "Infrascriptos," 3.

103. Mariano Payeras to Esteban Tapis, January 13, 1810, SBMA, p. 2.

104. Ibid., 1. See also Payeras to Guardian of San Fernando College, February 2, 1820, AGN, Colección de Documentos para la Historia de Mexico, 1st series, vol. 2, fols. 86–88, and Father Lasúen's concerns over the small number of live births in his "Refutation of Charges," June 19, 1801, in Kenneally, *Writings,* 2:209–10.

105. Payeras to Tapis, January 13, 1810, SBMA, p. 2.

106. James A. Sandos, "Christianization among the Chumash: An Ethnohistoric Perspective," *AIQ* 15:1 (Winter 1991): 73.

107. Cited in Manuel Servín, "Costansó's 1791 Report," *CHSQ* 49 (Sept. 1970): 227.

108. Ibid.

109. Bancroft, *California Pastoral,* 312.

110. Bancroft, *History of California,* 2:160.

111. Ibid., 614.

112. Florence Shipek, *Delfina Cuero: Her Autobiography, An Account of Her Last Years and Her Ethnobotanic Contributions by Florence Connolly Shipek* (Menlo Park, Calif.: Ballena Press, 1991), 43–44.

113. Ibid., 39.

114. Ibid., 42–43.

115. Arch. of Calif., vol. 2, BL, p. 78.

116. Kostromitonov, "Notes," 10.

117. Ibid.

118. Monroy, "They Didn't Call Them 'Padre' for Nothing," 435.

119. Tibesar, *Writings,* 4:63. See also Edwin A. Beilharz, *Felipe de Neve: First Governor of California* (San Francisco: California Historical Society, 1971), 55–63.

120. Joseph Antonio Rengel to Don Pedro Fages, Chihuahua, March 13, 1785, p. 1, SBMA, CMD (copy from Arch. of Calif.).

121. Pedro Fages to Diego González, "Sobre subordinar a los oficiales y tropa,"

Monterey, July 1, 1785, BL, Arch. of Calif., vol. 54, State Papers, Sacramento, vol. 2, p. 43.

122. Branciforte to Borica, "Sobre escoltas a los religiosos," October 5, 1795, Mexico, BL, Arch. of Calif., vol. 7, Prov. St. Pap., vol. 13, p. 256. See also BL, Arch. of Calif., vol. 5, Prov. St. Pap., vol. 9, pp. 107, 121 (1789), and vol. 10, p. 151ff. (1791); Governor to Commanders of Presidios, "Excesos de la tropa con las Indias, su corrección," Monterey, April 11, 1796, BL, Arch. of Calif., vol. 23, Prov. Rec., vol. 3, pp. 421–22.

123. José Ramón Valdés, "Memorias," San Buenaventura, February 15, 1878, MS, BL, fol. 18.

124. Ibid.

125. This topic is notably absent, however, from Julio César, "Recollections of My Youth at San Luis Rey Mission," *Touring Topics* 22 (Nov. 1930): 42–43; and Minna and Gordon Hewes, eds., "Indian Life and Customs at Mission San Louis Rey: A Record of California Mission Life by Pablo Tac, an Indian Neophyte, Written at Rome about 1835," reprinted in *Americas* 9:1 (1952): 87–106.

126. Remarks by Asisara in this paragraph are from Asisara, "Memorias," 99–100.

127. Geiger, *Franciscan Missionaries*, 105. Geiger mistakenly attributed authorship of these charges to Pedro Amador; it was Lorenzo Asisara who made them.

128. Zephyrin Engelhardt, *Mission San Luis Obispo in the Valley of the Bears* (Santa Barbara: Mission Santa Barbara, 1933): 199.

129. Bancroft, *History of California,* 2:387–89.

130. Argüello to Arrillaga, "Muerte de un misionero," October 13, 1812, San Francisco, extract, BL, Arch of Calif., vol. 12, Prov. St. Pap., vol. 19, p. 322.

131. In a letter dated October 2, 1814, Durán wrote, "Those of the house [mission] murdered him [Quintana] in so barbarous a manner that I doubt if such cruelty has ever been resorted to in the most barbarous nations for they tortured him *in pudendis* [involving the genitalia] and suffocated him at the same time with the cloths used in administering extreme unction." Quoted in Geiger, *Franciscan Missionaries,* 205. (The original is held in a private collection.)

132. See Amador, "Memorias," 58–113. For English translations, see Asisara, "Narrative," 45–48, and Lorenzo Asisara, "The Assassination of Padre Andres Quintana by the Indians of Mission Santa Cruz in 1812: The Narrative of Lorenzo Asizara," *CH* 68 (Fall 1989): 116–25.

133. Amador, "Memorias," 73.

134. Nunis and Castillo, "California Mission Indians," 209.

135. See note 131.

136. Nunis and Castillo, "California Mission Indians," 210.

137. Quotations from Librado are from Travis Hudson, ed., *Breath of the Sun: Life in Early California as Told by a Chumash Indian, Fernando Librado, to John P. Harrington* (Banning, Calif.: Malki Museum Press, 1979), 52–53.

138. Sir George Simpson, *Narrative of a Voyage to California Ports in 1841–42* (Fairfield, Wash.: Ye Galleon Press, 1988), 106.

139. Bancroft, *California Pastoral,* 197.

Chapter 7. Resistance

1. George Harwood Phillips, *Chiefs and Challengers: Indian Resistance and Cooperation in Southern California* (Berkeley: University of California Press, 1975), 22.

2. Pangua, letter, June 3, 1776, in Mexico, AGN, Calif., vol. 72, exp. 24, fols. 245–53; and Junípero Serra, "Nota Previa," in San Diego mission, "Libros de Misión," BL, 1878, p. 4.

3. Bancroft, *History of California,* 1:253.

4. See Ernest J. Burrus, S.J., *Diario del Comandante Fernando de Rivera y Moncada,* part 2 (Madrid: Ediciones José Porrúa Turanzas, 1967); Vicente Fuster to Serra, November 28, 1775, San Diego (original in Stephens Collection, Austin; typescript copy in SBMA, Junípero Serra Collection); Junípero Serra, "Nota Previa"; and Vicente Fuster, "Registro de defunciones desde la fundación," January 26, 1777, in San Diego mission, "Libros de Misión," BL, pp. 3–4, 71.

5. See the inquest documents "Diligencias que de orden del Govor practico el Sargento Jph Ingo Olivera contra un Yndio Neofito dela Misión de San Gabriel llamado Nicolás Josef, y otros dos Yndios y una Yndia Gentiles acusados de ser Cavezillas de la Sublevación qe hicieron contra los Padres, y Escolta de dha Misión la noche del 25 de octubre de 1785," AGN, Prov. Int., vol. 120, exp. 2, fols. 34–50v.

6. Ignacio Olivera, "Diligencia," AGN, Prov. Int., vol. 120, exp. 2, fols. 37v–38.

7. Castañeda, "Presidarias y pobladoras," 253.

8. Thomas Workman Temple II, "Toypurina the Witch and the Indian Uprising at San Gabriel," *Masterkey for Indian Lore and History* 32:5 (Sept.–Oct. 1958): 152.

9. Pedro Amador to Governor Borica, San José, July 8, 1797, extract, BL, Arch. of Calif., Prov. St. Pap., vol. 15, pp. 371–73; Borica to Amador, Monterey, July 10, 1797, BL, Arch. of Calif., vol. 9, Prov. St. Pap., vol. 16, pp. 71–72; Amador, "Diario," 1797, in AGN, Calif., vol. 65, exp. 1, fol. 93.

10. BL, Arch. of Calif., vol. 3, Prov. St. Pap., vol. 5, p. 118.

11. Argüello, "Relación que formó de las declaraciones de los Indios Cristianos huidos de la Misión de San Francisco," 1797, cited in Bancroft, *History of California,* 1:711.

12. Ibid., 1:712.

13. [Pedro de] Alberni to [California interim governor José Joaquín de] Arrillaga, "Sobre sospechas de envenenamiento por indios de San Miguel a dos ministros de aquella, y otros dos de San Francisco y San Carlos," Monterey, April 7, 1801, extract, BL, Arch. of Calif., vol. 11, Prov. St. Pap., vol. 18, pp. 62–65. See also Bancroft, *History of California,* 2:146–7.

14. Martín and Martínez to Carrillo, April 27, 1802, San Miguel mission, extract, BL, Arch. of Calif., vol. 11, Prov. St. Pap., vol. 18, pp. 205–6.

15. Carrillo to Arrillaga, June 5, 1802, extract, BL, Arch. of Calif., vol. 11, Prov. St. Pap., vol. 18, p. 203. Bancroft's account of this incident is somewhat misleading, for it implies that the priests, not Carrillo, favored punishing the accused. Bancroft, *History of California,* 2:150.

16. Geiger, *Franciscan Missionaries,* 150.

17. Bancroft, *History of California,* 2:147.

18. Ibid., 2:137 and 2:146–7.

19. Ibid., 2:345.

20. Alberni to Arrillaga, "Sublevación de Indios del Carmelo; intentos de asesinar al Padre e incendiar la Misión," extract, Monterey, February 9, 1801, BL, Arch. of Calif., vol. 11, Prov. St. Pap., vol. 18, pp. 63–64.

21. Sánchez to Argüello, January 16, 1805, San José mission, Arch. of Calif., vol. 12, Prov. St. Pap., vol. 19, pp. 34–35. The documents all say Cuevas, but Bancroft lists the priest as Cueva. Bancroft also notes the possibility that a ranchería other than that destined for the visit might have attacked the group. Bancroft, *History of California,* 2:34.

22. A Spanish soldier later recalled that Cuevas was on his way to instruct gentile Indians. Amador, "Memorias."

23. Luis Peralta, "Sobre heridas a un Padre Misionero," Santa Clara, February 29, 1805, extract, BL, Arch. of Calif., vol. 12, Prov. St. Pap., vol. 19, p. 29.

24. Iturrigaray to Governor of Californias, "Acusa recibo de su oficio de 11 marzo participando el atentado de los gentiles contra el misionero de San José," Mexico, April 22, 1805, extract, BL, Arch. of Calif., vol. 12, Prov. St. Pap., vol. 19, p. 51. See also Arrillaga to Viceroy, March 11, 1805, Loreto, AGN, Calif., vol. 9, fols. 452–53. Bancroft cited a report by Father President Estevan Tapis, "Informe general de misiones, 1803–4 [*sic*]," MS, 77, which indicated that "a neophyte treacherously guided Cueva [*sic*] to the wrong ranchería." This suggests that some priests may have attributed perfidious motives to the Indians following the investigation. Bancroft, *History of California,* 2:34–35.

25. [Alférez] Luis Argüello to José Argüello, "Sobre un plan de Indios para quemar la misión de Sta Clara y matar a los Padres," May 10, 1805, extract, BL, Arch. of Calif., vol. 12, Prov. St. Pap., vol. 19, p. 30.

26. Argüello to Arrillaga, "Espedición en solicitud de indios prófugos," May 30, 1805, Arch. of Calif., vol. 12, Prov. St. Pap., vol. 19, p. 42.

27. For an analysis of flight as resistance, see Adriaan C. van Oss, *Catholic Colonialism: A Parish History of Guatemala, 1524–1821* (Cambridge: Cambridge University Press, 1986).

28. Beechey, *Narrative,* 1:360.

29. Hugo Reid, "First Missionary Proceedings," no. 18, n.p.

30. Ibid.

31. Cook, *Conflict,* 58–61; Cook, "Population Trends" 27. For examples of the persecution of mission fugitives, see Rodríguez to Arrillaga, letters, June 20, 1806, July 25, 1806, August 29, 1806, San Diego, BL, Arch. of Calif., vol. 12, Prov. St. Pap., vol. 19, pp. 123, 125–26, 157; BL, Arch. of Calif., vol. 4, Prov. St. Pap., pp. 7–8, 74, 75, 92–93, 77–78. In 1795, 280 Christian Indians fled the San Francisco mission; see BL, Arch. of Calif., vol. 7, p. 320. See also Governor Pablo Vicente de Solá, letter, January

20, 1816, BL, C-C 1:172–73; BL, Arch. of Calif., vol. 3, Prov. St. Pap., pp. 5–6, 432–33; and Jackson, *Indian Population Decline,* 207.

32. Kenneally, *Writings,* 2:203.

33. Remaining quotations in this paragraph are from Tapis to Arrillaga, SBMA, CMD, 676, March 1, 1805, p. 1.

34. Quotations in this paragraph are from Carobeth Laird, *Encounter with an Angry God: Recollections of My Life with John Peabody Harrington* (Banning, Calif.: Malki Museum Press, 1975), 18.

35. García, "Hechos históricos," 34–37, 80.

36. Quotations in this paragraph are from Amador, "Memorias," 107.

37. The response from La Purísima Concepción has not been found. San Rafael and San Francisco Solano (Sonoma) missions had not yet been established at the time of the questionnaire. The other responses, ranging from two to sixteen manuscript pages from each mission, can be found in the Santa Barbara Mission Archive. For an English translation of the SBMA manuscripts, see Geiger and Meighan, *As the Padres Saw Them.* The Bancroft Library holds transcripts of these originals, made by E. G. Murray in 1877, which omit significant portions of the originals. José Señán, "Contestación al Interrogatorio," in BL, AMSB, Pap. Misc., vol. 7, 112–216. The San Diego responses may be found in BL, AMSB, Inf. y Corr., 1802–22, vol. 3, pp. 27–37. See Alfred L. Kroeber, "A Mission Record of the California Indians from a Manuscript in the Bancroft Library," *UCPAAE* 8:1 (May 28, 1908): 1–27.

38. The debate over the use of force had plagued Spanish conquests in America since the sixteenth century. See Lewis Hanke, *The Spanish Struggle for Justice in the Conquest of America* (Philadelphia: University of Pennsylvania Press, 1949); Silvio Zavala, *La filosofía política en la conquista de América* (Mexico: Fondo de Cultura Económica: 1947): 42–77; and Sabine MacCormack, " 'The Heart Has Its Reasons': Predicaments of Missionary Christianity in Early Colonial Peru," *HAHR* 65:3 (Aug. 1985): 443–66.

39. Carvajal, "Ynterrogatorio," 1.

40. The responses to this question, the ninth in the questionnaire, can be found in BL, AMSB, Pap. Misc., vol. 7, pp. 154–57.

41. Ramón Olbés, "Respuesta," December 31, 1813, Santa Barbara mission, SBMA, p. 1.

42. Martín and Cabot to Señán, April 5, 1814, San Miguel mission, SBMA, p. 1. In this context, I interpret *gente de razón,* "people of reason," to mean Christian or Spaniard. See Miranda, "Racial and Cultural Dimensions of *Gente de Razón* Status," 265–78.

43. Fernando Martín and José Sánchez, "Responden los infrafirmados Ministros de la Misión de Sn Diego de Nipaguai," December 23, 1814, San Diego mission, SBMA, p. 3.

44. Sancho and Cabot to Señán, February 26, 1814, San Antonio de Padua mission, SBMA, p. 2.

45. Summaries of the replies to this question can be found in BL, AMSB, Pap. Misc., vol. 7, pp. 138–42.

46. Marcelino Marquínez and Jayme Escudé, "Los Ministros Evangélicos, y Predicadores Apostólicos de la Misn. de Sta Cruz en la Calif. Septentrional," April 30, 1814, Mission Santa Cruz, SBMA, p. 2.

47. Susan Lee Painter and Don Dutton, "Patterns of Emotional Bonding in Battered Women: Traumatic Bonding," *International Journal of Women's Studies* 8:4 (Sept.–Oct. 1985): 363–75.

48. James C. Scott, *Domination and the Arts of Resistance* (New Haven: Yale University Press, 1990), 138. See also his *Weapons of the Weak: Everyday Forms of Peasant Resistance* (New Haven: Yale University Press, 1985).

49. Marquínez and Escudé, "Ministros Evangélicos," p. 4.

50. Ibid.

51. Juan Amorós, "Respuesta que dan al Interrogatorio Los P.P. Misioneros Apostólicos hijos del Colegio de S. Fernando de Mexico, Ministros de esta Misión de S. Carlos de Monterrey de la Alta California," February 3, 1814, San Carlos de Monterey mission, p. 2.

52. Magín Catalá and José Viader, "Respuestas que los PPs. Mintros de la Mn de Sta Clara de la Alta Calif. dan al interrogatorio del Govierno," November 4, 1814, Santa Clara mission, 2.

53. Durán and Fortuny, "Infrascriptos," 1.

54. José Señán, "Confesionario," Mission San Buenaventura, before 1823, SBMA, p. 6. See Madison S. Beeler, ed. *The Ventureño Confesionario of José Señán, O.F.M.* (Berkeley: University of California Press, 1967).

55. Arlene Hirschfelder and Paulette Molin, *The Encyclopedia of Native American Religions* (New York: Facts on File, 1992); Leslie Spier, *Yuman Tribes of the Gila River* (Chicago: University of Chicago Press, 1933), passim.

56. Margolin, *The Way We Lived*, 7.

57. Cora DuBois, "The 1870 Ghost Dance," in Robert E. Heizer and M. A. Whipple, eds., *The California Indians: A Source Book* (Berkeley: University of California Press, 1971): 496–99.

58. Boscana, *Chinigchinich*, 41–42; José de Zúñiga to Tte. Cor. Pedro Fages, December 17, 1782, San Diego, BL, Arch. of Calif., 2:78.

59. Tapis to Arrillaga, March 1, 1805, Santa Barbara mission, SBMA, CMD, pp. 2–3.

60. Father Olbés recorded the name of the Chupa deity as *sup,* who was considered to be identical to Achup or Chupu of the Purísima Chumash. Campbell Grant, "Eastern Coastal Chumash," in Robert Heizer, ed., *Handbook of North American Indians, vol. 8: California* (Washington, D.C.: Smithsonian Institution Press, 1978): 509–19.

61. John P. Harrington, "Culture Element Distributions, 19: Central California Coast," *University of California Anthropological Records* 7:1 (1942): 1–46. Also see Grant, "Eastern Coastal Chumash."

62. Robert Spott and Alfred L. Kroeber, eds., *Yurok Narratives, UCPAAE,* 35:9 (Berkeley: University of California, 1942), 158–63.

63. Culleton, *Indians,* 222.

64. Willoughby, *Division of Labor,* 57–61.

65. Quotations are from Carter, "Duhaut-Cilly's Account," 315.

66. Múñoz and Nuez, "Respuesta," 1.

67. Alfred L. Kroeber, *Handbook of the Indians of California* (Berkeley: California Book Company, 1953), 622–23.

68. Constance G. DuBois, "The Religion of the Luiseño Indians," *UCPAAE* 8 (1908): 69–173.

69. Raymond White, "Religion and Its Role among the Luiseño," in Lowell J. Bean and Thomas C. Blackburn, eds., *Native Californians: A Theoretical Retrospective* (Ramona, Calif.: Ballena Press, 1976), 360–64.

70. Riane Eisler, *The Chalice and the Blade: Our History, Our Future* (San Francisco: Harper and Row, 1987); Pamela Berger, *The Goddess Obscured: Transformation of the Grain Protectress from Goddess to Saint* (Boston: Beacon Press, 1985).

71. Amorós, "Respuesta," p. 3.

72. Felipe Arroyo de la Cuesta, "Respuesta qe. los P.P. Ministros de Sn. Juan Bauta. dan," May 1, 1814, San Juan Bautista mission, p. 6.

73. Rodríguez and Martínez to Señán, February 20, 1814, San Luís Obispo mission, p. 2.

74. Remaining quotations in this paragraph are from José Señán, "Respuesta, qe. dan los Ministros de esta Misión de Sta. Barbara al interrogatorio, qe. por medio del Yllmo. Sr. Obispo de Sonora, dirigio el Exmo Sr. Dn. Ciriaco Gonzalez Carbajal Secrio interino de la Governacion de Ultramar," December 31, 1813, Santa Barbara mission, pp. 4–5.

75. Francisco Suñer and Antonio Peyri, "A la circular que nos remitió nutro P. Presidente Fr Jose Señan," December 12, 1814, San Luís Rey mission, p. 2.

76. Ibid.

77. Boscana, *Chinigchinich,* 235.

78. Estevan Tapis and Francisco Xavier Uría, "Contestacion de los PP Mntros infraescritos de la misión de Sta Ynes en la N. California," March 8, 1814, Santa Inés mission, p. 2.

79. Brady, Crome, and Reese, "Resist!" 147.

80. Tapis and Uría, "Respuesta," 2.

81. Marquínez and Escudé, "Ministros Evangélicos," 4.

82. DuBois, "Religion"; Martha Voght, "Shamans and Padres: The Religion of the Southern California Mission Indians," *PHR* 36:4 (1967): 363–73.

83. Remaining quotations in this paragraph are from Laird, *Encounter,* 91–93.

84. Literally, "shout so you may not idle." Suñer and Peyri, "A la circular," 1.

85. Martín and Sánchez, "Responden," 2.

86. Marquínez and Escudé, "Ministros Evangélicos," 4.

87. For background on church-state relations during the Bourbon dynasty, see

David Brading, *Church and State in Bourbon Mexico: The Diocese of Michoacán, 1749–1810* (Cambridge: Cambridge University Press, 1994).

88. "R.C. [*Real Cédula*] para que en los Reinos de las Indias se destierren los diferentes idiomas de que se usa, y solo se hable castellano," Aranjuez, May 10, 1770, in Konetzke, *Colección de documentos,* 3:2, 364–68. Original in AGI, Indif. 540, lib. 17, fol. 131. See also AGN, RCD, 1770, vol. 136; AGN, RCD, n.d., vol. 166, fols. 185, 190; Borica to Goycochea, July 23, 1793, BL, Arch. of Calif., 1795, 8:61.

89. Remaining quotations in this paragraph are from "Real Cédula," May 10, 1770, in Konetzke, *Colección de documentos,* 3:1, 364–65.

90. Serra to Palou, August 18, 1772, Monterey, in Tibesar, *Writings,* 1:267.

91. See AMSB, Pap. Misc., vol. 7, pp. 112–216, passim; AGN, RCD, 1778, vol. 146, fols. 27 and 209.

92. Antonio Jayme, "Ynforme ó respuestas al interrogatorio," June 20, 1814, Soledad mission, p. 1.

93. AMSB, Pap. Misc., vol. 7, pp. 112–216, passim.

94. Arroyo de la Cuesta, "Respuesta," 1–2.

95. Felipe Arroyo de la Cuesta, "Extracto de la Gramática Mutsún, o de la Lengua de los Naturales de la misión de San Juan Bautista" (New York: Cramoisy Press, 1861). This manuscript contains a note on its cover that reads: "Copia de la lengua Mutsún en estilo Catalán a causa la escribió un Catalán. La Castellana usa de la fuerza de la pronunciación de letras de otro modo en su alfabeto. Ve el original intitulado Gramática California." Original is a 76-page small quarto MS belonging to the College of Santa Inez and forwarded to the Smithsonian Institution.

96. Buenaventura Sitjar, *Vocabulario de la lengua de los naturales de la misión de San Antonio, Alta California,* Shea's Library of American Linguistics, no.7 (1797, reprint, New York, 1861).

97. Mariano Payeras to Estevan Tapis, January 13, 1810, SBMA, CMD, p. 1.

98. Señán, "Confesionario."

99. Lasúen to Pangua, San Diego, December 6, 1780, MS, Mexico, INHA, FF, vol. 66, no. 1640, fols. 185–86v.

100. Vicente Francisco de Sarria, Circular letter, San Carlos de Monterey, January 25, 1817, in SBMA, CMD, no. 692/1373.

101. Serra to Palou, June 21, 1771, in Tibesar, *Writings,* 1:241; Serra to Miguel de Petra, August 4, 1773, in Tibesar, *Writings,* 1:393.

102. Tapis and Uría, "Respuesta," 1.

103. Carlo Tagliavini, "L'Evangelizzazione e i costumi degli Indi Luiseños secondo la narrazione di un chierico indigeno," in *Proceedings of the Twenty-Third International Congress of Americanists, 1928* (New York, 1930): 633–48.

104. The treatise ("Conversión de los San Luiseños de la Alta California") and the lexicon have been annotated and published. See Carlo Tagliavini, "L'Evangelizzazione," and Tagliavini, "Frammento d'un dizionarietto Luiseño-Spagnuolo scritto da un indigeno," in *Proceedings of the Twenty-Third International Congress of American-*

ists, 1928 (1930): 633–48, 905–17. The original is "Lingua Californese," Fondo Mezzofanti, Biblioteca dell'Archiginnasio, Bologna, Italy. Tac's account has been translated into English by Minna and Gordon Hewes, *Indian Life and Customs*. See also Carlo Tagliavini, "La lingua degli Indi Luiseños (Alta California) secondo gli appunti grammaticali inediti di un chierico indigeno," *Biblioteca dell'Archiginnasio,* series 2, vol. 31 (Bologna, 1926).

105. "R.C. que se pongan escuelas," May 30, 1691, in Konetzke, *Colección de documentos,* 3:1, 11–12.

106. Gil and Zalvidea, "Respuesta," 2.

107. "R.C. que se pongan escuelas," May 30, 1691, in Konetzke, *Colección de documentos,* 3:1, 11–12.

108. See prior discussion and Sarria and Abella, "Libro de Patentes," n.p.; Sarria, January 25, 1817, pp. 2–3.

109. Antonio Rodríguez and Luís Antonio Martínez to José Señán, February 20, 1814, San Luís Obispo mission, p. 2.

110. Tagliavini, "L'Evangelizzazione," 642–43.

111. Rodríguez and Martínez to Señán, February 20, 1814, p. 1.

112. Ibid.

113. Suñer and Peyri, "Respuesta," 1.

114. Mariano Payeras to Father President Estevan Tapis, January 13, 1810, Purísima mission, p. 1; CMD, SBMA.

115. Karen Spalding, *Huarochirí: An Andean Society under Inca and Spanish Rule* (Stanford: Stanford University Press, 1984).

116. Silverblatt, *Moon, Sun, and Witches.*

117. Martín and Sánchez, "Responden," 2.

118. Durán and Fortuny, "Infrascriptos," 1.

119. See Scott, *Weapons of the Weak.*

120. Juan Martín and Juan Cabot to José Señán, April 5, 1814, San Miguel mission, p. 2.

121. AMSB, Pap. Misc., vol. 7, pp. 181–83.

122. Múñoz and Nuez, "Respuesta," 2.

123. Señán, "Contestación," 9.

124. Amorós, "Respuesta," 4–4v.

125. Señán, "Contestación," 12.

126. Catalá and Viader, "Respuestas," 3.

127. Arroyo de la Cuesta, "Respuesta," 4.

128. Amorós, "Respuesta," 5.

129. Durán and Fortuny, "Infrascriptos," 4.

130. Olbés, "Respuesta," 4.

131. Amorós, "Respuesta," 6.

132. Abella and Sainz de Lucio, "Respuesta," 11.

133. Olbés, "Respuesta," 4.

134. Rodríguez and Martínez to Señán, February 20, 1814, San Luís Obispo mission, pp. 5–6.

Chapter 8. Partial Truths

1. James Clifford and George E. Marcus, eds., *Writing Culture: The Poetics and Politics of Ethnography* (Berkeley: University of California Press, 1986), 7.

2. Neither the petitions of María de León nor that of María Encarnación de Castro appears in Herbert E. Bolton's voluminous index for materials in the Mexican archives for the history of the United States. María de León's 1783 letter was found in a volume that was indexed by Bolton as "California. Correspondencia del Capitan Rivera con el Virrey"; her 1776 letter was indexed under the heading, "Transportation of the family of the lieutenant of the presidio of San Francisco at the expense of the treasury." María de la Encarnación Castro's letter (Manuel Ramón de Goya to the Fiscal de Real Hacienda, Mexico, July 17, 1783, AGN, Calif., vol. 31, exp. 37, fols. 318–21v) was in a volume indexed as including "Correspondence of the commissar, the commandant of marine, the treasurer, and the calker (*calafate*) of San Blas, concerning the affairs of the department." Herbert E. Bolton, *Guide to the Materials for United States History in the Archives of Mexico* (Washington, D.C.: Carnegie Institution of Washington, 1913), 125, 139, 149. In this chapter I cite a handful of other examples found by careful perusal of the Provincias Internas section of the Archivo General de la Nación. Another case is Prov. Int. vol. 210, exp. 7, fols. 186–92, also noted as "Minor affairs" in Bolton, *Guide to Materials,* 127.

3. G. Carrillo to Captain Pedro Fages, June 4, 1773, Archivo del Arzobispado de San Francisco, vol. 1, part 4, p. 6, indexed in Alexander Smith Taylor, "Chronological Index to the 5 Volumes of the Manuscript Letters of the Catholic Missionaries of California from 1772–1849," Monterey, 1859, MS, BL, C-C 212.

4. Hubert Howe Bancroft, *California Pioneer Register and Index 1542–1848* (Baltimore: Regional Publishing Co., 1964).

5. In order to distinguish between the Santa Barbara Mission Archives (SBMA) and the Bancroft Library transcripts of these same archives, I have retained the Spanish designation Archivo de la Misión de Santa Barbara (AMSB) to refer to the latter.

6. Though all of the extant journals and related correspondence from Anza's 1775–76 expedition have been published in English translation, thanks in large part to the monumental work of Herbert Bolton, I am aware of none that has been published in Spanish. Thus the researcher wishing to consult the original Spanish texts is forced to work with microfilms and manuscript copies. Bolton, *Anza's California Expeditions.*

7. Richard Price, *First-Time: The Historical Vision of an Afro-American People* (Baltimore: Johns Hopkins University Press, 1983), 5.

8. L. P. Condé and S. M. Hart, *Feminist Readings on Spanish and Latin-American Literature* (New York: Edwin Mellen Press, 1991), viii.

9. Greg Sarris, "Reading Narrated American Indian Lives: Elizabeth Colson's Autobiographies of Three Pomo Women," in *Keeping Slug Woman Alive: A Holistic Approach to American Indian Texts* (Berkeley: University of California Press, 1993), 81.

10. Ibid.

11. Price, *First-Time,* 7.

Bibliography

Archives

Archivo General de la Nación, Mexico, D.F. (AGN)
Bancroft Library, University of California, Berkeley
Beinecke Library, Yale University (New Haven, Conn.)
Instituto Nacional de Historia e Antropología, Mexico, D.F.
Monterey Historical Society (Monterey, Calif.)
Santa Barbara Mission Archives-Library
Smithsonian Museum of Natural History Anthropological Archives

Primary Sources

Amador, José María. "Memorias sobre la historia de California." Dictated to Thomas Savage, Whiskey Hill (San Luis Obispo), 1877. BL, HHBC, C-D 28.

Arenal, Electa, and Stacey Schlau. *Untold Sisters: Hispanic Nuns in Their Own Works.* Albuquerque: University of New Mexico Press, 1989.

Asisara, Lorenzo. "The Assassination of Padre Andres Quintana by the Indians of Mission Santa Cruz in 1812: The Narrative of Lorenzo Asisara." Ed. Edward D. Castillo. *CH* 68 (Fall 1989): 116–25.

———. "An Indian Account of the Decline and Collapse of Mexico's Hegemony over the Missionized Indians of California." Ed. Edward D. Castillo. *AIQ* 13 (1989): 391–408.

———. "Narrative of a Mission Indian." In *History of Santa Cruz County, California,* pp. 45–48. Ed. Edward S. Harrison. San Francisco: Pacific Press Publishing Company, 1892.

Avila, María Inocenta Pico. "Cosas de California." Dictated to Thomas Savage. 1878. BL, HHBC, C-D 34.

Avila de Ríos, Catarina. "Recuerdos." By Thomas Savage and Vicente Gómez. Santa Clara, June 20, 1877. BL, HHBC, C-D 35.

Bancroft, Hubert H. *The History of California.* 7 vols. San Francisco: History Company, 1890.

————. *History of Mexico.* 6 vols. San Francisco: Bancroft, 1883–89.

Bandini, José. "Descrisión de l'Alta California." 1828. BL, Cowan Collection.

Beechey, Frederick William. *Narrative of a Voyage to the Pacific and Beering's [sic] Strait to Cooperate with the Polar Expedition in the Years 1825, 26, 27, 28.* 2 vols. London: H. Colburn and R. Bentley, 1831.

Beeler, Madison S., ed. *The Ventureño Confesionario of José Señán, O.F.M.* Berkeley: University of California Press, 1967.

Betanzos, Juan de. *Narrative of the Incas.* Trans. and eds. Roland Hamilton and Dana Buchanan. Austin: University of Texas Press, 1996.

Bolton, Herbert E., trans. and ed. *Anza's California Expeditions.* 5 vols. New York: Alfred A. Knopf, 1930–39.

————, ed. *Spanish Exploration in the Southwest, 1542–1706.* New York: Barnes and Noble, 1963 [1908].

Boscana, Gerónimo. *Chinigchinich: A Historical Account of the Origin, Customs, and Traditions of the Indians at the Missionary Establishment of St. Juan Capistrano, Alta California.* Trans. Alfred Robinson. New York: Wiley and Putnam, 1846.

Bowman, J. N., and R. F. Heizer. *Anza and the Northwest Frontier of New Spain.* Southwest Museum Papers, no. 20. Los Angeles: Southwest Museum, 1967.

Browning, Peter, ed. *The Discovery of San Francisco Bay: The Portolá Expedition of 1769–1770. The Diary of Miguel Costansó in Spanish and English.* Lafayette, Calif.: Great West Books, 1992.

Burrus, Ernest J., S.J. *Diario del Comandante Fernando de Rivera y Moncada,* Part 2. Colección Chimalistac de Libros y Documentos acerca de la Nueva España. Madrid: Ediciones José Porrúa Turanzas, 1967.

Carrasco y Guisasola, Francisco. *Documentos referentes al reconocimiento de las costas de las Californias en los años 1584 a 1602.* Madrid: Dirección de Hidrografía, 1882.

Carter, Charles Franklin, trans. "Duhaut-Cilly's Account of California in the Years 1827–1828." Part 1: *CHSQ* 8 (June 1929): 130–66; part 2: *CHSQ* 8 (Sept. 1929): 214–50; part 3: *CHSQ* 8 (Dec. 1929): 306–36.

Carvajal, Gaspar de. *Relación del nuevo descubrimiento del famoso río Grande de las Amazonas.* 1541–42. Mexico: Fondo de Cultura Económica, 1955.

Casas, Bartolomé de las. *Brevísima relación de la destruycion de las Indias: colegidas por el Obispo do[n] fray Bartolomé de las Casas/o Casaus de la orden de Sa[n]cto Domingo.* Seville: Sebastián Trugillo, 1553.

————. *Historia de las Indias.* 3 vols. Eds. Agustín Millares Carlo and Lewis Hanke. Mexico: Fondo de Cultura Económica, 1951.

Cerruti, Henry. "Ramblings in California." 1874. Bancroft Library.

————, ed. "Relación de la entrevista que tuve con Isidora viuda del Principe Solano." In *Pioneer Sketches,* no. 12, April 9, 1874. BL.

César, Julio. "Cosas de Indios de California," May 1878. BL, HHBC, C-D 109.

———. "Recollections of My Youth at San Luis Rey Mission." *Touring Topics* 22 (Nov. 1930): 42–43.

Colón, Cristóbal. *Los cuatro viajes. Testamento,* ed. Consuelo Varela. Madrid: Alianza Editorial, 1986.

———. *Textos y documentos completos.* Ed. Consuelo Varela. Madrid: Alianza, 1982.

Colson, Elizabeth. *Autobiography of Three Pomo Women.* 1941. Berkeley: University of California Archeological Research Facility, Department of Anthropology, 1974.

Coronel, Don Antonio Franco. "Cosas de California." 1877. BL, HHBC, C-D 61.

Costansó, Miguel. "Diario Histórico de los Viages de Mar, y Tierra Hechos al Norte de la California," Mexico, October 24, 1770, BL, fols. 53–54.

Covarrubias Horozco, Sebastián. *Tesoro de la Lengua Castellana o española según la impresión de 1611, con las adiciones de Benito Remigio Noydens.* 1674. Facsimile edition, Barcelona: S. A. Horta, 1943.

Cutter, Donald. *The California Coast: Documents from the Sutro Collection.* 1891. Reprint, Norman: University of Oklahoma Press, 1969.

del Portillo y Diez de Sollano, Alvaro. *Descubrimiento y exploración en las costas de California.* Madrid: Consejo Superior de Investigaciones Científicas, 1947.

Díaz del Castillo, Bernal. *Historia verdadera de la conquista de la Nueva España.* Ed. Miguel León-Portilla. Madrid: Historia 16, 1985.

Eastwood, Alice, ed. "Menzies' California Journal." *CHSQ* 2 (Jan. 1924): 265–340.

Fages, Pedro. *Breve descripción histórica política y natural de la Alta California 1770–1774.* Ed. Andrés Henestrosa. 1775. Reprint, Mexico: Fondo Pagliai, 1973.

———. *A Historical, Political, and Natural Description of California.* Trans. and ed., Herbert Ingram Priestley. Berkeley: University of California Press, 1937.

Figueroa, José. *Manifesto to the Mexican Republic.* Translated with introduction and notes by C. Alan Hutchinson. Berkeley: University of California Press, 1978.

Font, Pedro. "Diario que forma el P. Fr. Pedro Font Pdo^r Ap^{co} del Colegio de la Sta Cruz de Queretaro, sacado del borrador que escrivio en el camino del viage que hizo à Monterey y Puerto de S^n. Francisco." Horcasitas. September 29, 1775–June 23, 1776. BL, Cowan Collection.

———. "Diario que formó el P. Pdo. Apco. Fr. Pedro Font Missionero . . . en el viage que hizo à Monterey," Horcasitas, September 29, 1775–Tubutama, May 11, 1777, original in John Carter Brown Library, Brown University, Providence, R.I., photocopy in BL, Bolton Papers, no. 137, carton 11, fol. 15.

———. "Font's Complete Diary: A Chronicle of the Founding of San Francisco." In *Anza's California Expeditions.* 5 vols. Ed. Herbert E. Bolton. Berkeley: University of California Press, 1933.

García, Inocente. "Hechos Históricos de California, Relatados por Inocente García, Vecino de San Luis Obispo, 1878, Apuntados por Thomas Savage." San Luis Obispo. April 12–15, 1878. BL, HHBC, C-D 84.

Geiger, Maynard, ed. "Fray Antonio Ripoll's Description of the Chumash Revolt at Santa Barbara in 1824." *SCQ* 52 (Dec. 1970): 345–64.

———, ed. *The Letter of Luis Jayme, O.F.M., San Diego, October 17, 1772.* Los Angeles: Glen Dawson, 1970.

———, ed. "Questionnaire of the Spanish Government in 1812 concerning the Native Culture of the California Mission Indians." *Americas* 5 (Apr. 1949): 474–90.

Geiger, Maynard, and Clement Meighan, eds. *As the Padres Saw Them: California Indian Life and Customs as Reported by the Franciscan Missionaries, 1813–1815.* Santa Barbara: Santa Barbara Mission Archive Library, 1976.

Guerra de Hartnell, María Teresa de la. "Narrativa de la distinguida matrona californiana Doña Teresa de la Guerra de Hartnell dictada el día doce de marzo de 1875 en el rancho del Alizal y reprendada el día 21 del mismo mes y año en el mismo rancho." By Enrique Cerruti. Monterey, March 1875. BL, C-E 67:2

Hammond, George P., and Agapito Rey. *Narratives of the Coronado Expedition, 1540–1542.* Albuquerque: University of New Mexico Press, 1940.

Harrington, John P. *The Eye of the Flute: Chumash Traditional History and Ritual as Told by Fernando Librado Kitsepawit to John P. Harrington.* Banning, Calif.: Malki Museum Press, 1981.

Hartnell, Margaret. "The Grandmother We Never Met." Typescript, n.d. Monterey Historical Society Collection.

Heizer, Robert F., ed. *Hugo Reid, The Indians of Los Angeles County.* Los Angeles: Southwest Museum, 1968.

———, ed. "Missionaries' Replies to the Interrogatorio of 1812." In *The Costanoan Indians,* pp. 45–69. Local History Studies, no. 18. Cupertino, Calif.: California History Center, De Anza College, 1974.

Hernández Sánchez-Barba, Mario, ed. *Cartas de relación.* Madrid: Historia 16, 1985.

Herrera, Antonio de. *Historia general de los hechos de los Castellanos.* 4 vols. Madrid: En la Emplentarea, 1601–15.

Hewes, Minna, and Gordon Hewes, eds. "Indian Life and Customs at Mission San Louis Rey: A Record of California Mission Life by Pablo Tac, an Indian Neophyte, Written at Rome about 1835." Reprinted in *Americas* 9:1 (1952): 87–106.

Hudson, Travis, ed. *Breath of the Sun: Life in Early California as Told by a Chumash Indian, Fernando Librado, to John P. Harrington.* Banning, Calif.: Malki Museum Press, 1979.

———, ed. "The Chumash Revolt of 1824: Another Native Account from the Notes of John P. Harrington." *JCGBA* 2 (Summer 1980): 123–26.

Kenneally, Finbar K., trans. and ed. *Writings of Fermín Francisco de Lasúen.* 2 vols. Washington, D.C.: Academy of American Franciscan History, 1965.

Khlebnikov, Kirill Timofeevich. "Memoirs of California." Trans. Anatole G. Mazour. *PHR* 9 (Sept. 1940): 307–36.

Konetzke, Richard, ed. *Colección de documentos para la historia de la formación social de Hispanoamérica, 1493–1810.* 3 vols. in 5. Madrid: Consejo Superior de Investigaciones Científicas, 1953.

Kostromitonov, P. "Notes on the Indians in Upper California." In *Ethnographic*

Observations on the Coast Miwok and Pomo by Contre-Admiral F. P. Von Wrangell and P. Kostromitonov of the Russian Colony Ross, 1839. Trans. Fred Stross. Berkeley: University of California, Department of Anthropology, 1974.

Kroeber, Alfred L. "A Mission Record of the California Indians from a Manuscript in the Bancroft Library," *UCPAAE* 8:1 (May 28, 1908): 1–27.

Laird, Carobeth. *Encounter with an Angry God: Recollections of My Life with John Peabody Harrington.* Banning, Calif.: Malki Museum Press, 1975.

Langsdorff, Georg von. *Voyages and Travels in Various Parts of the World, during the years 1803, 1804, 1805.* 2 vols. London: B. Clarke, 1813–14.

Leese, Rosalia. "History of the Bear Party." June 27, 1874. BL, C-E 65-10.

Lorenzana, Apolinaria. "Memorias de Doña Apolinaria Lorenzana 'La Beata' Vieja de unos setenta y cinco años." Santa Barbara, 1878. BL, HHBC, C-D 116.

Lugo, José del Carmen. "Vida de un ranchero: Los Angeles." October 30, 1877. BL, HHBC, C-D 118.

Machado, Juana Alipaz de Ridington. "Los Tiempos Pasados de la Alta California." Dictated to Thomas Savage. North San Diego. January 11, 1878. BL, HHBC, C-D 119.

———. "Times Gone By in Alta California: Recollections of Señora Doña Juana Machado Alipaz de Ridington." Ed. Raymond S. Brandes. *HSSCQ* 41 (Sept. 1959): 195–240.

Margolin, Malcolm, ed. *Monterey in 1786: The Journals of Jean François de la Perouse.* Berkeley: Heyday Books, 1989.

———, ed. *The Way We Lived: California Indian Reminiscences, Stories, and Songs.* Berkeley: Heyday Books, 1981.

Mills, Elaine L., and Ann J. Brickfield. *A Guide to the Field Notes: Native American History, Language, and Culture of Southern California/Basin.* Vol. 3 of *The Papers of John Peabody Harrington in the Smithsonian Institution, 1907–1957.* 9 vols. White Plains, N.Y.: Kraus International, 1986.

Mills, Kenneth, and William B. Taylor, eds. *Colonial Spanish America: A Documentary History.* Wilmington, Del.: Scholarly Resources, 1998.

Ministerio de Fomento. *Cartas de Indias.* Madrid: Impresa de M. G. Hernández, 1877.

Möllhausen, H. B. *Diary of a Journey from the Mississippi to the Coasts of the Pacific with a U.S. Exploring Expedition,* 2 vols. London, 1860.

Mollins, Margaret, and Virginia E. Thickens, eds. "Ramblings in California: The Adventures of Henry Cerruti." Typescript. Berkeley: Friends of the Bancroft Library, 1954.

Nebrija, Antonio de. *Gramática castellana: Reproduction phototypique de l'edition princeps (1492).* Ed. E. Walberg. Halle: M. Niemeyer, 1909.

Ord, Angustias de la Guerra. "Ocurrencias en California." Santa Barbara. 1878. BL, HHBC, C-D 134.

Ord, Rebecca R. "Recuerdos," as told by her mother, Angustias de la Guerra Ord.

December 31, 1880. Trans. Luis Moreno. Santa Barbara, TS, Santa Barbara Trust for Historic Preservation.

Ordóñez de Montalvo, Garcí. *The Labors of the Very Brave Knight Esplandián.* Trans. William Thomas Little. Binghamton, N.Y.: State University of New York, Center for Medieval and Early Renaissance Studies, 1992.

———. *Las sergas de Esplandián.* Biblioteca de Autores Españoles, Libros de Caballerías, vol. 40. 1857. Reprint, Madrid: M. Rivadeneyra, 1874, 1880.

Oviedo, Gonzalo Fernández de. *Historia general y natural de las Indias.* 4 vols. Ed. José Amador de los Ríos. Written in 1548, first published in 1557. Reprint, Madrid: Ediciones Atlas, 1959.

Pacheco, Joaquín, Francisco de Cárdenas, and Luis Torres de Mendoza, eds. *Colección de documentos inéditos, relativos al descubrimiento, conquista y organización de las antiguas posesiones españolas de América y Oceania.* 42 vols. Madrid: Imprenta de Fias y compañía, Misericordia, 1867.

Palou, Francisco, O.F.M. *Noticias de la Nueva California.* 4 vols. San Francisco: California Historical Society, 1874.

———. *Relación histórica de la vida y apostólicas tareas del venerable padre Fray Junipero Serra.* Ed. Miguel León-Portilla. Mexico: Editorial Porrúa, 1970.

Pérez, Eulalia. "Una vieja y sus recuerdos dictados a la edad avanzada de 139 años." Dictated to Thomas Savage. San Gabriel, Calif., 1877. BL, HHBC, C-D 139. Facsimile published in *Three Memoirs of Mexican California.* Berkeley: Friends of the Bancroft Library, University of California, 1988.

Perouse, Comte Jean François de Galaup de la. *Voyage de La Perouse autour du monde.* Paris: Imprimerie de la Republique, 1791.

Petit-Thouars, Abel du. *Voyage autour du monde sur la fregate la Venus, pendant les années 1836–1839: Publié par ordre du roi.* Paris: Gide, 1840–55.

Porrúa Turanzas, José, ed. *Noticias y documentos acerca de las Californias, 1764–1795.* Colección Chimalistac de Libros y Documentos acerca de la Nueva España, no. 5. Madrid: Porrúa Turanzas, 1959.

Powers, Stephen. *Tribes of California.* Contributions to North American Ethnology Series, no. 3. Washington, D.C.: Government Printing Office, 1877.

Prescott, William H. *History of the Conquest of Mexico, with a Preliminary View of the Ancient Mexican Civilization, and the Life of the Conquerer, Hernando Cortes.* 2 vols. London: Routledge, Warre, and Routledge, 1865.

Priestley, Herbert I., ed. and trans. *The Colorado River Campaign, 1781–1782: Diary of Pedro Fages.* Publications of the Academy of Pacific Coast History, vol. 3, no. 2. Berkeley: University of California Press, 1913.

Purchas, Samuel. *Hakluytus Posthumus, or Purchas his Pilgrimes: Contayning a History of the World in Sea Voyages and Lande Travells by Englishmen and Others.* 20 vols. Glasgow: J. MacLehose and Sons, 1905–7.

Recopilación de leyes de los reynos de las Indias. 4 vols. Madrid: A. Ortega, 1774.

Richardson, H. D. "History of the Foundation of the City of Vallejo." Sketches of California Pioneers Series. 1874. BL, C-E 65:3.

Rima de Vallbona, ed. *Vida i sucesos de la monja alférez: Autobiografía atribuida a Doña Catalina de Erauso.* Tempe: Center for Latin American Studies, Arizona State University, 1992.

Rodríguez Cermenho, Sebastián. *The Voyage to California of Sebastián Rodríguez Cermeño in 1595.* Trans. Henry R. Wagner. San Francisco: California Historical Society, 1924.

Rollins, M. "Philological and Pathological Memoir on the Americans, by M. Rollins, M.D., Surgeon Major of the Boussole Frigate." In *The Voyage of La Perouse Round the World, in the Years 1785, 1786, 1787, and 1788, with the Nautical Tables,* vol. 2, pp. 260–79. London: J. Stockdale, 1798.

Savage, Thomas. "Report of Labors in Archives and Procuring Material for History of California." 1876–79. BL, C-E 191.

Shipek, Florence. *Delfina Cuero: Her Autobiography, An Account of Her Last Years and Her Ethnobotanic Contributions by Florence Connolly Shipek.* Menlo Park, Calif.: Ballena Press, 1991.

Simpson, Sir George. *Narrative of a Voyage to California Ports in 1841–1842.* Fairfield, Wash.: Ye Galleon Press, 1988.

Simpson, Lesley Byrd. *The Letters of José Señán, O.F.M., Mission San Buenaventura, 1796–1823.* San Francisco: John Howell Books, 1962.

Sitjar, Buenaventura. *Vocabulario de la lengua de los naturales de la mision de San Antonio, Alta California.* Shea's Library of American Linguistics, no. 7. 1797. Reprint, New York, 1861.

Smith, Buckingham. *Colección de varios documentos para la historia de la Florida y tierras adyacentes,* vol. 1. London: Trubner y Compañía, 1857.

Smith, Donald, and Frederick Teggart, eds. *Diary of Gaspar de Portolá during the California Expedition of 1769–1770.* Publications of the Academy of Pacific Coast History, 1:3. Berkeley: University of California Press, 1909.

Solano, Isidora. "My Years with Chief Solano." Trans. Nellie Van de Grift Sánchez. *Touring Topics* 22 (Feb. 1930): 39, 52.

Soulé, Frank, John H. Gihon, and James Nisbet. *The Annals of San Francisco: Containing a Summary of the History of the First Discovery, Settlement, Progress, and Present Condition of California, and a Complete History of All the Important Events Connected with Its Great City.* San Francisco: Montgomery Street, 1855.

Spott, Robert, and Alfred A. Kroeber, eds. *Yurok Narratives.* UCPAAE 35:9. Berkeley: University of California Press, 1942.

Tagliavini, Carlo. "L'Evangelizzazione e i costumi degli Indi Luiseños secondo la narrazione di un chierico indigeno." In *Proceedings of the Twenty-Third International Congress of Americanists, 1928* (New York, 1930): 633–48.

———. "Frammento d'un dizionarietto Luiseño-Spagnuolo scritto da un indigeno."

In *Proceedings of the Twenty-Third International Congress of Americanists, 1928* (New York, 1930): 905–17.

———. "La lingua degli Indi Luiseños (Alta California) secondo gli appunti grammaticali inediti di un chierico indigeno." *Biblioteca dell'Archiginnasio,* series 2, vol. 31 (Bologna, 1926).

Tarakanoff, Vassilli Petrovitch. *Statement of My Captivity among the Californians.* Trans. Ivan Petroff. Early California Travels Series, no. 14. Los Angeles: Glen Dawson, 1953.

Taylor, Alexander Smith. "Chronological Index to the Five Volumes (Bound in 8 Volumes) of the Manuscript Letters of the Catholic Missionaries of California from 1772–1849." Monterey, Calif., MS, 1859. BL, C-C 212.

———. *The First Voyage to the Coast of California, made in the Years 1542 and 1543, by Juan Rodríguez Cabrillo and His Pilot Bartolomé Ferrelo.* San Francisco: Le Count and Strong, 1853.

Tibesar, Antonine, ed. and trans. *Writings of Junípero Serra.* 4 vols. Academy of American Franciscan Historical Documentary Series, nos. 4–7. Washington, D.C.: Academy of American Franciscan History, 1955–66.

Torquemada, Juan de. *The Voyage of Sebastián Vizcaíno to the Coast of California, Together with a Map & Sebastián Vizcaíno's Letter Written at Monterey, December 28, 1602.* San Francisco: Book Club of California, 1933.

Valdés, José Ramón. "Memorias." San Buenaventura, February 15, 1878. BL, HHBC, C-D 164.

Valdez, Dorotea. "Reminiscences." June 27, 1874. Bancroft Library, HHBC, C-E 65:8.

Vallejo, Guadalupe. "Ranch and Mission Days in Alta California." *Century Magazine* 41 (Dec. 1890): 186–87.

Vancouver, George. *A Voyage of Discovery to the North Pacific Ocean, and Round the World; in which the Coast of North-West America Has Been Carefully Examined and Accurately Surveyed. Undertaken by His Majesty's Command, Principally with a View to Ascertain the Existence of any Navigable Communication between the North Pacific and North Atlantic Oceans; and Performed in the Years 1790, 1791, 1792, 1793, 1794, and 1795, in the Discovery Sloop of War, and Armed Tender Chatham, under the Command of Captain George Vancouver.* 3 vols. London: Printed for G. G. and J. Robinson, Paternoster Row; and J. Edwards, Pall-Mall, 1798.

Wagner, Henry R. *Spanish Voyages to the Northwest Coast of America in the Sixteenth Century.* San Francisco: California Historical Society, 1929.

Weber, Francis J. *Prominent Visitors to the California Missions.* Los Angeles: Glen Dawson, 1991.

Secondary Sources

Adorno, Rolena. "Reconsidering Colonial Discourse for Sixteenth- and Seventeenth-Century Spanish America." *LARR* 28:3 (1993): 135–45.

Almaraz, Felix Jr. *The San Antonio Missions and Their System of Land Tenure.* Austin: University of Texas Press, 1989.

Alonso, Ana María. *Thread of Blood: Colonialism, Revolution, and Gender on Mexico's Northern Frontier.* Tucson: University of Arizona Press, 1995.

Altamira, Rafael, ed. "El texto de las leyes de Burgos de 1512." *RHA* 4 (1938): 5–79.

Andrien, Kenneth, and Rolena Adorno. *Transatlantic Encounters: Europeans and Andeans in the Sixteenth Century.* Berkeley: University of California Press, 1991.

Archibald, Robert. *The Economic Aspects of the California Missions.* Washington, D.C.: Academy of American Franciscan History, 1978.

———. "The Economy of the Alta California Mission, 1803–1821." *SCQ* 58 (Summer 1976): 227–40.

———. "Indian Labor at the California Missions: Slavery or Salvation?" *JSDH* 24 (Spring 1978): 172–82.

Armitage, Susan. "Women and Men in Western History: A Stereoptical Vision." *WHQ* 16 (Oct. 1985): 381–95.

Armitage, Susan, and Elizabeth Jameson. *The Women's West.* Norman: University of Oklahoma Press, 1987.

Arrom, Silvia. *The Women of Mexico City, 1790–1857.* Stanford, Calif.: Stanford University Press, 1985.

Axtell, James L. "The European Failure to Convert the Indians: An Autopsy." In *Proceedings of the Sixth Algonquin Conference,* pp. 146–91. Mercury Series. Ottawa: National Museum of Man, 1975.

Bancroft, Hubert H. *California Pioneer Register and Index, 1542–1848.* Baltimore: Regional Publishing Company, 1964 [1886].

———. *The Works of Hubert Howe Bancroft, vols. 18–21: The History of California.* San Francisco: A. L. Bancroft, 1884–86.

———. *The Works of Hubert Howe Bancroft, vols. 22–24: The History of California.* San Francisco: History Co., 1886–90.

———. *The Works of Hubert Howe Bancroft, vol. 34: California Pastoral, 1769–1848.* San Francisco: A. L. Bancroft, 1888.

Bannon, John Francis. "The Mission as a Frontier Institution: Sixty Years of Interest and Research." *WHQ* 10 (July 1979): 302–22.

Bataille, Gretchen M., and Kathleen Mullen Sands. *American Indian Women, Telling Their Lives.* Lincoln: University of Nebraska, 1984.

Bean, Lowell J. "Social Organization in Native California." In *Antap: California Indian Political and Economic Organization,* pp. 11–34. Eds. Lowell J. Bean and T. F. King. Menlo Park, Calif.: Ballena Press, 1974.

———. "Social Organization in Native California." In *Native Californians: A Theoretical Retrospective,* pp. 99–123. Eds. Lowell J. Bean and Thomas C. Blackburn. Ramona, Calif.: Ballena Press, 1976.

Bean, Walton, and James J. Rawls. *California: An Interpretive History.* San Francisco: McGraw-Hill, 1988.

Bee, Robert L. *Crosscurrents along the Colorado: The Impact of Government Policy on the Quechan Indians.* Tucson: University of Arizona Press, 1981.

Beilharz, Edwin A. *Felipe de Neve: First Governor of California.* San Francisco: California Historical Society, 1971.

Berger, Pamela. *The Goddess Obscured: Transformation of the Grain Protectress from Goddess to Saint.* Boston: Beacon Press, 1985.

Billington, Ray Allen. *America's Frontier Heritage.* New York: Holt, Rinehart and Winston, 1966.

Blackburn, Thomas, ed. "The Chumash Revolt of 1824: A Native Account." *JCA* 2 (Winter 1975): 223–27.

Blok, Josine H. *The Early Amazons: Modern and Ancient Perspectives on a Persistent Myth.* New York: E. J. Brill, 1995.

Bolton, Herbert E. *Guide to the Materials for United States History in the Archives of Mexico.* Washington, D.C.: Carnegie Institution of Washington, 1913.

——. "The Mission as a Frontier Institution in the Spanish-American Colonies." *AHR* 23 (Oct. 1917): 42–61.

——. *Outpost of Empire.* Berkeley: University of California Press, 1930.

Bouvier, Virginia M. "Women, Conquest, and the Production of History: Hispanic California, 1542–1840." Ph.D. diss., University of California, Berkeley, 1995.

Bowman, Jacob N. "Prominent Women in Provincial California." *HSSCQ* 39 (June 1957): 149–67.

——. *Ranchos of California.* Fresno, Calif.: Academy Library Guild, 1956.

——. "The Resident Neophytes (Existentes) of the California Missions, 1769–1834." *HSSCQ* 40 (June 1958): 138–46.

Bowser, Frederick. "The African in Colonial Spanish America: Reflections on Research Achievements and Priorities." *LARR* 7:1 (1972): 77–94.

Boxer, Charles R. *Mary and Misogyny: Women in Iberian Expansion Overseas, 1415–1815.* London: Duckworth, 1975.

Boyer, Richard. *Lives of the Bigamists: Marriage, Family, and Community in Colonial Mexico.* Albuquerque: University of New Mexico Press, 1995.

Brading, David. *Church and State in Bourbon Mexico: The Diocese of Michoacán, 1749–1810.* Cambridge: Cambridge University Press, 1994.

——. *The First America: The Spanish Monarchy, Creole Patriots, and the Liberal State 1492–1867.* New York: Cambridge University Press, 1991.

Brady, Victoria, Sarah Crome, and Lyn Reese. "Resist! Survival Tactics of Indian Women." *CH* 63 (Spring 1984): 141–51.

Brink, Jean R., Maryanne C. Horowitz, and Allison P. Coudert, eds. *Playing with Gender: A Renaissance Pursuit.* Urbana: University of Illinois Press, 1991.

Brown, Jennifer S. H. *Strangers in Blood: Fur Trade Company Families in Indian Country.* Vancouver: University of British Columbia Press, 1980.

——. "Women as Centre and Symbol in the Emergence of Métis Communities." *Canadian Journal of Native Studies* 3 (1983).

Brown, Lester B., ed. *Two Spirit People: American Indian Lesbian Women and Gay Men.* New York: Haworth, 1997.

Burkett, Elinor. "Indian Women and White Society: The Case of Sixteenth-Century Peru." In *Latin American Women: Historical Perspectives,* pp. 101–28. Ed. Asunción Lavrín. Westport, Conn.: 1978.

Burnett, Georgellen. *We Just Toughed It Out: Women in the Llano Estacado.* Southwestern Studies, no. 90. University of Texas at El Paso: Texas Western Press, 1990.

Callender, Charles, and Lee M. Kochems. "The North American Berdache." In *Culture and Human Sexuality: A Reader,* pp. 367–97. Eds. David N. Suggs and Andrew W. Miracle. Pacific Grove, Calif.: Brooks/Cole Publishing Company, 1993.

Campbell, Ena. "The Virgin of Guadalupe and the Female Self-Image: A Mexican Case History." In *Mother Worship: Theme and Variations,* pp. 5–24. Ed. James J. Preston. Chapel Hill: University of North Carolina Press, 1982.

Campbell, Leon. "The First Californios: Presidial Society in Spanish California, 1769–1822." *JW* 11 (Oct. 1972): 582–95.

Caplan, Pat. *The Cultural Construction of Sexuality.* New York: Tavistock, 1987.

Castañeda, Antonia. "Comparative Frontiers: The Migration of Women to Alta California and New Zealand." In *Western Women: Their Land, Their Lives,* pp. 283–301. Eds. Lillian Schlissel, Vicki L. Ruiz, and Janice Monk. Albuquerque: University of New Mexico Press, 1988.

———. "Engendering the History of Alta California, 1769–1848: Gender, Sexuality, and the Family." *CH* 76:2–3 (Summer–Fall 1997): 230–59.

———. "Gender, Race, and Culture: Spanish-Mexican Women in the Historiography of Frontier California." *Frontiers* 11 (1990): 8–20.

———. "Marriage: The Spanish Borderlands." In *Encyclopedia of North American Colonies,* vol. 2, pp. 727–38. Eds. Jack Ernest Cooke et al. New York: Scribner's Sons, 1993.

———. "Presidarias y Pobladoras: Spanish-Mexican Women in Frontier Monterey, Alta California, 1770–1821." Ph.D. diss., Stanford University, 1990.

Castillo, Edward D., ed. *Native American Perspectives on the Hispanic Colonization of Alta California.* Spanish Borderlands Source Book, no. 26. New York: Garland, 1991.

Castillo, Edward, and Doyce Nunis, Jr. "California Mission Indians: Two Perspectives." *CH* 70 (Summer 1991): 206–15, 236–38.

Cevallos-Candau, Francisco Javier, Jeffrey A. Cole, Nina M. Scott, and Nicomedes Suárez-Araúz, eds. *Coded Encounters: Writing, Gender, and Ethnicity in Colonial Latin America.* Amherst: University of Massachusetts Press, 1994.

Chapman, Charles. *A History of California: The Spanish Period.* New York: Macmillan, 1921.

Christian, William O., Jr. *Local Religion in Sixteenth-Century Spain.* Princeton, N.J.: Princeton University Press, 1981.

Clendinnen, Inga. *Ambivalent Conquest: Mayan and Spanish in Yucatan, 1517–1570.* Oxford: Oxford University Press, 1987.

——. "Yucatec Maya Women and the Spanish Conquest: Role and Ritual in Historical Reconstruction." *JSH* 15 (1982): 427–42.

Clifford, James, and George E. Marcus, eds. *Writing Culture: The Poetics and Politics of Ethnography.* Berkeley: University of California Press, 1986.

Cline, Howard F., ed. *Latin American History: Essays on Its Study and Teaching, 1898–1965.* 2 vols. Austin: University of Texas Press, 1967.

Condé, L. P., and S. M. Hart, eds. *Feminist Readings on Spanish and Latin-American Literature.* New York: Edwin Mellen Press, 1991.

Cook, Sherburne F. *The Aboriginal Population of the North Coast of California.* Berkeley: University of California Press, 1956.

——. *The Conflict between the California Indian and White Civilization.* Ibero-Americana, no. 21. 1943. Reprint, Berkeley: University of California Press, 1963.

——. *Expeditions to the Interior of California's Central Valley, 1820–1840.* Anthropological Records, vol. 20, no. 5. Berkeley: University of California Press, 1962.

——. *The Population of the California Indians, 1769–1970.* Berkeley: University of California Press, 1976.

——. *Population Trends among the California Mission Indians.* Ibero-Americana, no. 17. Berkeley: University of California Press, 1940.

Cook, Sherburne F., and Woodrow Borah. "Mission Registers as Sources of Vital Statistics: Eight Missions of Northern California." In *Essays in Population History: Mexico and California.* Eds. Sherburne F. Cook and Woodrow Borah. Berkeley: University of California Press, 1979.

Cook, Warren. *Flood Tide of Empire: Spain and the Pacific Northwest, 1543–1819.* New Haven, Conn.: Yale University Press, 1973.

Cope, R. Douglas. *The Limits of Racial Domination: Plebeian Society in Colonial Mexico City, 1660–1720.* Madison: University of Wisconsin Press, 1994.

Cortés Alonso, Vicente. "Los esclavos domésticos en América." *AEA* 24 (1967): 955–83.

——. "La imagen del otro: Indios, blancos y negros en el México del siglo XVI." *Revista de Indias* 51 (May–Aug. 1991): 259–92.

Costello, Julia G., ed. *Documentary Evidence for the Spanish Missions of Alta California.* Spanish Borderlands Sourcebooks, no. 14. New York: Garland, 1991.

——. Variability among the Alta California Missions: The Economics of Agricultural Production." In *Columbian Consequences, vol. 3: The Spanish Borderlands in Pan-American Perspectives,* pp. 435–50. Ed. David Hurst Thomas. Washington, D.C.: Smithsonian Institution Press, 1991.

Costo, Rupert, and Jeannette Costo, eds. *The Missions of California: A Legacy of Genocide.* San Francisco: Indian Historian Press, 1987.

Couturier, Edith. "Women and the Family in Eighteenth-Century Mexico: Law and Practice." *JFH* 8 (Fall 1985): 294–304.

Culleton, James. *Indians and Pioneers of Old Monterey: Being a Chronicle of the Religious History of Carmel Mission.* Academy of California Church History Series, no. 2. Fresno: Academy of California Church History, 1950.

Cutter, Donald C. "Sources of the Name 'California.'" *Arizona and the West* 3 (Autumn 1961): 233–43.

Cypess, Sandra Messinger. "Los géneros re/velados in *Los empeños de una casa* de Sor Juana Inés de la Cruz." *Hispamérica* (1993): 177–85.

———. *La Malinche in Mexican Literature: From History to Myth.* Austin: University of Texas Press, 1991.

Dakin, Susanna Bryant. *Rose, or Rose Thorn? Three Women of Spanish California.* Berkeley: Friends of the Bancroft Library, 1963.

———. *A Scotch Paisano: Hugo Reid's Life in California, 1832–1852, Derived from His Correspondence.* Berkeley: University of California Press, 1939.

Del Castillo, Adelaida R. *Between Borders: Essays on Mexicana/Chicana History.* Encino, Calif.: Floricanto Press, 1990.

Demarest, Donald, and Coley Taylor. *The Dark Virgin: The Book of Our Lady of Guadalupe.* Freeport, Maine: Coley Taylor, 1956.

Deutsch, Sandra McGee. *No Separate Refuge: Culture, Class, and Gender on an Anglo-Hispanic Frontier, 1880–1940.* New York: Oxford University Press, 1987.

———. "Women and Intercultural Relations: The Case of Hispanic New Mexico and Colorado." *Signs* 12 (Summer 1987): 719–39.

Devens, Carol. *Countering Colonization: Native American Women and Great Lakes Missions, 1630–1900.* Berkeley: University of California Press, 1992.

———. "Separate Confrontations: Gender as a Factor in Indian Adaptation to European Colonization in New France." *AQ* 38 (Bibliography Issue, 1986): 461–80.

Downs, Jane, and Nancy Baker Jones. *Women and Texas History: Selected Essays.* Austin: Texas State Historical Association, 1993.

DuBois, Constance G. "The Religion of the Luiseño Indians." *UCPAAE* 8 (1908): 69–173.

DuBois, Cora. "The 1870 Ghost Dance." In *The California Indians: A Source Book,* pp. 496–99. Eds. Robert E. Heizer and M. A. Whipple. Berkeley: University of California Press, 1971.

DuBois, Ellen Carol, and Vicki L. Ruiz, eds. *Unequal Sisters: A Multicultural Reader in U.S. Women's History.* New York: Routledge, 1990.

Dysart, Jane. "Mexican Women in San Antonio, 1830–1860: The Assimilation Process." *WHQ* 7 (Oct. 1976): 365–75.

Eisler, Riane. *The Chalice and the Blade: Our History, Our Future.* San Francisco: Harper and Row, 1987.

Eldredge, Zoeth Skinner, ed. *History of California.* 5 vols. New York: Century History, 1915.

Elstob, Winston, and Helen Shropshire. *Handbook for the Re-enactment of the Juan Bautista de Anza Expedition, 1775–1776.* Monterey: California Heritage Guides, 1975.

Engelhardt, the Reverend Zephyrin, O.F.M. "Miscellany: Interrogatorio y Respuestas of Fr. Jose Señán, August 11, 1815." *Catholic Historical Review* 5 (April 1919): 55–70.

————. *Mission La Concepción Purísima de María Santísima.* Santa Barbara: Mission Santa Barbara, 1932.

————. *Missions and Missionaries of California.* 2 vols. 2d ed. Santa Barbara: Santa Barbara Mission Archive-Library, 1930.

————. *Mission San Luis Obispo in the Valley of the Bears.* Santa Barbara: Mission Santa Barbara, 1933.

————. *San Gabriel Mission and the Beginnings of Los Angeles.* San Gabriel, Calif.: Mission San Gabriel, 1927.

Etienne, Mona, and Eleanor Leacock, eds. *Women and Colonization: Anthropological Perspectives.* New York: J. F. Bergin, 1980.

Exley, Jo Ella Powell. *Texas Tears and Texas Sunshine: Voices of Frontier Women.* College Station: Texas A&M University Press, 1984.

Faragher, John Mack. "The Custom of the Country: Cross-Cultural Marriage in the Far Western Fur Trade." In *Western Women: Their Land, Their Lives,* pp. 199–215. Eds. Lillian Schlissel, Vicki L. Ruiz, and Janice Monk. Albuquerque: University of New Mexico Press, 1988.

Farriss, Nancy. *Mayan Society under Colonial Rule: The Collective Enterprise of Survival.* Princeton, N.J.: Princeton University Press, 1984.

Feldman, Lawrence H. *Indian Payment in Kind: The Sixteenth-Century Encomiendas of Guatemala.* Lancaster, Calif.: Labyrinthos, 1992.

Fernández Duro, Cesáreo. *La mujer española en Indias.* Madrid: Estab. tip. de la viuda e hijos de M. Tello, 1902.

Fischer, Christiane. *Let Them Speak for Themselves: Women in the American West, 1849–1900.* Hamden, Conn.: Archon Books, 1977.

Foote, Cheryl J. *Women of the New Mexico Frontier, 1846–1912.* Niwot, Colo.: University Press of Colorado, 1990.

Forbes, Jack D. "Black Pioneers: The Spanish-Speaking Afroamericans of the Southwest." In *Minorities in California,* pp. 20–33. Eds. George E. Frakes and Curtis B. Solberg. New York: Random House, 1971.

————. "Frontier in American History and the Role of the Frontier Historian." *Ethnohistory* 15 (Spring 1968): 203–35.

————. "Hispano-Mexican Pioneers of the San Francisco Bay Region: An Analysis of Racial Origins." *Aztlán* 14 (Spring 1983): 175–89.

————. *Warriors of the Colorado: The Yumas of the Quechan Nation and Their Neighbors.* Norman: University of Oklahoma Press, 1965.

Forde, C. Daryll. *Ethnography of the Yuma Indians.* UCPAAE 28:4. Berkeley: University of California Press, 1931.

Frakes, George E., and Curtis B. Solberg, eds. *Minorities in California.* New York: Random House, 1971.

Francis, Jessie Davis. *An Economic and Social History of Mexican California.* New York: Arno Press, 1976.

Gallatin, Albert. "Notes on the Semi-Civilized Nations of Mexico, Yucatan, and

Central America." *Transactions of the American Ethnological Society.* 3 vols. New York: Bartlett and Welford, 1845–1853.

Gandía, Enrique de. *Historia crítica de los mitos de la conquista americana.* Madrid: Sociedad General Española de Librería, 1929.

Garate, Donald. "Notes on Anza." Unpublished MS. Tumacácori National Historical Park: National Park Service, November 15, 1994.

Garber, Marjorie. *Vested Interests: Cross-Dressing and Cultural Anxiety.* New York: Routledge, 1992.

Garr, Daniel. "Planning, Politics, and Plunder: The Missions and Indian Pueblos of Hispanic California." *SCQ* 54 (Winter 1972): 291–312.

———. "A Rare and Desolate Land: Population and Race in Hispanic California." *WHQ* 6 (April 1975): 133–48.

Geiger, Maynard. "The 1824 Chumash Revolt." *SCQ* 7 (Dec. 1970): 345–64.

———. *Franciscan Missionaries in Hispanic California, 1769–1848: A Biographical Dictionary.* San Marino, Calif.: Huntington Library, 1969.

———, trans. and ed. "Instructions concerning the Occupation of California, 1769." *SCQ* 47 (June 1965): 209–15.

———. "Six Census Records of Los Angeles and Its Immediate Area between 1804 and 1823." *SCQ* 54 (Winter 1972): 313–42.

Gibson, Charles. *Spain in America.* New York: Harper and Row, 1966.

Gil, Juan. *Mitos y utopías del descubrimiento, vol. 2: El Pacífico.* Madrid: Alianza Editorial, 1989.

Giles, Mary E., ed. *Women in the Inquisition: Spain and the New World.* Baltimore: Johns Hopkins University Press, 1999.

Gleeson, William. *History of the Catholic Church in California.* 2 vols. San Francisco: A. L. Bancroft, 1872.

Goldschmidt, Walter. *Nomlaki Ethnography. UCPAAE* 42:4 (1951). Berkeley: University of California Press.

Goldwert, Marvin. *Machismo and Conquest: The Case of Mexico.* Lanham, Md.: University Press of America, 1983.

González, Deena. *Refusing the Favor: The Spanish-Mexican Women of Santa Fe, 1820–1880.* New York: Oxford University Press, 1999.

———. "Spanish-Mexican Women on the Santa Fe Frontier: Patterns of Their Resistance and Accommodation, 1820–1880." Ph.D. diss., University of California, Berkeley, 1985.

———. "The Widowed Women of Santa Fe: Assessments on the Lives of an Unmarried Population, 1850–1889." In *On Their Own: Widows and Widowhood in the American Southwest, 1848–1939,* pp. 65–90. Ed. Arlene Scadron. Urbana: University of Illinois Press, 1988.

González Montes, Soledad, ed. *Mujeres y relaciones de género en la antropología latinoamericana.* Mexico: Colegio de México, 1993.

González Stephan, Beatriz, and Lúcia Helena Costigan, eds. *Crítica y descolonización:*

El sujeto colonial en la cultura latinoamericana. Caracas: Universidad de Simón Bolívar and Ohio State University, 1992.

Gosner, Kevin, and Deborah E. Kanter, eds. "Special Issue: Women, Power, and Resistance in Colonial Mesoamerica." *Ethnohistory* 42:4 (Fall 1995).

Grant, Campbell. "Eastern Coastal Chumash." In *Handbook of North American Indians, vol. 8: California,* pp. 509–19. Ed. Robert Heizer. Washington, D.C.: Smithsonian Institution Press, 1978.

Grant, Helen F. "The World Upside-Down." In *Studies in Spanish Literature of the Golden Age Presented to Edward M. Wilson,* pp. 103–35. Ed. R. O. Jones. London: Tamesis, 1973.

Griswold del Castillo, Richard. "Neither Activists nor Victims: Mexican Women's Historical Discourse—The Case of San Diego, 1820–1850." *CH* (Fall 1995): 230–43.

———. "Patriarchy and the Status of Women in the Late Nineteenth Century Southwest." In *The Mexican and Mexican American Experience in the Nineteenth Century,* pp. 85–99. Ed. Jaime E. Rodriguez. Tempe, Ariz.: Bilingual Press/Bilingue Press, 1989.

Grivas, Theodore. "Alcalde Rule: The Nature of Local Government in Spanish and Mexican California." *CHSQ* 40 (March 1961): 11–32.

Grumet, Robert Steven. "Sunksuaws, Shamans, and Tradeswomen: Middle Atlantic Coastal Algonkian Women during the Seventeenth and Eighteenth Centuries." In *Women and Colonization,* pp. 43–62. Eds. Mona Etienne and Eleanor Leacock. New York: Praeger, 1980.

Gruzinski, Serge. *The Conquest of Mexico: The Incorporation of Indian Societies into the Western World, Sixteenth–Eighteenth Centuries.* Cambridge: Polity Press, 1993.

Guest, Francis F. "Cultural Perspectives on California Mission Life." *SCQ* 65 (Spring 1983): 1–65.

———. "An Examination of the Thesis of S. F. Cook on the Forced Conversion of Indians in the California Missions." *SCQ* 61 (Spring 1979): 1–78.

———. "An Inquiry into the Role of the Discipline in California Mission Life." *SCQ* 71 (Spring 1989): 1–68.

Gutiérrez, Ramón A., "Contested Eden: An Introduction." *CH* 76: 2–3 (Summer–Fall 1997): 1–11.

———. *When Jesus Came, the Corn Mothers Went Away: Marriage, Sexuality, and Power in New Mexico, 1500–1846.* Stanford, Calif.: Stanford University Press, 1991.

Gutiérrez, Ramón A., and Richard J. Orsi, eds. *Contested Eden: California before the Gold Rush.* Berkeley: University of California Press, 1998.

Haas, Lisbeth. *Conquest and Historical Identities in California, 1769–1936.* Berkeley: University of California Press, 1995.

Hale, Edward Everett. *The Queen of California: The Origin of the Name of California with a Translation from the Sergas of Esplandián.* 1862. Reprint, San Francisco: Colt Press, 1945.

Hanke, Lewis. *The Spanish Struggle for Justice in the Conquest of America.* Philadelphia: University of Pennsylvania Press, 1949.

Harrington, John P. "Culture Element Distributions, 19: Central California Coast." *University of California Anthropological Records* 7:1 (1942): 1–46.

Heizer, Robert F. *The California Indians: A Source Book.* Berkeley: University of California Press, 1957.

———. "A California Messianic Movement of 1801 among the Chumash." *American Anthropologist* 43 (Jan.–Mar. 1941): 128–29.

———, ed. *California's Oldest Historical Relic?* Berkeley: University of California, Robert H. Lowie Museum of Anthropology, 1972.

Heizer, Robert F., and Albert B. Elsasser. *The Natural World of the California Indians.* California Natural History Guides, no. 46. Berkeley: University of Calfornia Press, 1980.

Hernández, Salomé. "No Settlement without Women: Three Spanish California Settlement Schemes, 1790–1800." *SCQ* 72 (Fall 1990): 203–78.

Herren, Ricardo. *La conquista erótica de las Indias.* Barcelona: Planeta, 1991.

Hilton, Sylvia L. *La Alta California Española.* Madrid: Editorial MAPFRE, 1992.

Himelblau, Jack J., ed. *The Indian in Spanish America: Centuries of Removal, Survival, and Integration. A Critical Anthology.* 2 vols. Lancaster, Calif.: Labyrinthos, 1994.

Himmerich y Valencia, Robert. *The Encomenderos of New Spain, 1521–1555.* Austin: University of Texas Press, 1991.

Hirschfelder, Arlene, and Paulette Molin. *The Encyclopedia of Native American Religions.* New York: Facts on File, 1992.

Hittell, Theodore. *History of California.* 4 vols. San Francisco: N. J. Stone, 1885–97.

Hoganson, Kristin. *Fighting for American Manhood: How Gender Politics Provoked the Spanish-American and Philippine-American Wars.* New Haven, Conn.: Yale University Press, 1998.

Horn, Rebecca. *Postconquest Coyoacán: Nahua-Spanish Relations in Central Mexico, 1519–1650.* Stanford, Calif.: Stanford University Press, 1997.

Hornbeck, David. "Economic Growth and Change at the Missions of Alta California, 1769–1846." In *Columbian Consequences, vol. 1: Historical and Archaeological Perspectives on the Spanish Borderlands West,* pp. 423–33. Ed. David Hurst Thomas. Washington: Smithsonian Institution Press, 1989.

———. "Land Tenure and Rancho Expansion in Alta California, 1784–1846." *JHG* 4 (Dec. 1978): 371–90.

Hudson, Travis. "Chumash Canoes of Mission Santa Barbara: The Revolt of 1824." *JCA* 3 (Winter 1976): 5–15.

Hulme, Peter. *Colonial Encounters: Europe and the Native Caribbean, 1492–1797.* London; New York: Methuen.

Hunt, Rockwell D. "Great Women of California." *HSSCQ* 31 (Sept. 1949): 197–211.

Hurtado, Albert. *Intimate Frontiers: Sex, Gender, and Culture in Old California.* Albuquerque: University of New Mexico Press, 1999.

Hutchinson, Cecil Alan. *Frontier Settlement in Mexican California: The Híjar-Padrés Colony and Its Origins, 1769–1835.* Yale Western Americana Series, no. 21. New Haven, Conn.: Yale University Press, 1969.

———. "The Mexican Government and the Mission Indians of Upper California, 1821–35." *Americas* 21 (1965): 335–62.

———. "An Official List of the Members of the Híjar-Padrés Colony for Mexican California, 1834." *PHR* 42 (Aug. 1973): 407–18.

Icaza, Francisco A. de. *Diccionario autobiográfico de conquistadores y pobladores de Nueva España.* 2 vols. Madrid: Imp. de "El Adelantado de Segovia," 1923.

Irving, Washington. *The History of the Life and Voyages of Christopher Columbus.* New York: G. P. Putnam's Sons, 1895–97.

Jackson, Robert H. "Disease and Demographic Patterns at Santa Cruz Mission, Alta California." *JCGBA* 5:1–2 (1983): 33–57.

———. "Gentile Recruitment and Population Movements in the San Francisco Bay Area Missions." *JCGBA* 6 (Winter 1984): 225–39.

———. *Indian Population Decline: The Missions of Northwestern New Spain, 1687–1840.* Albuquerque: University of New Mexico Press, 1994.

Jackson, Robert H., and Edward Castillo. *Indians, Franciscans, and Spanish Colonization: The Impact of the Mission System on California Indians.* Albuquerque: University of New Mexico Press, 1995.

Jameson, Elizabeth. "Toward a Multicultural History of Women in the Western U.S." *Signs* 13 (Summer 1988): 761–91.

Jeffrey, Julie Roy. *Frontier Women: The Trans-Mississippi West, 1840–1880.* New York: Hill and Wang, 1979.

Jensen, Joan M. *With These Hands: Women Working on the Land.* New York: Feminist Press, 1981.

Jensen, Joan M., and Gloria Ricci Lothrop. *California Women: A History.* San Francisco: Boyd and Fraser, 1987.

Jensen, Joan M., and Darlis A. Miller. "The Gentle Tamers Revisited: New Approaches to the History of Women in the American West." *PHR* 49 (May 1980): 173–214.

Johnson, John. "The Chumash and the Missions." In *Columbian Consequences, vol. 1: Archeological and Historical Perspectives on the Spanish Borderlands West,* pp. 365–75. Ed. David Hurst Thomas. Washington, D.C.: Smithsonian Institution Press, 1989.

Johnson, Lyman, and Sonya Lipsett-Rivera. *The Faces of Honor: Sex, Shame, and Violence in Colonial Latin America.* Albuquerque: University of New Mexico Press, 1998.

Jones, Grant D. *The Conquest of the Last Maya Kingdom.* Stanford, Calif.: Stanford University Press, 1998.

Jones, Howard Mumford. *Ideas in America.* Cambridge, Mass.: Harvard University Press, 1944.

Jordan, Constance. *Renaissance Feminism: Literary Texts and Political Models*. Ithaca, N.Y.: Cornell University Press, 1990.

Karttunen, Frances E. *Between Worlds: Interpreters, Guides, and Survivors*. Rutgers, N.J.: Rutgers University Press, 1994.

Keen, Benjamin. "Main Currents in United States Writings on Colonial Spanish America, 1884–1984." *HAHR* 65:4 (Nov. 1985): 658–82.

Keith, Robert G. "Encomienda, Hacienda, and Corregimiento in Spanish America: A Structural Analysis." *HAHR* 51:3 (Aug. 1971): 431–46.

Kellogg, Susan. *Law and the Transformation of Aztec Culture, 1500–1700*. Norman: University of Oklahoma, 1995.

Kelsey, Harry. *Juan Rodríguez Cabrillo*. San Marino, Calif: Huntington Library, 1986.

———. "Mapping the California Coast: The Voyages of Discovery, 1533–1543." *Arizona and the West* 26 (Winter 1984): 307–24.

Kicza, John E., ed. *The Indian in Latin American History: Resistance, Resilience, and Acculturation*. Jaguar Books on Latin America, no. 1. Wilmington, Del.: Scholarly Resources, 1993.

Kidwell, Clara Sue. "Indian Women as Cultural Mediators." *Ethnohistory* 39 (Spring 1992): 97–107.

King, Laura. "Hugo Reid and His Indian Wife." *Annual Publication of the Historical Society of Southern California* vol. 4, part 2 (1898): 111–113.

Klein, Laura F., and Lillian A. Ackerman, eds. *Women and Power in Native North America*. Norman: University of Oklahoma Press, 1995.

Kolodny, Annette. *The Land Before Her: Fantasy and Experience of the American Frontiers, 1630–1860*. Chapel Hill: University of North Carolina Press, 1984.

Konetzke, Richard. "La emigración de mujeres españolas a América durante la época colonial." *RIS* 9 (Jan.–Mar. 1945): 123–50.

Krell, Dorothy. *The California Missions: A Pictorial History*. Menlo Park, Calif.: Sunset Publishing, 1991.

Kroeber, Alfred L. *Handbook of the Indians of California*. Bureau of American Ethnology Bulletin no. 78. Washington, D.C.: Government Printing Office, 1925. Reprint. Berkeley: California Book Company, 1953.

Kuznesof, Elizabeth. "The Construction of Gender in Colonial Latin America." *CLAR* 1, nos. 1–2 (1992): 253–70, 268.

Kuznesof, Elizabeth, and Robert Oppenheimer. "The Family and Society in Nineteenth-Century Latin America: An Historiographical Introduction." *JFH* 10:3 (Fall 1985): 215–35.

Lafaye, Jacques. *Quetzalcoatl y Guadalupe: La formación de la conciencia en México (1531–1813)*. Trans. Ida Vitale. Mexico: Fondo de Cultura Económica, 1983.

Langellier, J. Phillip, and Daniel Bernard Rosen. *A History under Spain and Mexico, 1776–1846*. Denver: U.S. Dept. of the Interior, National Park Service, Denver Service Center, 1992.

Langer, Erick D., and Robert H. Jackson. "Colonial and Republican Missions Compared: The Cases of Alta California and Southeastern Bolivia." *Society for Comparative Study of Society and History* (1988): 286–311.

———, eds. *The New Latin American Mission History.* Lincoln: University of Nebraska Press, 1995.

Lara-Cea, Helen. "Notes on the Use of Parish Registers in the Reconstruction of Chicana History in California prior to 1850." In *Between Borders: Essays on Mexican/ Chicana History,* pp. 131–59. Ed. Adelaida R. Del Castillo. Encino: Floricanto Press, 1990.

Larson, Catherine. "New Clothes, New Roles: Disguise and the Subversion of Convention in Tirso and Sor Juana." *Romance Languages Annual* 1 (1989): 500–503.

Lavrín, Asunción. *Sexuality and Marriage in Colonial Latin America.* Lincoln: University of Nebraska Press, 1989.

Leacock, Eleanor Burke. "Montagnais Women and the Jesuit Program for Colonization." In *Women and Colonization,* pp. 25–42. Eds. Mona Etienne and Eleanor Leacock. New York: Praeger, 1980.

———. *Myths of Male Dominance: Collected Articles on Women Cross-Culturally.* New York: Monthly Review Press, 1981.

Leacock, Eleanor, and Richard Lee, eds. *Politics and History in Band Societies.* New York: Cambridge University Press, 1982.

Lecompte, Janet. "The Independent Women of Hispanic New Mexico, 1821–1846." *WHQ* 12 (Jan. 1981): 17–35.

Leighly, John. *California as an Island.* San Francisco: Book Club of California, 1972.

Leonard, Irving. *Books of the Brave: Being an Account of Books and of Men in the Spanish Conquest and Settlement of the Sixteenth Century.* Cambridge, Mass.: Harvard University Press, 1949.

———. "Conquerors and Amazons in Mexico." *HAHR* 24 (Nov. 1944): 561–79.

Lockhart, James. "Encomienda and Hacienda: The Evolution of the Great Estate in the Spanish Indies." *HAHR* 49:3 (Aug. 1969): 411–29.

———. *The Men of Cajamarca: A Social and Biographical Study of the First Conquerors of Peru.* Austin: University of Texas Press, 1972.

———. *The Nahuas after the Conquest: A Social and Cultural History of the Indians of Central Mexico, Sixteenth through Eighteenth Centuries.* Stanford, Calif.: Stanford University Press, 1992.

———. *Postconquest Central Mexican History and Philology.* Stanford, Calif.: Stanford University Press, 1991.

———. "The Social History of Colonial Spanish America: Evolution and Potential." *LARR* 7:1 (1972): 6–46.

Lockhart, James, and Stuart B. Schwartz. *Early Latin America: A History of Colonial Spanish America and Brazil.* New York: Cambridge University Press, 1983.

Lothrop, Gloria Ricci. "Reminiscences of a Princess, Isidora Solano," *The Californians* 11:3 (1994): 24–28.

———. "Westering Women and the Ladies of Los Angeles: Some Similarities and Differences." *South Dakota Review* 19 (Spring–Summer 1981): 41–67.

MacCormack, Sabine. "'The Heart Has Its Reasons': Predicaments of Missionary Christianity in Early Colonial Peru." *HAHR* 65:3 (August 1985): 443–66.

Malone, Ann Patton. *Women on the Texas Frontier: A Cross-Cultural Perspective.* Southwestern Studies, Monograph 70. University of Texas at El Paso: Texas Western Press, 1983.

Manocchio, Regina Teresa. "Tending Communities, Crossing Cultures: Midwives in Nineteenth-Century California." Master's thesis, Yale University School of Nursing, 1998.

Margolin, Malcolm. *The Ohlone Way: Indian Life in the San Francisco–Monterey Bay Area.* Berkeley: Heyday Books, 1978.

Marshall, C. E. "The Birth of the Mestizo in New Spain." *HAHR* 19 (May 1939): 161–84.

Martín, Luis. *Daughters of the Conquistadores: Women of the Viceroyalty of Peru.* Albuquerque: University of New Mexico Press, 1983.

Martínez-Alier, Verena. *Marriage, Class and Colour in Nineteenth-Century Cuba: A Study of Racial Attitudes and Sexual Values in a Slave Society.* Ann Arbor: University of Michigan Press, 1974.

Mathes, W. Michael. *Vizcaíno and Spanish Expansion in the Pacific Ocean, 1580–1630.* San Francisco: California Historical Society, 1968.

Maura, Juan F. "Esclavas españolas en el Nuevo Mundo: Una nota histórica." *CLAHR* 2 (Spring 1993): 185–94.

———. *Women in the Conquest of the Americas.* Trans. John F. Deredita. New York: Peter Lang, 1997.

Mayberry, Nancy K. "The Role of the Warrior Women in *Amazonas en las Indias.*" *Bulletin of the Comediantes* 29 (Spring 1977): 38–44.

Maynarde, Thomas. *Sir Francis Drake His Voyage, 1595.* London: Hakluyt Society, 1849.

McCarty, Kieran. "The Colorado Massacre of 1781: María Montielo's Report." *JAH* 16 (Autumn 1975): 221–25.

McDowell Craver, Rebecca. *The Impact of Intimacy: Mexican-Anglo Intermarriage in New Mexico, 1821–1846.* Southwestern Studies, no. 66. University of Texas at El Paso: Texas Western Press, 1982.

McGarry, Daniel D. "Educational Methods of the Franciscans in Spanish California." *Americas* 6 (Jan. 1950): 335–58.

McKendrick, Malveena. *Women and Society in the Spanish Drama of the Golden Age: A Study of the* Mujer Varonil. New York: Cambridge University Press, 1974.

Medicine, Beatrice, and Patricia Albers, eds. *The Hidden Half: Studies of Plains Indian Women.* Lanham, Md.: University Press of America, 1983.

Meighan, Clement. "Indians and California Missions." *SCQ* 69 (Fall 1987): 187–201.

Michel, Sonya, and Robyn Muncy, eds. *Engendering America: A Documentary History, 1865 to the Present.* New York: McGraw-Hill College, 1999.

Miller, Darlis A. "Cross-Cultural Marriages in the Southwest: The New Mexico Experience, 1846–1900." *NMHR* 57 (Oct. 1982): 335–59.

Milliken, Randall. "An Ethnohistory of the Indian People of the San Francisco Bay Area from 1770 to 1810." Ph.D. diss., University of California, Berkeley, 1991.

Miranda, Gloria. "Racial and Cultural Dimensions of *Gente de Razón* Status in Spanish and Mexican California." *SCQ* 70 (Fall 1988): 265–78.

Molina, Ida, and Oleg Zinam. "The Historical Role of a Woman in the Chicano's Search for Ethnic Identity: The Case of Doña Marina." *Quarterly Journal of Ideology* 14:1 (1990): 39–53.

Monroy, Douglas. "They Didn't Call Them 'Padre' For Nothing: Patriarchy in Hispanic California." In *Between Borders: Essays on Mexicana/Chicana History,* pp. 433–46. Ed. Adelaida R. del Castillo. Encino, Calif.: Floricanto Press, 1990.

———. *Thrown among Strangers: The Making of Mexican Culture in Frontier California.* Berkeley: University of California Press, 1990.

Moorhead, Max L. *The Presidio: Bastion of the Spanish Borderlands.* Norman: University of Oklahoma Press, 1975.

Mora, Magdalena, and Adelaida R. del Castillo, eds. *Mexican Women in the U.S.: Struggles of Past and Present.* Los Angeles: Chicano Studies Research Center, University of California, 1980.

Moynihan, Ruth, Susan Armitage, and Christiane Fischer Dichamp, eds. *So Much to Be Done: Women Settlers on the Mining and Ranching Frontier.* Lincoln: University of Nebraska Press, 1990.

Murphy, Lucy Eldersveld. "Autonomy and the Economic Roles of Indian Women of the Fox-Wisconsin Riverway Region, 1763–1832." In *Negotiators of Change,* pp. 72–89. Ed. Nancy Shoemaker. New York: Routledge, 1995.

Myers, Kathleen A. "Broader Canon, Interdisciplinary Approaches: Recent Works in Colonial Latin American Literary Studies." *LARR* 33:2 (1998): 258–70.

Myres, Sandra. "Victoria's Daughters: English-Speaking Women on Nineteenth-Century Frontiers." In *Western Women: Their Land, Their Lives,* pp. 261–83. Eds. Lillian Schlissel, Vicki L. Ruiz, and Janice Monk. Albuquerque: University of New Mexico Press, 1988.

———. *Westering Women and the Frontier Experience, 1880–1915.* Albuquerque: University of New Mexico Press, 1982.

Namias, June. *White Captives: Gender and Ethnicity on the American Frontier.* Chapel Hill: University of North Carolina Press, 1993.

Nash, June. "Aztec Women: The Transition from Status to Class in Empire and Colony." In *Women and Colonization,* pp. 134–148. Eds. Mona Etienne and Eleanor Leacock. New York: Praeger, 1980.

Navas Ruiz, Ricardo. "La Malinche: Hacia una semiótica de la conquista." In *Ensayos de literatura europea e hispanoamericana,* pp. 353–58. Ed. Félix Menchacatorre. San Sebastián, Spain: Universidad del País Vasco, 1990.

Newton, Janet. *Las Positas: The Story of Robert and Josefa Livermore.* Livermore, Calif.: Janet Newton, 1969.

Nizza da Silva, Maria Beatriz, ed. *Families in the Expansion of Europe, 1500–1800.* Brookfield, Vt.: Ashgate, 1998.

Northrop, Marie E. "Padrón of Monterey, 1790." *HSSCQ* 62 (June 1960): 210–11.

———. *Spanish-Mexican Families of Early California: 1769–1850.* 2 vols. Burbank, Calif.: Southern California Genealogical Society, 1987.

Nunis, Doyce, and Edward D. Castillo. "California Mission Indians: Two Perspectives." *CH* 70 (Summer 1991): 206–215, 236–238.

Ogden, Annegret. "Go West, Young Women." Part 1: *The Californians* 3 (May–June 1985): 6–7; Part 2: *The Californians* 3 (July–Aug. 1985): 6, 51.

O'Gorman, Edmundo. *La idea del descubrimiento de América: Historia de esa interpretación y crítica de sus fundamentos.* Mexico: Centro de Estudios Filosóficos, Universidad Nacional Autónoma de México, 1951.

O'Meara, Walter. *Daughters of the Country: The Women of the Fur Traders and Mountain Men.* New York: Harcourt, Brace and World, 1968.

O'Sullivan-Beare, Nancy. *Las mujeres de los conquistadores: La mujer española en los comienzos de la colonización americana.* Madrid: Compañía Bibliográfica Española [1956].

Ots Capdequí, José María. *Instituciones sociales de la América española en el período colonial.* La Plata, Argentina: Imprenta López, 1934.

Padilla, Genaro. " 'Yo sola aprendí': Contra-patriarchal Containment in Women's Nineteenth-Century California Personal Narratives." *Americas Review* 16 (Fall–Winter 1988): 91–109.

Painter, Susan Lee, and Don Dutton. "Patterns of Emotional Bonding in Battered Women: Traumatic Bonding." *IJWS* 8 (Sept.–Oct. 1985): 363–75.

Papachristou, Judith. "American Women and Foreign Policy, 1898–1905: Exploring Gender in Diplomatic History." *Diplomatic History* 14 (Fall 1990): 493–509.

Pascoe, Peggy. "Introduction: The Challenge of Writing Multicultural Women's History." *Frontiers* 12:1 (1991): 1–4.

Pastor Bodmer, Beatriz. *The Armature of Conquest: Spanish Accounts of the Discovery of America, 1492–1589.* Stanford, Calif.: Stanford University Press, 1992.

———. *Discursos narrativos de la conquista: Mitificación y emergencia.* Hanover, N.H.: Ediciones del Norte, 1988.

Patch, Robert. *Maya and Spaniard in Yucatán, 1648–1812.* Stanford, Calif.: Stanford University Press, 1993.

Perry, Mary Elizabeth. "From Convent to Battlefield: Cross-Dressing and Gendering the Self in the New World of Imperial Spain." In *Queer Iberia: Sexualities, Cultures, and Crossings from the Middle Ages to the Renaissance,* pp. 394–419. Eds. Josiah Blackmore and Gregory S. Hutcheson. Durham: Duke University Press, 1999.

Peterson, Jacqueline. "The People in Between: Indian-White Marriage and the Genesis of a Métis Society and Culture in the Great Lakes Region, 1680–1830." Ph.D. diss., University of Illinois, Chicago, 1981.

————. "Women Dreaming: The Religiopsychology of Indian-White Marriages and the Rise of a 'Métis' Culture." In *Western Women: Their Land, Their Lives,* pp. 49–68. Eds. Lillian Schlissel, Vicki L. Ruiz, and Janice Monk. Albuquerque: University of New Mexico Press, 1988.

Peterson, Jacqueline, and Jennifer Brown, eds. *The New Peoples: Being and Becoming Métis in North America.* Lincoln: University of Nebraska Press, 1985.

Pfefferkorn, Ignaz. *Sonora: A Description of the Province.* Ed. George P. Hammond; trans. Theodore E. Treutlein. Coronado Cuarto Centennial Publications, 1540–1940, no. 12. Albuquerque: University of New Mexico Press, 1949.

Phelan, John Leddy. "Authority and Flexibility in the Spanish Imperial Bureaucracy." *Administrative Science Quarterly* 5 (1960): 47–65.

Phillips, George Harwood. "The *Alcaldes:* Indian Leadership in the Spanish Missions of California." Newberry Library Occasional Papers in Curriculum Series, no. 11. Chicago: D'Arcy McNickle Center, 1989.

————. *Chiefs and Challengers: Indian Resistance and Cooperation in Southern California.* Berkeley: University of California Press, 1975.

Phillips, Lynne. "Rural Women in Latin America: Directions for Future Research." *LARR* 25:3 (1992): 89–107.

Piette, Charles J. G. *Le secret de Junípero Serra: Fondateur de la Californie-Nouvelle, 1769–1784.* 2 vols. Washington, D.C.: Academy of American Franciscan History, 1949.

Platt, Tristan. "Simón Bolívar, the Sun of Justice, and the Amerindian Virgin: Andean Conceptions of the *Patria* in Nineteenth-Century Potosí." *JLAS* 25 (Feb. 1993): 159–85.

Pratt, Mary Louise. *Imperial Eyes: Travel Writing and Transculturation.* New York: Routledge, 1992.

Prescott, William H. *History of the Conquest of Mexico and History of the Conquest of Peru.* New York: Modern Library [1900?].

Price, Richard. *First-Time: The Historical Vision of an Afro-American People.* Baltimore: Johns Hopkins University Press, 1983.

Priestley, Herbert I. *José de Gálvez, Visitor-General of New Spain, 1765–1771.* Berkeley: University of California Press, 1916.

Putnam, Ruth. "California: The Name." *University of California Publications in History* 4:4 (1917): 289–365.

Ramírez, Susan Elizabeth. *The World Upside Down: Cross-Cultural Contact and Conflict in Sixteenth-Century Peru.* Stanford, Calif.: Stanford University Press, 1996.

Rawls, James J. *Indians of California: The Changing Image.* Norman: University of Oklahoma Press, 1984.

Restall, Matthew. "Central Issues: Social History and the Recent Study of Colonial Central America." *LARR* 33:2 (1998): 207–20.

————. *Maya Conquistador: Yucatec Perceptions of the Spanish Conquest.* Boston: Beacon, 1998.

————. *The Maya World: Yucatec Culture and Society, 1550–1850.* Stanford, Calif.: Stanford University Press, 1997.

Reynolds, Keld J. "The Reglamento for the Hijar y Padres Colony of 1834." *HSSCQ* 28:4 (Dec. 1946): 142–75.

Richman, Irving B. *California under Spain and Mexico, 1535–1847.* Boston: Houghton Mifflin, 1911.

Riley, Glenda. *The Female Frontier: A Comparative View of Women on the Prairie and the Plains.* Lawrence: University Press of Kansas, 1988.

————. *Women and Indians on the Frontier, 1825–1915.* Albuquerque: University of New Mexico Press, 1984.

Ripodas Ardanaz, Daisy. *El matrimonio en Indias: Realidad social y regulación jurídica.* Buenos Aires: Fundación para la Educación, la Ciencia, y la Cultura, 1977.

Robinson, W. W. *Land in California.* Berkeley: University of California Press, 1948.

Ronda, James P. " 'We Are Well as We Are': An Indian Critique of Seventeenth-Century Christian Missions." *William and Mary Quarterly* 34 (Jan. 1977): 66–82.

Root, Maria P. P., ed. *Racially Mixed People in America.* Newbury Park, Calif.: Sage Publications, 1992.

Roscoe, Will. "Bibliography of Berdache and Alternative Gender Roles among North American Indians." *Journal of Homosexuality* 14:3–4 (1987): 81–171.

————. "How to Become a Berdache: Toward a Unified Analysis of Gender Diversity." In *Third Sex, Third Gender: Beyond Sexual Dimorphism in Culture and History,* pp. 329–72. Ed. Gilbert Herdt. New York: Zone Books, 1994.

Rothschild, Mary Aickin, and Pamela Claire Hronek. *Doing What the Day Brought: An Oral History of Arizona Women.* Tucson: University of Arizona Press, 1992.

Rudnick, Lois. "Re-Naming the Land: Anglo Expatriate Women in the Southwest." In *The Desert Is No Lady: Southwestern Landscapes in Women's Writing and Art,* pp. 10–26. Eds. Vera Norwood and Janice Monk. New Haven: Yale University Press, 1987.

Ruiz, Vicki L. "Dead Ends or Gold Mines? Using Missionary Records in Mexican-American Women's History." *Frontiers* 12:1 (1991): 33–56.

Samara, Eni de Mesquita, and Dora Isabel Paiva da Costa. "Family, Patriarchalism, and Social Change in Brazil." *LARR* 32:1 (1997): 212–25.

Sánchez, Rosaura, and Rosa Martínez Cruz, eds. *Essays on La Mujer.* Los Angeles: Chicano Studies Center, University of California, 1977.

Sánchez, Rosaura, Beatrice Pita, and Barbara Reyes. "Nineteenth-Century *Californio* Testimonials." Special edition of *Crítica,* Spring 1994.

Sandos, James A. "Christianization among the Chumash: An Ethnohistoric Perspective." *AIQ* 15:1 (Winter 1991): 65–89.

————. "Levantamiento! The Chumash Uprising Reconsidered." *SCQ* 67 (Summer 1985): 109–33.

Sarris, Greg. *Keeping Slug Woman Alive: A Holistic Approach to American Indian Texts.* Berkeley: University of California Press, 1993.

Scadron, Arlene, ed. *On Their Own: Widows and Widowhood in the American Southwest, 1843–1939.* Urbana: University of Illinois Press, 1988.

Scheper, George L. "Re-Reading the 'Conquest of Mexico': Whose Story?" In *Semiotics 1990,* pp. 195–210. Proceedings of the Fifteenth Annual Meeting of the Semiotic Society of America. New York: University Press of America, 1993.

Schlissel, Lillian. *Women's Diaries of the Westward Journey.* New York: Schocken Books, 1982.

Schlissel, Lillian, Vicki L. Ruiz, and Janice Monk, eds. *Western Women: Their Land, Their Lives.* Albuquerque: University of New Mexico Press, 1988.

Schroeder, Susan, Stephanie Wood, and Robert Haskett, eds. *Indian Women of Early Mexico.* Norman: University of Oklahoma Press, 1997.

Schwartz, Seymour I., and Ralph E. Ehrenberg. *The Mapping of America.* New York: Abrams, 1980.

Schwartz, Stephen. *From East to West: California and the Making of the American Mind.* New York: Free Press/Simon and Schuster, 1998.

Scott, James C. *Domination and the Arts of Resistance.* New Haven, Conn.: Yale University Press, 1990.

———. *Weapons of the Weak: Everyday Forms of Peasant Resistance.* New Haven, Conn.: Yale University Press, 1985.

Scott, Joan Wallach. *Gender and the Politics of History.* New York: Columbia University Press, 1988.

Seed, Patricia. *Ceremonies of Possession in Europe's Conquest of the New World, 1492–1640.* New York: Cambridge University Press, 1995.

———. "Colonial and Postcolonial Discourse," *LARR* 26:3 (1991): 181–200.

———. "'Failing to Marvel': Atahualpa's Encounter with the Word." *LARR* 26:1 (1991): 1–12.

———. "More Colonial and Postcolonial Discourses." *LARR* 28:3 (1993): 146–52.

———. "Taking Possession and Reading Texts: Establishing the Authority of Overseas Empires." *William and Mary Quarterly* 49 (April 1992): 183–209.

———. *To Love, Honor, and Obey in Colonial Mexico: Conflicts over Marriage Choice, 1574–1821.* Stanford, Calif.: Stanford University Press, 1988.

Servín, Manuel P. "California's Hispanic Heritage." In *New Spain's Far Northern Frontier: Essays on Spain in the American West, 1540–1821,* pp. 117–133. Ed. David Weber. Albuquerque: University of New Mexico Press, 1979.

———. "Costansó's 1791 Report." *CHSQ* 49 (Sept. 1970): 221–32.

———. "The Secularization of the California Missions: A Reappraisal." *SCQ* 47 (June 1965): 133–49.

Shay, Anthony. "Fandangos and Bailes: Dancing and Dance Events in Early California." *SCQ* 64 (Fall 1977): 245–50.

Shipek, Florence C. "California Indian Reactions to the Franciscans." *Americas* 41:4 (1985): 480–91.

———. "A Native American Adaptation to Drought: The Kumeyaay as Seen in the San Diego Mission Records, 1770–1798." *Ethnohistory* 28:4 (1981): 295–312.

Shoemaker, Nancy, ed. *Negotiators of Change: Historical Perspectives on Native American Women.* New York: Routledge, 1995.

Showalter, Elaine. *Speaking of Gender.* New York: Routledge, 1989.

Silverblatt, Irene. *Moon, Sun, and Witches: Gender Ideologies and Class in Inca and Colonial Peru.* Princeton, N.J.: Princeton University Press, 1987.

———. "'The Universe has turned inside out . . . There is no justice for us here': Andean Women under Spanish Rule." In *Women and Colonization,* pp. 149–85. Eds. Mona Etienne and Eleanor Leacock. New York: Praeger, 1980.

Socolow, Susan Migden. "La población de la América colonial." In *Descubrimiento, conquista y colonización de América a quinientos años,* pp. 218–48. Ed. Carmen Bernand. Mexico City: Consejo Nacional para la Cultura y las Artes/Fondo de Cultura Económica, 1994.

———. "Spanish Captives in Indian Societies: Cultural Contact along the Argentine Frontier, 1600–1835." *HAHR* 72 (Feb. 1992): 73–99.

Spalding, Karen. "The Colonial Indian: Past and Present Research Perspectives." *LARR* 7:1 (1972): 47–75.

———. *Huarochirí: An Andean Society under Inca and Spanish Rule.* Stanford, Calif.: Stanford University Press, 1984.

Spier, Leslie. *Yuman Tribes of the Gila River.* Chicago: University of Chicago Press, 1933.

Stern, Steve J. *The Secret History of Gender: Women, Men, and Power in Late Colonial Mexico.* Chapel Hill: University of North Carolina Press, 1995.

Stodder, Ann Lucy Wiener. *Mechanisms and Trends in the Decline of the Costanoan Indian Population of Central California: Nutrition and Health in Pre-contact California and Mission Period Environments.* Salinas, Calif.: Coyote Press, 1986.

Stoner, K. Lynn. *Latinas of the Americas: A Source Book.* New York: Garland, 1989.

Stratton, Joanna L. *Pioneer Women: Voices from the Kansas Frontier.* New York: Simon and Schuster, 1981.

Suggs, David N., and Andrew W. Miracle, eds. *Culture and Human Sexuality: A Reader.* Pacific Grove, Calif.: Brooks/Cole Publishing Co., 1993.

Tamayo Sánchez, Jesús. *La ocupación española de las californias.* Mexico: Plaza y Valdés, 1992.

Taufer, Alison. "The Only Good Amazon Is a Converted Amazon: The Woman Warrior and Christianity in the Amadís Cycle." In *Playing with Gender: A Renaissance Pursuit,* pp. 35–51. Eds. Jean R. Brink, Maryanne C. Horowitz, and Allison P. Coudert. Chicago: University of Illinois Press, 1991.

Taylor, William B. *Magistrates of the Sacred: Parish Priests and Indian Parishioners in Eighteenth-Century Mexico.* Stanford, Calif.: Stanford University Press, 1996.

———. "The Virgin of Guadalupe in New Spain: An Inquiry into the Social History of Marian Devotion." *American Ethnologist* 14 (1987): 9–33.

Temple, Thomas Workman II. "The Founding of Misión San Gabriel Arcángel." Part 1: *Masterkey* 33 (July–Sept. 1959): 103–12; part 2: *Masterkey* 33 (Oct.–Dec. 1959): 153–61.

———. "Toypurina the Witch and the Indian Uprising at San Gabriel." *Masterkey* 32 (Sept.–Oct. 1958): 136–52.

Thomas, David Hurst, ed. *Columbian Consequences, vol. 1: Historical and Archaeological Perspectives on the Spanish Borderlands West.* Washington, D.C.: Smithsonian Institution Press, 1989.

———, ed. *Columbian Consequences, vol. 2: Historical and Archaeological Perspectives on the Spanish Borderlands East.* Washington, D.C.: Smithsonian Institution Press, 1990.

———, ed. *Columbian Consequences, vol. 3: The Spanish Borderlands in Pan-American Perspectives.* Washington, D.C.: Smithsonian Institution Press, 1991.

Todorov, Tzvetan. *The Conquest of America.* New York: HarperPerennial, 1984.

Torchiana, H. A. Van Coenen. *Story of the Mission Santa Cruz.* San Francisco: P. Elder, 1933.

Torre Revello, José. "Esclavas blancas en las indias occidentales." *BIIH* 6 (1927–28): 263–71.

Trexler, Richard. "From the Mouths of Babes: Christianization by Children in Sixteenth-Century New Spain." In *Religious Organization and Religious Experience,* pp. 115–35. Ed. John Davis. Association of Social Anthropologists, no. 21. New York: Academic Press, 1982.

———, ed. *Gender Rhetorics: Postures of Dominance and Submission in History.* Medieval and Renaissance Texts and Studies, no. 113. Binghamton, N.Y.: Center for Medieval and Early Renaissance Studies, State University of New York at Binghamton, 1994.

———. "Infanticide in Florence: New Sources and First Results." *History of Childhood Quarterly* 1 (Summer 1973): 98–116.

Tuñon Pablos, Julia. *Women in Mexico: A Past Unveiled.* Trans. Alan Hynds. Austin: University of Texas Press, 1999.

Turner, Frederick Jackson. *The Frontier in American History.* New York: H. Holt, 1920.

Tuthill, Franklin. *The History of California.* San Francisco: H. H. Bancroft, 1866.

Uchmany, Eva Alexandra. "El mestizaje en el siglo XVI novohispano." *Historia Mexicana* 37:1 (1987): 29–48.

Vallejo, Guadalupe. "Ranch and Mission Days in Alta California." *Century Magazine* 41 (Dec. 1890): 183–92.

Van de Grift Sánchez, Nellie. *Spanish Arcadia.* San Francisco: Powell Publishing, 1929.

Van Kirk, Sylvia. *Many Tender Ties: Women in Fur-Trade Society in Western Canada, 1670–1870.* Norman: University of Oklahoma Press, 1983.

Van Nostrand, Jeanne. *A Pictorial and Narrative History of Monterey . . . 1770–1847.* San Francisco: California Historical Society, 1968.

van Oss, Adriaan C. *Catholic Colonialism: A Parish History of Guatemala, 1524–1821.* Cambridge: Cambridge University Press, 1986.

Van Young, Eric. "Mexican Rural History since Chevalier: The Historiography of the Colonial Hacienda." *LARR* 18:3 (1983): 5–61.

———. "The Raw and the Cooked: Elite and Popular Ideology in Mexico, 1800–1821." In *The Middle Period in Latin America,* pp. 75–102. Ed. Mark D. Szuchman. Boulder, Colo.: Lynne Reiner, 1984.

Varón Gabai, Rafael. *Francisco Pizarro and His Brothers: The Illusion of Power in Sixteenth-Century Peru.* Norman: University of Oklahoma Press, 1997.

Vidal, Hernán. "The Concept of Colonial and Postcolonial Discourse: A Perspective from Literary Criticism." *LARR* 28:3 (1993): 113–19.

Villa, Eduardo W. *Historia del estado de Sonora.* 2d ed. Hermosilla, Sonora: Editorial Sonora, 1951.

Villafane, María Teresa. "La mujer española en la conquista y colonización de América." *Cuadernos Hispanicos* 59 (1964): 125–42.

Voght, Martha. "Shamans and Padres: The Religion of the Southern California Mission Indians." *PHR* 36:4 (1967): 363–73.

Wagner, Henry R. *Juan Rodríguez Cabrillo: Discoverer of the Coast of California.* San Francisco: California Historical Society, 1941.

Waldman, Carl. *Who Was Who in Native American History: Indians and Non-Indians From Early Contacts through 1900.* New York: Facts on File, 1990.

Wall, Steve, ed. *Wisdom's Daughters: Conversations with Women Elders of Native America.* New York: HarperCollins, 1993.

Wallace, Edith. "Sexual Status and Role Differences." In *Handbook of North American Indians, vol. 8: California,* pp. 683–89. Ed. Robert F. Heizer. Washington, D.C.: Smithsonian Institution Press, 1978.

Washburn, Wilcomb E. "The Meaning of 'Discovery' in the Fifteenth and Sixteenth Centuries." *AHR* 68 (1962–63): 1–21.

Waters, Willard O. *Franciscan Missions of Upper California as Seen by Foreign Visitors and Residents: A Chronological List of Printed Accounts, 1786–1848.* Early California Travels Series, no. 24. Los Angeles: Glen Dawson, 1954.

Weber, David, ed. *New Spain's Far Northern Frontier: Essays on Spain in the American West, 1540–1821.* Albuquerque: University of New Mexico Press, 1979.

Weber, Francis J. *Vignettes of California Catholicism.* Mission Hills, Calif.: Libra Press, 1988.

Weimer, Christopher Brian. "Sor Juana as Feminist Playwright: The *Gracioso's* Satiric Function in *Los empeños de una casa.*" *LATR* (1992): 91–98.

White, Hayden. *Tropics of Discourse: Essays in Cultural Criticism.* Baltimore: Johns Hopkins University Press, 1978.

White, Raymond. "Religion and Its Role among the Luiseño." In *Native Californians: A Theoretical Retrospective,* pp. 355–77. Eds. Lowell J. Bean and Thomas C. Blackburn. Ramona, Calif.: Ballena Press, 1976.

Whitehead, Richard S. *Citadel on the Channel: The Royal Presidio of Santa Barbara, Its Founding and Construction, 1782–1798.* Santa Barbara Trust for Historic Preservation. Spokane, Wash.: Arthur H. Clark, 1996.

Willoughby, Nona Christiansen. *Division of Labor among the Indians of California.* University of California Archaeological Survey Reports, no. 60. Berkeley: University of California Archaeological Survey, 1963.

Wilson, Joan H., and Lynn B. Donovan. "Women's History: A Listing of West Coast Archival and Manuscript Sources." *CHSQ* 55 (Spring–Summer 1976): 74–83, 170–84.

Wilson, Terry P. "Blood Quantum: Native American Mixed Bloods." In *Racially Mixed People,* pp. 108–125. Ed. Maria P. P. Root. Newbury Park, Calif.: Sage Publications, 1992.

Wolf, Eric R. "The Virgen de Guadalupe: A Mexican National Symbol." *JAF* 71 (Jan.–Mar. 1958): 34–39.

Woodward, Arthur. "An Early Account of the Chumash." *Masterkey* 8:4 (1934): 118–23.

Zavala, Silvio. *La filosofía política en la conquista de América.* Mexico: Fondo de Cultura Económica: 1947.

Zulawski, Ann. "Social Differentiation, Gender, and Ethnicity: Urban Indian Women in Colonial Bolivia, 1640–1725," *LARR* 25:2 (1990): 93–113.

Index

About the Author

Virginia M. Bouvier is an assistant professor of Latin American Literature in the Department of Spanish and Portuguese at the University of Maryland in College Park. She received her doctorate in Latin American Studies from the University of California at Berkeley and has published articles and monographs on female narratives on the California frontier, democracy and culture in Latin America, U.S.–Latin American relations, Sor Juana Inés de la Cruz, and human rights issues. She attended the Institute for the Editing of Historical Documents in 1994 and worked as a National Historical Publications and Records Commission intern on a documentary edition of the writings and correspondence of Emma Goldman. She teaches courses on colonial Latin American literature and culture and gender studies.